Challenge of the Congo

CHALLENGE
OF THE CONGO

KWAME NKRUMAH

INTERNATIONAL PUBLISHERS ★ NEW YORK

Published simultaneously in London
by Thomas Nelson and Sons Ltd.,
36 Park Street, London, W.1 and in New York
by International Publishers Co., Inc.,
381 Park Avenue South, New York, N.Y. 10016

Printed in Great Britain by
Thomas Nelson (Printers) Ltd, London and Edinburgh

A Ahmed Sékou Touré, Mon Frère de Combat
Au Bureau Politique National du Parti Démocratique
de Guinée et au Vaillant Peuple de Guinée
Aux Peuples Africains et aux Courageux
Militants pour la Cause Sacrée
du Progrès Africain dans la
Liberté et l'Unité du Continent

Contents

Preface

SINCE writing the final chapters of this book, Ghana has temporarily fallen victim to the same external forces which have, for six years, tried to prevent progress towards real independence in the Congo.

On 24 February 1966, certain members of the army and police, acting in co-operation with neo-colonialists seized power while I was on my way to Hanoi with proposals for ending the cruel war being waged in Vietnam. Ghana has been laid open once more to the foreign exploitation we had fought so hard to overcome since independence was achieved on 6 March 1957.

Only the deliberately blind could fail to see this latest example of imperialist interference in Africa as a part of the world-wide struggle being waged between, on the one hand, the independent developing states, and on the other, the neo-colonialist, imperialist countries trying to exert pressure on them. The struggle takes different forms in the various areas. In the Congo, where the conflict has been long drawn out, foreign interference has operated mainly in the economic sphere and has at times been less obvious because of internal subversive activity. In Ghana, however, the issues have been exposed with sudden and dramatic clarity by a seizure of power backed by frustrated neo-colonialists who see no other way of achieving their aims to dominate and exploit. Ghana, in the forefront of the struggle for a free and united Africa and on the brink of a great industrial breakthrough which would have given true economic independence, had become too dangerous an example to the rest of Africa to be allowed to continue under a socialist-directed government.

The tragedy in Ghana, and the threat to set back the African Revolution which it entails is only temporary. Yet this does not minimise the crime. These men have betrayed not only Ghanaians and Africans everywhere but indirectly, all the poor and oppressed people in the world.

Since coming to Conakry, I have received hundreds of letters from men and women in practically every country, expressing sympathy and support. These letters have touched me deeply. They have also cheered me since they show an awareness of the true nature of the struggle taking place in Africa and the world between the forces of progress and those of reaction, which in the final analysis is the fight of the common man against injustice and privilege. For we live in a world in which one quarter of the people are becoming richer and richer, while the rest grow poorer and poorer. This situation can only be remedied by world socialism. For as long as imperialism, the common enemy of mankind, goes unchecked, there will always be exploitation, an ever-widening gap between the haves and have-nots, and all the evils of imperialism and neo-colonialism which breed and sustain wars.

It is ironic that the army and police action in Ghana should have occurred while I was flying to Hanoi with proposals for ending the war in Vietnam—a war in which imperialist aggression is seen in its most blatant and tragic form. Since the 1950s when U.S. aid to the Saigon government was limited to training the South Vietnamese army and giving advice and help in the political and economic spheres, the American commitment has risen sharply. In 1960 there were some 2,000 U.S. troops in South Vietnam; by 1963, when Diem was assassinated, there were 15,500. Today there are no less than 280,000 Americans fighting a senseless, protracted war which is costing the people of the United States at least two million dollars daily, and which can only delay, but not prevent, the Vietnamese people from working out their own future free from foreign inter-ference and domination.

I had arrived in Peking when news reached me of the 'coup' in Ghana and I decided to return to Africa without completing my mission. It is sad that events in Ghana forced me to abandon my mission to Hanoi, but these same events have taught progressive Africa a great lesson. There are likely to be more coups and rebellions in Africa as long as imperialists and neo-colonialists are able to exploit our weaknesses. Unless we unite and deal with neo-colonial-ism on a Pan-African basis, they will continue to try to undermine our independence, and draw us again into spheres of influence comparable to the original carve-up of Africa arranged at the Berlin Conference of 1884.

Because attempts to achieve political and economic independence and to advance on the road towards continental unity have been consistently and insidiously sabotaged by neo-colonialist manoeuvres it is no longer possible, indeed it would be suicidal to combat such dangerous and ruthless forces by the old methods of peaceful persuasion and compromise. For years, a virtual state of war has existed in Africa between the developing, independent states, and the foreign interests determined to maintain and even strengthen their stranglehold on the economic life of our continent. This 'war' must now come into the open, and be fought and won in the military sense, if Africa is ever to achieve her full development. The movement for total liberation from imperialism and neo-colonialism is entering a new phase, the phase of an All-African Peoples' Revolutionary armed struggle.

Foreign powers already have military bases in various, strategically important parts of our continent. There are in Africa at present, seventeen air bases owned and operated by individual members of the North Atlantic Treaty Organisation (NATO). There are nine naval bases encircling the continent from the north coast of Africa right round the south coast to the east. There are foreign military missions, for example in Kenya, Morocco, Liberia, Libya, South Africa, Senegal and Ivory Coast. Furthermore, they possess three rocket sites, and an atomic testing range in North Africa. There are mines being exploited for the production of raw materials for the manufacture of nuclear weapons. Some of these mines are situated in the Congo, Angola, South Africa, Mozambique and Rhodesia. In the context of the imperialist plan to prevent Africa from achieving complete political and economic independence and an All-African Union Government, these foreign military bases present a serious threat to the African revolutionary struggle.

In striking contrast to the military preparedness of foreign powers is the present military weakness of the Independent States of Africa. The total strength of African forces is estimated to be about 480,000 (excluding Rhodesia and South Africa), and just over one-third of these forces belong to African-governed States south of the Sahara. But their effectiveness in any joint action is minimised by lack of arms standardisation and training, and the absence of any combined high command. When the question of direct armed intervention to put an end to Ian Smith's illegal government in Rhodesia was debated in the Organisation of African Unity, in December 1965, it was decided that this was not feasible. Instead, members voted to break off diplomatic relations with Britain, a step quite inadequate to deal with the situation.

Other crises will occur as the African revolutionary struggle continues to gain momentum. We must be prepared to deal with them. Now is the time to make a concerted and sustained effort to achieve an All-African Union Government, without which final victory of the African revolution will be incomplete. This is the challenge of the Congo.

KWAME NKRUMAH

Conakry, 22 June 1966

Republic of the Congo

Introduction

The disintegration and liquidation of the colonial system has reached its final stage. Within a decade the African Revolution and its liberation movements have shattered the colonial empires which took centuries to establish.

The upheavals in the Congo, the resurgence and restlessness pervading Africa, and the magnetic attraction which the concept of freedom and independence from colonialism and foreign domination have had, make it necessary in this introduction to give a concise account of how the African struggle and revolution started.

The birth of the United Nations Organisation with its Declaration of Human Rights and the struggle for freedom as a result of the last two world wars brought new hope to the oppressed and colonised peoples of the world. The granting of independence to India, Pakistan, Burma and a large part of South East Asia produced a ferment and an upsurge in Africa. The period after the Second World War was therefore one of intensified political activity in the liberation movement in Africa.

It was during this period that a number of the present leaders returned to Africa. The spirit of their return was motivated by the 5th Pan-African Congress which took place in Manchester, England, in 1945. They returned determined to organise and lead their people in a massive struggle against colonialism and imperialism. The same upsurge and the dominant wish to return to Africa was also evident in the French-speaking African colonies.

I went to Paris in 1946 and spent a hectic five days in consultation with the then French African leaders who were Members or Deputies of the French National Assembly. I met Senghor of Senegal, Houphouet-Boigny of Ivory Coast, Apithy of Dahomey, Coulibali of

Mali—in fact I met all the twelve outstanding Deputies who were then representing French Africa in the National Assembly. We all agreed on one objective: that Africa must be free. How and when we could not forecast.

In spite of the national enthusiasm everywhere, there was no planning and directing centre to co-ordinate these movements for all Africa. Centres of the liberation struggle were set up in each territory with very little effective co-ordination between them. The Rassemblement Démocratique Africain was in process of bringing French-speaking Africa together. Among the English colonial territories there was a dearth of any unified political organisation. Thus the struggle for colonial freedom in Africa was fragmented and was confined to individual colonies. The domestic factor in the upsurge of the national liberation movement in Africa is significant in its relation to later development of the African liberation movement as a whole.

It is true to say that during the period 1945 to 1958 the African Revolution had no strategy. It had no programme. While each territory was fighting its own battle and taking little more than academic interest in events in other African territories, the colonialist powers were maintaining effective co-ordination and liaison among themselves. For instance, the armed forces for the maintenance of law and order throughout the British West African colonies were based in Accra, with regiments in each British colony. The era of collective imperialism and neo-colonialism had begun. It was a time when there was complete lack of understanding of the struggle against colonialism by some African leaders. The cramping circumstances imposed by the colonial rule everywhere and the general obstruction of contacts between leaders of the various nations of the liberation movement were responsible for the political chaos. The free states of Africa could not give the much needed unified guidance to the struggle of African freedom, independence and unity.

The break-through came in 1957. Ghana achieved her independence and declared to the whole world that the independence of Ghana was meaningless unless it was linked up with the total liberation of the African continent. As long as one square inch of African soil was under colonial or foreign rule, Africa was not free or secure. The independence of Ghana was the first crack in the seemingly impregnable armour of imperialism in Africa. It created and furnished the bridgehead for organised assaults upon colonialism in Africa.

A year after Ghana's independence I called the first ever Conference of Independent African States. It was held in Accra from 15 to 22 April 1958. All the Heads of State of the independent states in Africa at that time—eight in all—attended. Today the independent states number 36, and there are others waiting to be free as the liberation struggle of the African freedom fighters unfolds itself. The countries which attended the Conference in 1958 were Morocco, Tunisia, Libya, Egypt, Sudan, Ethiopia, Liberia and Ghana.

The Conference of Independent African States of 1958 was a tremendous success. Unanimously the eight African States adopted resolutions which defined a new positive approach to the African problem and the colonial question. It put forward an all-African approach to the problem of fighting colonialism in all its forms. It blazed a new path in Africa for African affairs and world politics. It even declared itself 'the vanguard of the complete emancipation of Africa'. The continental struggle for Africa's total liberation from imperialism and neo-colonialism had begun.

Barely six weeks after the Accra Conference, I toured all the countries which had participated in the Conference. By the time I returned to Accra from this tour, the foundations for united and concerted action by the independent African States had been laid.

In the same year, from 5 to 13 December, I invited freedom movements and political parties in Africa to a conference in Accra. Delegates came from British, French, Belgian, Portuguese and Spanish colonial territories. This was the first All-African Peoples' Conference. What I had in mind was to give the forces of the liberation movement the strategy to move into action and the tactics for that strategy. It was to put meat on the bones of the resolutions of the Conference of the African Heads of State. It was to sound the clarion call for the advance and final assault on imperialism and the complete eradication of colonial oppression in Africa. Freedom fighters came from all over the continent, and those who were then unknown are now the leaders, presidents and prime ministers of the colonised territory they represented. My object again was to infuse into the African Revolution new spirit and a new dynamism; and to create these where they were lacking.

Jomo Kenyatta, even though in prison, was invited: naturally he could not attend. And so, after the Conference, Tom Mboya, Oginga-Odinga and Koinange returned to Kenya; Nyerere to Tanganyika; Karume to Zanzibar; Banda to Nyasaland; Kaunda and Nkumbula to Northern Rhodesia; Joshua Nkomo to Southern Rhodesia; Lumumba and others to the Congo, Angola, Portuguese and Spanish Guinea and Cape Verde Islands. The battle against imperialism and neo-colonialism was joined. The African Revolution had started in earnest. In two years, from 1958 to 1960, the number of independent

African States rose from 8 to 15. By 1965 this figure had risen to 36, and the struggle of the freedom fighters was more than intensified. It now remains for a continental Union Government of Africa to seal for ever the fate and doom of imperialism and colonialism in Africa.

While it is true that none of us in the independent African States can survive for long without the protection afforded by the central direction of our combined political, military and economic resources under a continental Union Government, the Congo, for historical reasons and owing to certain geographical factors, is more vulnerable than most of us. The Congo's vast economic resources and the insatiable avidity of the imperialists makes this so. Because of this, it must be stated also that the Congo provides fertile ground for the operation of the cold war and of limited wars.

Although the struggle for national independence in the Congo has yet to be won, I see no alternative for the future of the Congo, except in the arms of a united Africa within the framework of a continental Union Government. Until this is achieved, the dangers facing the Congo will not only multiply but will be complicated by many factors which will involve the whole of Africa.

It may be asked why I have taken it upon myself to write about a sister African State. The reasons are straightforward. The history of independent Congo has been unusual right from the achievement of independence in 1960. It was faced with unusual trials and temptations, and the independent African States (including Ghana) were called upon to give it much needed assistance. Furthermore, the events that have taken place in the Congo since its independence constitute a turning-point in the history of Africa. If we allow the independence of the Congo to be compromised in any way by the imperialists and neo-colonialists, the whole of Africa will be exposed to grave risk.

There must also be an African solution to the crisis in Rhodesia to bring an end to the oppression of its people. Moreover, the continuance of minority rule in this strategically important area of Africa, as in the Congo, represents an obstacle which must be overcome swiftly if the forward march of the African revolutionary struggle is to maintain its increasing momentum.

The troubles of the Congo are therefore our troubles, and her struggles are those of the independent states of Africa. I make no apology in examining critically, for all to see, the influences that have been at work in the Congo, influences which are designed to subvert and imperil its freedom and independence.

1 Before Independence

In the year 1482, three small Portuguese ships set out from Elmina in Ghana. Their mission was to find a route round Africa which would outflank the Arab States which controlled North Africa. The Portuguese hoped to reach the legendary kingdom of that supposed great African Christian monarch, Prester John. This fleet, commanded by Diogo Cam, never rounded the tip of Africa but it did discover the ancient kingdom of the Congo, and the long history of European intervention in Central Africa had begun.

The Portuguese were already established in a number of forts along the African West Coast, of which the Fort of St George at Elmina (1481), from which the expedition started, was the largest and best equipped. The African States of this coast and hinterland were well organised politically, militarily and economically. They controlled the produce of the interior and sold it on their own terms. They did not need to enter any military or economic alliance with the Portuguese, who were tolerated solely as traders.

In the Congo, however, it was different. The King of the Congo, the Mani Congo, was in reality only a feudal overlord and he was engaged, as had been the Portuguese monarchy eighty years before, in a life and death struggle with his nominal vassals. The Portuguese therefore were welcomed by the Mani Congo as potential allies. The Portuguese on their side saw the opportunity of establishing a Christian State as a bastion against Islamic intrusion and as a link with the Kingdom of Prester John. The first consignment of technical aid, consisting of priests and skilled craftsmen with the tools of their trade and a variety of religious objects, arrived in 1490.

From then onwards there was a small but steady flow of European technicians, who included, in 1492, two German printers. Considering that printing had been established in England only fifteen years before and had not yet been established in Spain, the provision of printers is a remarkable tribute to the level of civilisation reached in the Congo. The Portuguese, with the support of the Mani Congo, set out on a systematic policy of westernisation in the Congo. At this point emerged the contradiction that has haunted European and African relations ever since.

The Congolese wanted to secure, through trade with Europe, foreign exchange in the form of gold and silver, capital equipment like merchant ships and printing presses, and above all European specialists in medicine, teaching, shipbuilding and navigation. The Portuguese on the other hand were determined to exploit the economic superiority which they had derived from their specialised naval knowledge, their large merchant fleet and their command of the sea. This command of the sea involved alliances with those who controlled the approaches to the Congo and beyond. Such an alliance was fatal to any real partnership between the Congo and Portugal. The centre of Portuguese naval power in the Central and South Atlantic was the island of São Tome, originally colonised as a Portuguese penal settlement in the very year the first group of priests and technicians were sent to the Congo. It was ruled by a Lord Proprietor, whose goodwill the Portuguese had to maintain at all costs.

The Lord Proprietor of São Tome had one overriding interest— the slave trade. Once Portugal began to develop Brazil she became herself dependent on the slaves sold through the São Tome slaving organisations.

The development of all this was in the future. At the time, it appeared on paper that Portugal and the Congo treated each other as equal states. The Mani Congo, who ascended the Ivory Throne in 1506, became a Christian as part of a concerted policy of westernisation. Much of the correspondence of this remarkable king, Dom Affonso, with the Kings of Portugal has survived and it is clear that he looked on the Portuguese alliance as the most effective method of modernising his kingdom. Before we condemn his lack of realism in this regard, it is necessary to remember that there are African rulers today who are pursuing a similar policy. What subsequently happened in the Congo should be an object lesson to them.

In much the same way as modern colonialist powers provided their colonial territories with model constitutions, so King Manoel of Portugal provided a constitution for the Congo. This famous document, known as the Regimento of 1512, can perhaps be described as the first essay in neo-colonialism. It provided that the Portuguese should help the King of the Congo in organising his kingdom. The Portuguese were to introduce a system of European law and to train the Congolese Army in their methods of warfare. They were to teach the royal court the correct etiquette to observe and they were to build churches and to provide missionaries. In return for this the Congo would fill the Portuguese ships with valuable cargo. In his letter of instruction to the Ambassador who was to present the Regimento, the King of Portugal wrote:

This expedition has cost us much; it would be unreasonable to send it home with empty hands. Although our principal wish is to serve God and the pleasure of the King of the Congo, none the less you will make him understand, as though speaking in our name, what he should do to fill the ships, whether with slaves or copper or ivory.

The mention of copper is interesting as showing that the products of the Zambia and Katanga copper belt were already well known. At this time, surviving records show that Katanga copper was also being marketed on the East Coast, though the main African trade in the metal was internal. Dom Affonso accepted the Regimento and provided the Portuguese with 320 slaves. Thus began an unequal trade between the Congo and the West. The evil effect of this trade was not immediately apparent and the Kingdom of the Congo was at first able to treat other European nations on equal terms. In 1513 a mission from the Mani Congo led by his son, who had been baptised Dom Henrique, visited the Pope, travelling overland from Portugal and carrying with them gifts of ivory, rare skins and the fine woven raffia textiles then manufactured in the Congo. Dom Henrique, who was at this time 18 years old, was able to address the Pope in Latin and five years later, on the formal proposal of four Cardinals, he was elevated to the rank of Bishop of the Congo.

In the end Dom Affonso was prepared to sacrifice all Portuguese trade if he could suppress slaving. In 1526 he wrote to the King of Portugal:

We cannot reckon how great the damage is, since the above mentioned merchants daily seize our subjects, sons of the land and sons of our noblemen and vassals and our relatives. . . . Thieves and men of evil conscience take them because they wish to possess the things and wares of this Kingdom. . . . They grab them and cause them to be sold: and so great, Sir, is their corruption and licentiousness that our country is being utterly depopulated. And to avoid (them), we need from (your) Kingdoms no other than priests and people to teach in schools, and no other goods but wine and flour for the holy sacrament: that is why we beg of Your Highness to help and assist us in this matter, commanding your factors that they should send here neither merchants nor wares, because it is our will that in these kingdoms (of Congo) there should not be any trade in slaves nor market for slaves.

But by then his power had been undermined. The traders of São Tome went over his head to his nominal vassals from whom they procured the slaves, even fomenting civil wars in which Portuguese subjects served on both sides. Thus whichever way the war went, an ample supply of captives was assured for sale to São Tome and Brazil.

With Dom Affonso's death the Congo Kingdom broke up. Portuguese troops, acting under the terms of the alliance, drove out invaders in 1570 and the Mani Congo of the time acknowledged Portugal as the protecting power. The ancient Congo capital of São Salvador was raised to the rank of city and was made the seat of the Bishop of the diocese of the Congo and Angola. But by 1700 the Bishops had departed, its twelve churches were in ruins and São Salvador was a deserted city. The Portuguese turned their attention to the area farther south, the Portuguese colony now known as Angola.

The first attempt to construct an African State by an African leader in alliance with a European power had foundered in anarchy and confusion.

In the last official Handbook of the Congo published by the Belgian Government in 1959, the results of western slave trading are thus described:

By the end of the 17th century the slave trade, which had started as a Portuguese monopoly, had become a gigantic international undertaking. The places where slaves were kept became more and more numerous and profitable. The French appeared in their turn, drove the Portuguese away from the port of Cabinda and installed their slave markets chiefly beyond the north bank of the river toward Loango and Malemba, while the English traded in the estuary.

In the course of a single year, in 1778, 104,000 slaves had been exported from Africa; one third of them came from the Congo and Angola.

During the nineteenth century there began what is often described as 'the age of African exploration'. The term is misleading. The travels of great nineteenth-century European 'explorers' in Africa followed long-established lines of communication which had been in use by African peoples for hundreds of years. There was a network of well-defined trails from the Katanga copper mines along which the African-mined and smelted copper was distributed throughout Africa.

In 1877 one of these 'explorers', the United States journalist Henry Morton Stanley, arrived at Boma at the mouth of the Congo, having started from Zanzibar and in his journeying traced the course of the river from source to mouth. Stanley was typical of a class of nineteenth-century freebooters, very similar in outlook to the mercenaries who are operating in the Congo today. He was born in very poor circumstances in England, and his real name was John Rowlands. He worked his way across the Atlantic and acquired a wealthy American benefactor whose name he adopted. In the United States Civil War he served with the Confederate Army of the South. He was taken prisoner and in return for his freedom agreed to fight for the North. Later he served with various United States expeditions against the Red Indian people and then adopted the profession of journalist explorer. He had newspaper assignments in Tibet, the Caucasus and Ethiopia. He was asked by the *New York Herald* to go out to Africa to find the missing missionary David Livingstone. This he did in 1871 and stayed on in Africa. It was on behalf of his newspaper that he crossed the continent.

Stanley at once appreciated the possibilities of European exploitation of the Congo. 'I could prove to you', he wrote to the London *Daily Telegraph*, 'that the Power possessing the Congo . . . would absorb to itself the trade of the whole enormous basin behind. The river is and will be the grand highway to commerce to West Africa.'

Stanley's discovery was just what King Leopold II of Belgium was looking for. Some time earlier he had written:

Since history teaches that colonies are useful, that they play a great part in that which makes up the power and prosperity of States, let us strive to get one in our turn. Before pronouncing in favour of this or that system let us see where there are unoccupied lands . . . where are to be found peoples to civilise, to lead to progress in every sense, meanwhile assuring ourselves new revenues, to our middle classes the employment which they seek, to our army a little activity, and to Belgium as a whole the opportunity to prove to the world that it also is an imperial people capable of dominating and enlightening others.

He had already founded, as a cover for his colonialist ambitions, an international African Association and Stanley was employed by him to return to the Congo and make treaties with the local rulers as a preliminary to its take-over by the Belgian King.

Leopold's plan was to run the Congo as a private domain, uncontrolled by even the Belgian Government, and to exploit it on an international scale. He succeeded because the powers of Europe were unwilling to see any other among them control the Congo.

The British at one time hoped to establish a type of neo-colonialist state working through Portugal and Leopold's organisation. A treaty between Britain and Portugal handing over the Congo to Portugal had been signed in 1884. There was so much opposition from other powers excluded from this arrangement that finally the whole issue was referred to the Berlin Conference which sat from November 1884 to February 1885. At this Conference a compromise was worked out awarding the Congo to Leopold in a personal capacity but providing that it should be open to the trade of all those participating in the Berlin Conference. Thus the monarch of a small European State was made the absolute ruler over a territory equal to the area of Europe, excluding Russia. Leopold had never visited the Congo and was never to do so. Nevertheless, he was its sole lawmaker and the owner of all its land.

The Belgians declared that their first objective on entering the Congo was to suppress the slave trade. Up to the time of the Belgian occupation, some fifteen million Congolese had been shipped out by the western route alone. Ten million of them had died en route as a result of bad treatment.

In fact, the object of Leopold II of Belgium was not to suppress slavery, but to change its nature. His object was to make slavery more profitable by employing the slave in the Congo and thus avoid the difficulties caused by the international abolition of the trade in its old-fashioned form. That he was able to do this was due to the divisons between the Congolese people and the imperial rivalry between the European powers.

In a pamphlet *The Crime of the Congo* published in 1910 Sir Arthur Conan Doyle analysed the effects of Leopold's policy and denounced the European nations who refused to intervene.

He quoted extensively from Stanley's account of the Congo as he had found it in 1877 and contrasted it with its condition in 1910. He wrote:

One cannot let these extracts pass without noting that Bolobo, the first place named by Stanley, has sunk in population from 40,000 to 7,000; that Irebu, called by Stanley the populous Venice of the Congo, had in 1903 a population of fifty; that the natives who used to follow Stanley, beseeching him to trade, now, according to Consul Casement, fly into the bush at the approach of a steamer, and that the unselfish sentiment of King Leopold II has developed into dividends of 300 per cent per annum. Such is the difference between Stanley's anticipation and the actual fulfilment.

Describing Leopold's method of rule, Conan Doyle continued:

Having claimed, as I have shown, the whole of the land, and therefore the whole of its products, the State—that is, the King— proceeded to construct a system by which these products could be gathered most rapidly and at least cost. The essence of this system was that the people who had been dispossessed (ironically called 'citizens') were to be forced to gather, for the profit of the State, those very products which had been taken from them. This was to be effected by two means; the one, taxation, by which an arbitrary amount, ever growing larger until it consumed almost their whole lives in the gathering, should be claimed for nothing. The other, so called barter, by which the natives were paid for the stuff exactly what the State chose to give, and in the form the State chose to give it, there being no competition allowed from any other purchaser. This remuneration, ridiculous in value, took the most absurd shape, the natives being compelled to take it, whatever the amount, and however little they might desire it . . .

By this system some two thousand white agents were scattered over the Free State to collect the produce. The whites were placed in ones and twos in the more central points, and each was given a tract of country containing a certain number of villages. By the help of the inmates he was to gather the rubber, which was the most valuable asset. These whites, many of whom were men of low morale before they left Europe, were wretchedly paid, the scale running from 150 to 300 francs a month. This pay they might supplement by a commission or bonus on the amount of rubber collected. If their returns were large it meant increased pay, official praise, a more speedy return to Europe and a better chance of promotion. If, on the other hand, the returns were small it meant poverty, harsh reproof and degradation. No system could be devised by which a body of men could be so driven to attain results at any cost. It is not to the absolute discredit of Belgians that such an existence should have demoralised them, and, indeed, there were other nationalities besides Belgians in the ranks of the agents. I doubt if Englishmen, Americans or Germans could have escaped the same result had they been exposed in a tropical country to similar temptations.

And now, the two thousand agents being in place and eager to enforce the collection of rubber upon very unwilling natives, how did the system intend that they should set about it? The method was as efficient as it was absolutely diabolical. Each agent was given control over a certain number of savages drawn from the wild tribes but armed with firearms. One or more of these was placed in each village to ensure that the villagers should do their task. These are the men who are called 'Capitas', or head-men in the accounts, and who are the actual, though not moral, perpetrators of so many horrible deeds. Imagine the nightmare which lay upon each village while this barbarian squatted in the midst of it. Day or night they could never get away from him. He called for palm wine. He called for women. He beat them, mutilated them and shot them down at his pleasure. He enforced public incest in order to amuse himself by the sight. Sometimes they plucked up spirit and killed him. The Belgian Commission records that 142 Capitas had been killed in seven months in a single district. Then came the punitive expedition, and the destruction of the whole community. The more terror the Capita inspired, the more useful he was, the more eagerly the villagers obeyed him, and the more rubber yielded its commission to the agent. When the amount fell off, then the Capita was himself made to feel some of those physical pains which he had inflicted upon others. Often the white agent far exceeded in cruelty the barbarian who carried out his commissions. Often, too, the white man pushed the black aside, and acted himself as torturer and executioner.

The Report of Roger Casement, British Consul in the Congo, published in 1904, provides further information about the nature of Leopold's rule in the Congo.

. . . Perhaps the most striking change observed during my journey into the interior was the great reduction observable everywhere in native life. Communities I had formerly known as large and flourishing centres of population are today entirely gone, or now exist in such diminished numbers as to be no longer recognisable. The southern shores of Stanley Pool had formerly a population of fully 5,000 Batekas. These people some twelve years ago decided to abandon their homes, and in one night the great majority of them crossed over into French territory. Where formerly had stretched these populous native African villages, I saw today only a few scattered European houses.

Questioning some Congolese about the rubber trade, they told him they had to produce twenty baskets of rubber four times a month:

We got no pay. We got nothing . . . It used to take ten days to get the twenty baskets of rubber. We were always in the forest, and then when we were late we were killed. We had to go further and further into the forest to find the rubber vines, to go without food, and our women had to give up cultivating the fields and gardens. Then we starved. Wild beasts—the leopards—killed some of us when we were working away in the forest, and others got lost or died from exposure and starvation, and we begged the white man to leave us alone, saying we would get no more rubber, but the white men and their soldiers said, 'Go! You are only beasts yourselves; you are nyama (meat).' We tried, always going further into the forest, and when we failed and our rubber was short the soldiers came up our towns and shot us. Many were shot; some had their ears cut off . . . We fled because we could not endure the things done to us.

Professor Ritchie Calder in his book *The Agony of the Congo* has estimated that in the twenty-three years of Leopold's personal rule five to eight million Congolese had been killed by his security forces and agents engaged in the collection of rubber and ivory. When it is remembered that in 1960, when the Congo became independent, its population was around thirteen million, the extent of Leopold's tyranny and inhumanity can be realised. E. D. Morel in his famous book *Red Rubber, the Story of the Rubber Slave Trade of the Congo*, first published in 1906, has described in detail with innumerable quotations from actual observers the depopulation and the devastation of the country. It was not only that the inhabitants were massacred wholesale. Those who survived were often mutilated. It was a common practice to cut off a hand or a foot.

Public outcry against Leopold's personal rule reached such a height that by 1908 the Belgian Government had to take over the Congo, the state compensating the King handsomely for the loss that he had thus sustained. Before however relinquishing control Leopold had parcelled up the country into areas to be exploited by various international concerns.

Leopold was primarily a financier who employed any capital that came to hand and used any agent, whatever his nationality. It was thus that the Southern Rhodesian company, Tanganyika Concessions Ltd., came to be so closely concerned with investment in the Congo. The 'Tanganyika Concession' from which it takes its name was the transport concession which Rhodes wished to obtain on Lake Tanganyika for his proposed Cape to Cairo railway. Otherwise it has never had any connection with Tanganyika but was formed solely to exploit the mineral wealth of Northern Rhodesia and Katanga. The company established in 1899 was financed from Britain and one of Rhodes's associates, Sir Robert Williams, was its Chairman and Managing Director. On the formation of the Union Minière he became its Vice-President and Technical Manager. In order to export the Katanga copper he founded another English company, the Benguela Railway Company, to link Katanga with Atlantic ports of Portuguese Angola.

It was to consolidate these and other international interests that in 1906 Leopold set up the three great international companies which have dominated the Congo ever since.

These three great enterprises were known as 'the companies of 1906'. They were the Compagnie du Chemin de Fer du Bas-Congo (the BCK); the Société Internationale Forestière et Minière du Congo (Forminière); and L'Union Minière du Haut-Katanga.

The Belgian Government régime which succeeded that of Leopold, even if it wished to do so, could have done little to restore the devastation of the country or repair the exploitation of the preceding four hundred years. Actually Belgium had neither the will nor the means to redress the evil that had been done. Leopold's soldiers were recruited in the official Belgian Congolese Army, the 'force publique'. The same administrators remained in power and the same system continued, the worst abuses only being suppressed.

The First World War prevented further European criticism of Belgian policy. Belgium had been the victim of unprovoked aggression by Imperial Germany, and the Allied powers who won the war turned their attack on the German colonies which, as Conan Doyle had pointed out, were at least better administered than the Congo. Nevertheless this did not prevent Belgium being awarded a slice of former German colonial territory, the present states of Rwanda and Burundi. In the inter-war years the Congo was developed as a source of raw materials, copper and diamonds in particular. The need to industrialise and to employ African skilled labour made it impossible to continue repression in its old form. Instead the Belgians imposed a paternalist régime beneath the surface of which many of the old evils continued.

The Belgian system of colonial government differed in several ways from that of the British and French. A Governor-General was appointed, responsible to the Belgian Parliament, but he had no Legislative Council or Assembly to check his power, and no Congolese sat in the Belgian Parliament. Colonial law was made in Belgium by the King, acting on the advice of a minister for colonial affairs and a colonial council. Nobody in the Congo, white or black, could vote, and the Congolese had few, if any, civil rights. The essence of the Belgian colonial system, as later developed, was to buy off any discontent by giving a certain amount of material comfort. The Congo became a model colony.

Belgian district commissioners ruled their various localities in the same authoritarian manner as the Governor-General in Leopoldville. The Roman Catholic Church and big business were the other, no less powerful, rulers of the Congo. The Belgian Government, in fact, shared considerably in the investment holdings of the interlocking combines which monopolised the Congo's economy, often to the extent of as much as fifty per cent.

In 1957 the first elections, carefully controlled and limited municipal elections, were held in the Congo. They were a belated attempt by the Belgians to prevent rising national feeling from expressing itself in violence. By then the first Congolese parties demanding political liberty had already been formed. In 1958 several of these parties published programmes calling for independence and in the following year, after serious trouble in Leopoldville, the Belgian Government was compelled to face squarely the new situation. A Round Table Conference met in Brussels early in 1960 and passed resolutions, later approved by the Belgian Parliament, fixing the date of independence for 30 June 1960.

Prior to the assumption of independence by the Congo I sent two separate missions with the object of making known to the Belgian authorities my government's desire that progress to independence in the Congo should be orderly and peaceful, and that the Ghana Government was willing to do everything in its power to assist.

It will therefore be seen that Ghana's interest in the Congo's success and her transition to independence is of long standing.

If the political domination of the Congo by the Belgian Government between 1908 and 1960 was complete and the Congolese deprived of political experience, the economic stranglehold exercised by foreign firms was no less damaging to the interests of the Congolese people.

It was after 1908 that the great mining companies began to develop their power and influence. The Union Minière du Haut-Katanga (founded in 1906) produced its first ton of copper in 1911. Seventeen years later, in 1928, its copper output had reached seven per cent of world production. In 1907 diamonds were discovered in Kasai by a prospector of Forminière (Société International Forestière et Minière). By 1929 the Congo was the second largest producer of diamonds in the world, the largest being, of course, South Africa. Mineral products had by then taken the place of rubber as the mainstay of the Congo economy.

Today, the Congo produces sixty per cent of the world's output of cobalt, eight per cent of copper and four per cent of zinc. Among the most valuable commodities mined in the Congo are iron ore, coal, tin, uranium, radium, germanium, manganese, cadmium, gold and silver. There is hardly a country in Africa, Asia or Latin America which has such rich and varied mineral resources. Agricultural resources are no less great, and there are tremendous reserves of water power which can be used for the production of power and electricity.

Under Belgian rule, the Congo's wealth was used to serve the interests of foreign monopolists. With independence, the position remains much the same. Tanganyika Concessions, Société Générale de Belgique, L'Union Minière du Haut-Katanga, to name only a few, still make great profits and exert pressures on the young Republic which serve the interests not of the Congolese people but of foreign investors. The book *Trusts in the Congo*, published in Brussels in 1961, gives the net profit of the Union Minière between 1950 and 1959 as 31 billion Belgian francs. The shareholders of the corporation pocketed 30·5 million dollars in 1961 alone, reckoned to be a bad year for the firm because of the fighting in Katanga.

The comparatively recent entry of American big-business interests into the Congo has further strengthened the neo-colonialist hold on the country. American interests are particularly strong in Forminière, which besides participating in the mining of gold and silver owns vast plantations of cotton, oil-bearing palms, cocoa and rubber trees, as well as cattle stations and farms, forests, sawmills and even shops. When it is remembered also that in 1950 the American 'International Basic Economy Corporation' bought up 600,000 shares of Tanganyika Concessions it will be realised that this American firm created by the Rockefeller family group became a partner in the profits of the Union Minière.

Seen in the light of the vast complicated web of foreign economic interests in the Congo, the disastrous years since independence are not difficult to explain. The richer the natural resources of a country, the more determined the neo-colonialists to tighten, and extend if possible, their hold over it. Under the guise of 'aid', or in some cases, as in the Congo, by encouraging political disunity, they have sought to perpetuate the colonial-type economy in which Africa remains the great provider of primary materials for the industries of the metropolitan and other industrial powers.

Before independence, Belgian and British business interests predominated in the Congo and American capital was not able to penetrate very far. This explains to some extent the initial enthusiasm of the foreign business world for an independent Congo where it was hoped free competition would benefit private enterprise, and the subsequent disillusionment when Lumumba made it clear that he did not intend to become the puppet of any foreign interests.

But to leave for a moment the tangled economic situation in the Congo on the eve of independence and to turn to the way in which national sovereignty was achieved is to see that in this respect also the Congo was unique. No other country except the French colonies of Africa attained its independence so quickly, or was subjected to such suffering once independence had been achieved.

The revolt towards colonial freedom had begun in rather an unusual way through the formation of what may be described as Old Boys' Clubs. As political associations in the Congo were illegal under the Belgian colonial régime, the handful of educated *élites* made provision for their welfare through the ADEPES (Association des Anciens Elèves des Pères de Scheut) which followed a rather tranquil course from 1925. The activities of this association were fostered by other organisations, notably the Marist Brothers (UNELMA), the Christian Schools (ASAMEF), the school for the Jesuit Fathers, the UNISCO (l'Union des Intérêts Sociaux Congolais), whose members were mainly secondary school pupils. These bodies, which formed the circles of *évolués*, were devoted primarily to the study of religious and social questions, and the Belgian authorities and the Church naturally watched their development with great admiration. The only political organisations which flourished in the Congo were 'tribal' associations that occasionally emerged in the rural areas.

Thus for a long time 'independence' was a new word to the Congolese people, for no nationalists dared to use it in public. As one writer put it, 'Independence was released as a bullet into the brittle silence of Congo politics by a Belgian professor, Dr A. A. J. van Bilson', a liberal of the Christian Democratic wing of the Catholic Party in Brussels. Criticising Belgium, at first cautiously and later boldly, for allowing the Congo to be governed with virtually no parliamentary control, he attacked the unbalanced growth of agriculture and industry and the dismal state of Congolese social development. Congolese leaders were quick to seize this all-important opportunity to voice their grievances.

Independence for the Congo was, however, more than a national affair. It was part of the world ideological struggle. But it was more particularly an African affair from the colonial standpoint. To Africans everywhere the movement was part of the general drive towards freedom from colonial domination on the African continent. I have often said 'the independence of Ghana is meaningless unless it is linked up with the total liberation of Africa'. This in part explains why Ghana became a vigorous partner of the Congolese cause, especially at the time of their national crisis.

Ghana-Congo solidarity began with the All-African Peoples' Conference held at Accra in December 1958. Among the hundreds of delegates who attended the Conference were Patrice Lumumba, who became the President of the MNC (Congolese National Movement), and two associates of his party. It was at this memorable Conference that the Congolese nationalists had their baptism of fire as apostles of the impending struggle for Africa's liberation.

On returning home to Leopoldville, a mass meeting was convened on 3 January 1959 at which Lumumba with fiery oratory announced the objectives of immediate and total independence for his country. No doubt the new year was accompanied by new resolutions. Tension was already mounting in the Congolese capital. On 4 January some 30,000 riotous demonstrators, mainly unemployed workers, marched through the streets of Leopoldville and publicly demanded independence. The spontaneity of the event gave the impression that the whole nation had risen in concerted action.

Though certain political leaders, particularly those of the influential ABAKO party, had been arrested, it became abundantly clear that the Belgian colonial administration could no longer placate the rapidly growing political discontent. The All-African Peoples' Conference had made an immediate and dramatic impact on the Congo political scene. And there was no turning back.

Some diehard imperialists, after their usual fashion, sought to explain the riots in Leopoldville in terms of communist influence. In particular, a Belgian paternalist, Edward Mendiaux, went to the length of writing a book called *Moscow, Accra and the Congo*. Glorifying Belgian paternalism in the Congo as 'the greatest thing since Adam', and condemning the African personality as an instrument of international communism, he proudly asserted that 'in 50 years, Belgium has radically transformed the savage Congo into a modern state'. Students of colonial history are familiar with the outworn practice of branding all nationalist movements as communist-inspired. Even the Congo, which had been looked upon by the Belgians as a model colony in Africa, could not escape this label.

The year 1959 was an important year in the struggle for freedom in the Congo. Riots followed unrest in several parts of the country and whenever the colonial administration endeavoured to save the situation, the repressive measures were disproportionately brutal. In a declaration handed to the Press Agencies for communication to the United Nations, the Belgian Senate and King Baudouin, the Committee of the National Liberation Front, ABAKO, alleged that the Belgian Government, continuing its repressive measures, had threatened and forced the natives of the hinterland to sign the Belgian Ministerial Declaration of 13 January 1959. Soldiers, it was said, had occupied the whole of the Bakongo and Kwango districts and had made several indiscriminate arrests. Among the arrested were Chief Bahunhu, 'the uncontested owner of Leopoldville lands', formerly called Mpumbu, and Mr Gonda Samuel, a leader of the ABAKO African Democratic Party. Besides the arrests, searches had been made resulting in the seizure of vehicles and office materials belonging to the party, under the pretext of non-payment of taxes.

Such was the gravity of the situation that nationalist students of the Congo found it expedient to proceed to Ghana in September 1959 to mobilise public support for their just cause. A petition testifying the brutalities perpetrated by the Belgians in the Congo was presented to the Ghana Ministry of Foreign Affairs on 28 September, imploring me to use my good offices to communicate the contents to all independent African States, the Afro-Asian Movement and all world organisations sympathetic to their cause, urging immediate action:

1 To demand from the UNO an international commission to investigate the events in Leopoldville on 4 January 1959 and their consequences and further to examine the charges preferred by the Belgian Government against the ABAKO party;
2 To protest against the political activities of the Belgian Government on 13 January 1959 and the policy unilaterally decided upon by Belgium with the intention of creating a Belgium-Congo community contrary to the wishes of the Congolese people.
3 To protest against the proposed elections of 5 December 1959, forced upon the people for the purpose of implementing

the Belgian policy which would lead to the formation of a Belgian-Congolese community.

4 To send observers to the Congo in case the Belgian Government were to maintain and impose their will on the conduct of the December elections.

The long and explicitly written petition represented the sentiments of the Congolese *élite*, particularly of the ABAKO party, which at this time was the most important mouthpiece of the freedom fighters.

Ghana's support for the Congo took a new turn with the consolidation of the new and more dynamic party, the MNC (Congolese National Movement) led by Patrice Lumumba. The MNC from the end of 1958 became the forerunner of the smaller nationalist groups and parties. Its aims, in brief, were 'to prepare the masses and *élite* to take control of public affairs; to speed up the process of democratization; to implement the Declaration of Human Rights, and by peaceful negotiation, to do everything possible to free the Congo from colonialism and imperialism'.

The ABAKO party or the Association des Bakongo pour l'Unification, l'Expansion et la Défense de la Kilonga was led by Mr Joseph Kasavubu. Formed in 1950 by Edmond Nzeza-Landu, it was originally a purely cultural society which gained adherents partly because of the fear that the Bakongo tribe of the Lower Congo would be swamped by the influx of other tribes coming into the industrially booming Leopoldville and partly because of its dynamic leadership. The Bakongo had been averse to Belgian rule and, still conscious of their own identity, they had set up tribal and religious movements which sought to preserve their culture. Other tribal groups which maintained their own political interests were the Bangala of the Equatorial Province, the Balubas of Kasai and Katanga, the Balunda, Beyele and others.

Like the CPP of Ghana, Lumumba's MNC was the first Congolese political organisation to recognise the need for a national leader and a national movement in accordance with the principles of Pan-Africanism. Perhaps Patrice Lumumba's own peculiar advantage in organising a national movement was the fact that he hailed from a relatively unimportant tribe, the Batelela, a sub-group of the Mongo tribe which has affiliations in three of Congo's six provinces. From his boyhood he had been brought up by his Christian parents among the *évolués* of Stanleyville and was never under the influence of tribal affinities, nor tied down by any particular interest of a tribal character.

During the turbulent year of 1959, Patrice Lumumba, whose Pan-Africanist views had won the admiration of many Ghanaians, maintained close and continuous contact with me. In a dispatch dated 9 October 1959 he wrote through our Foreign Ministry, 'May I please ask the Prime Minister to give me the necessary guide in respect of the plan to follow in our struggle? His experience means a lot to us.' He went on to ask for copies of my political speeches for publication in the influential Congolese journal *Independence*.

Two main factors explain his request. The kind of divisions which beset political parties in the Congo soon after the Brussels Conference were not new to Ghana. The trends of national movements in both countries, though fundamentally different in points of detail, had certain basic characteristics in common; their struggle for national independence was to some extent the struggle between nationalism and tribalism; more explicitly, between a unitary system of government and federation. The situation which faced the Congo on the eve of independence did not differ profoundly from that which threatened Ghana's independence at the period of the ascendancy of the National Liberation Movement of Ashanti, the Togoland Congress, the Anlo Youth Association, the Northern People's Party and the Moslem Association, all of which were designed to destroy the CPP movement. As in Ghana, I was convinced that the Congo needed a strong unitary form of government. Events in the Congo since independence have only strengthened this conviction.

In the following chapters I hope, by publishing diplomatic documents and other material, to portray something of the real pressures behind the events which led to chaos in that vitally important region of our continent. An African solution to the problem of the Congo was, and still remains, the only hope for bringing about a lasting peace. Recent events in the Congo emphatically support this view.

2 Independence and the Intervention of the United Nations

On 10 May 1960 the Belgian Senate passed *La Loi Fondamentale sur les Structures de Congo*, which was signed by King Baudouin the following day. This Basic Law, as I will refer to it from now on, provided for the constitution of the new Republic of the Congo. There was to be a Head of State and 'Government directed by a Prime Minister', and a Parliament consisting of a Chamber of Representatives and a Senate. In each Province there was to be a Provincial Government directed by a President and a Provincial Assembly.

In the 259 articles of the Basic Law the powers of the various organs of government were clearly stated and provisions laid down for the division of powers between the central and provincial authorities. In view of Katanga's attempted secession, it is worth quoting one of the most important provisions:

Article 6   *The Congo constitutes, within its present boundaries, an indivisible and democratic state.*

Between 11 and 25 May elections were held in the Congo. The results showed a convincing win for Lumumba. His party, the MNC emerged as the strongest party in both the central and provincial elections, with 74 out of the 137 seats in the House of Representatives. The first National Government was formed on 24 June with Lumumba as Prime Minister and Kasavubu Head of State and here it must be noted that this government was approved by the Chamber by 74 votes to one with 5 abstentions. In all, 57 members were absent, including the majority of the members of the MNC (Kalonji Wing), of the Conakat (Tshombe's party) and of the Parti National du

Progrès. The Senate, however, approved the government by 60 votes to 12 with 8 abstentions, Mr Kasavubu being elected as Head of State on a joint vote of the two Houses by 159 votes to 43. The rival candidate was Mr Bolikango.

On 29 June, the day before independence was officially proclaimed, a Belgian-Congolese treaty of friendship was signed which stated that Belgian metropolitan troops stationed in bases in the Congo could only be used in the Congo at the request of the Congolese Minister of Defence. Like Article 6 of the Basic Law, this provision was soon to be violated.

Within two weeks of independence, mutinies and riots had occurred in various parts of the Congo, due initially to the refusal of the Belgian commander of the Congolese Army to consider any improvement in the pay and conditions of the troops. Panic-stricken Europeans began to leave the country as Belgian troops intervened, seizing Matadi and Leopoldville airport. Katanga announced its secession. Then came, on 12 July, the historic appeal by the Congolese Government for UN military assistance against Belgian aggression:

> The Government of the Republic of the Congo requests urgent dispatch by the United Nations of military assistance. This request is justified by the dispatch to the Congo of metropolitan Belgian troops in violation of the treaty of friendship signed between Belgium and the Republic of the Congo on 29 June 1960. Under the terms of that treaty, Belgian troops may only intervene on the express request of the Congolese Government. No such request was ever made by the Government of the Republic of the Congo, and we therefore regard the unsolicited Belgian action as an act of aggression against our country.
>
> The real cause of most of the disturbances can be found in colonialist machinations. We accuse the Belgian Government of having carefully prepared the secession of Katanga with a view to maintaining a hold of our country. The Government, supported by the Congolese people, refuses to accept a *fait accompli* resulting from a conspiracy between Belgian imperialists and a small group of Katanga leaders. The overwhelming majority of the Katanga population is opposed to secession, which means the disguised perpetuation of the colonialist régime. The essential purpose of the requested military aid is to protect the national territory of the Congo against the present external aggression which is a threat to international peace. We strongly stress the extremely urgent need for the despatch of United Nations troops to the Congo.

Joseph Kasavubu,
President of the Republic of the Congo and Supreme Comman-
der of the National Army;
Patrice Lumumba,
Prime Minister and Minister of National Defence.

The President and the Prime Minister of the Congo followed up
their appeal the next day with a telegram to the Secretary-General in
which they stated that they wanted military assistance *not* to restore
the internal situation in the Congo, 'but rather to protect the national
territory against acts of aggression committed by Belgian metropolitan troops'. They warned that if assistance was not sent without
delay they would have to ask the Bandung Treaty powers for help.

At the 873rd meeting of the Security Council held on 13/14 July,
Mr Slim, representing Tunisia, submitted a draft resolution calling on
the Belgian Government to withdraw its troops from the Congo and
authorising the Secretary-General to provide as quickly as possible the
military aid requested of the United Nations. After amendments
suggested by the Soviet representative, Mr Sobolev, condemning 'the
armed aggression by Belgium' and calling on the Belgians to withdraw
their troops from the Congo had been rejected, the Tunisian draft
resolution was put to the vote.

In favour: Argentina, Ceylon, Ecuador, Italy, Poland, Tunisia,
U.S.S.R., U.S.A.
Against: None
Abstaining: China, France, United Kingdom and Northern
Ireland

The British delegate explained his abstention by saying his government objected to the first paragraph of the draft resolution which
called on Belgium to withdraw its troops.

Because of the close and friendly personal relations established
before independence with the political leaders in the Congo and in
view of the importance of the Congo to the rest of Africa, I decided to
do all I could to help resolve the country's difficulties. In a letter dated
13 July 1960 I told Lumumba 'I am willing and anxious to help you in
any way I can, even to the extent of sending you a battalion of my
own army as a part of the United Nations Organisation, should you
deem this necessary.' I enclosed a copy of a statement which I made
the same day, expressing the view:

That the present difficulties in the Congo should be solved primarily
through the efforts of the independent African States within the

framework of the United Nations machinery. Intervention by Powers from outside the African continent, in the view of the Government of Ghana, is likely to *increase* rather than lessen tension.

The Government of Ghana has made this statement in the belief that the present situation in the Congo is one capable of peaceful and quick solution provided that rival outside powers do not interfere as a means of serving their own particular interests.

The Government of the Congo Republic asked Ghana for military aid and at 11 p.m. Ghana time on Wednesday, 13 July, I spoke by telephone to Mr Hammarskjöld, Secretary-General of the United Nations. I told him that the Congolese Government had asked Ghana for military aid and said that Ghana as an African State was ready and willing to send troops. Air transport, however, was needed urgently.

It was the same evening that the Security Council met and passed the resolution providing for the sending of UN forces to the Congo. Mr Hammarskjöld decided to make it a predominantly African operation although Sweden and Ireland, both unquestionably neutral, were asked to send troops. The Great Powers, excluded from the UN military force, provided air transport and on 15 July the first Tunisian soldiers, closely followed by Ghanaian troops, landed in the Congo. By then more Belgian soldiers had arrived in the Congo and on 14 July Lumumba and Kasabuvu broke off diplomatic relations with Belgium and both signed an appeal to Russia.

The day before UN troops arrived in the Congo the following message was received by the Ghana Ministry of Foreign Affairs:

To: The Ministry of Foreign Affairs
From: Elisabethville, Congo
For: The Minister of Foreign Affairs
Date: 15th July 1960

The people of Katanga consider that the United Nations Charter solemnly proclaims the right of all people to self determination. They consider that the tragic events which have cast a dark shadow over the birth of the Congo Republic demonstrate the inability of its leaders to guarantee respect for persons and property. They consider that the action taken by some of them is plunging the whole country into chaos and anarchy and compromising its destiny. They do not think that they can support the decision taken by Mr Lumumba to break off diplomatic relations with Belgium, to which they believe they are indebted for their economic and social development, their well being and prosperity. Through their elected representatives they solemnly appeal to all the countries of the free world to recognise without delay the independence of their territory. They pledge themselves to respect all the provisions of the Declaration of Human Rights and to contribute to the maintenance of peace in this part of the world.

TSHOMBE

Meanwhile, in spite of the Security Council resolution calling on Belgium to withdraw its troops, Belgian reinforcements continued to arrive in the Congo. Mr Kanza, representing the Congo Republic at the United Nations, reminded members of the Security Council of Article 6, paragraph 2, of the Treaty of Friendship signed just before independence by the Congolese and Belgian Governments:

The Belgian troops at present in the Congo shall not be used on Congolese national territory unless the Government of the Republic of the Congo, or the Congolese Minister for National Defence, explicitly so request.

Yet barely four days after independence the Belgian Government ordered Belgian troops to go into action on Congolese territory. In a long reply, the Belgian delegate, Mr Wigny, protested that Belgian troops had only intervened to save Belgian lives and that they would be willing to withdraw when a sufficiently large number of UN troops had arrived to take responsibility for the public peace. His speech convinced only those who wished to be convinced.

In a message to the Secretary-General delivered in New York on 20 July 1960 I again referred to the presence of Belgian troops in Katanga:

Yesterday I sent personal letters to Mr Kasavubu and Mr Lumumba urging moderation in the requests for outside military aid. I am strongly of the opinion that the intervention of any of the Great Powers would be likely to provoke a most dangerous situation. As you know, Mr Lumumba has made a declaration in accord with my personal request that he should withdraw his ultimatum.[1] However, I do consider that he is in the most difficult

---

[1] Lumumba and Kasavubu delivered an ultimatum from Stanleyville stating that if Belgian troops were not out of the Congo by 19 July they would appeal to Russia.

position and there is the gravest danger of outside Powers being involved unless the Belgians can be got out of Katanga . . . .

The attempt to detach Katanga appears to us here to have been entirely organised from outside. Mr Tshombe is well known to us in Ghana and the attitude he is now taking is quite contrary to what he advocated before Congo independence and is not in accord with the policy on which he fought the election. Indeed his whole policy seems to be dictated by the occupying Belgian troops.

We have tried to obtain clarification of the Belgian position from the Belgian Ambassador here and he says that it is the Belgian Government's intention to evacuate Katanga. I believe that if in fact this is so the situation could be immensely improved by the immediate removal of the Belgian troops from Elizabethville. I am absolutely certain that if the troops remain, there is the gravest danger of a situation developing which might cause armed conflict in Central Africa.

At its 879th meeting on 22 July the Security Council adopted unanimously a resolution, sponsored by Tunisia and Ceylon, which called upon the Belgian Government 'to implement speedily the Security Council resolution of 14 July 1960, on the withdrawal of their troops and authorises the Secretary-General to take all necessary action to this effect'. This resolution, like the one of 14 July, did not have the desired result. Belgian strength continued to increase and with it grew the confidence of Moise Tshombe.

Without Belgian support, Tshombe could never have maintained his position. He built up a large army officered by regular soldiers openly seconded from the Belgian Army. The financing of this was made possible by the paying to his rebellious régime of all the revenues, about £14 million a year, that the Union Minière should legally have paid to the Central Congolese Government. His supporters further provided Tshombe with a handsome bank account in Switzerland as an added inducement to serve their interests.

As might have been expected, Tshombe forbade the UN to send troops into Katanga and insisted that Belgian troops must stay there. He was supported by the Belgian Prime Minister, who said the UN should 'not intervene in the Congo's internal affairs' in regard to the Katanga problem. Sheltering behind 1,700 Belgian soldiers, Tshombe announced on 3 August that UN troops 'will have to fight their way in'.

Lumumba had already, in a letter to the President of the Security Council dated 31 July, expressed grave concern at the delay in the withdrawal of Belgian forces and the fact that, because of Belgian opposition, no United Nations troops had entered Katanga. He repeated again that the paramount problem was the removal of Belgian troops from the entire territory of the Republic. In a note transmitted on 1 August, the Ghana Minister for Foreign Affairs stated that if Belgium persisted in its policy, which had as its object not the protection of the lives of Belgian nationals but the detachment of Katanga from the rest of the Congo, the Government of Ghana would feel compelled to request the United Nations to declare Belgium an aggressor and to take appropriate action.

I sent a message to Tshombe three days later:

> In the interest of African solidarity and unity and in the interest of peace and security in the Congo and in Katanga in particular I appeal to you to assist in the peaceful entry of the United Nations troops.
>
> I am prepared to use my influence, if this is generally acceptable, to ensure that Ghana troops form the greater part of the contingent and you know you can rely on them to maintain order."

On the day this message was sent, the Secretary-General's Special Representative in the Congo, Mr Ralph Bunche, went to Elisabethville to arrange for the entry of UN troops. He returned to Leopoldville on 5 August reporting the unqualified and unyielding opposition of Tshombe and his colleagues to the sending of UN troops and their determination to resist by force any attempted entry. As a result of Bunche's report, Hammarskjöld cancelled his decision to send troops into Katanga and called for a new meeting of the Security Council to clarify his mandate.

I received Tshombe's reply to my message of 4 August three days later, on 7 August:

(Translation)

> Reference your telegram of the fourth, peace and order exist in Katanga. I regard the entry of United Nations troops as unnecessary. The entire population is opposed to occupation by these troops.
>
> Contrary to the statement made by the Lumumba Government, Katanga firmly desires African solidarity through a confederation of sovereign states forming the United States of the Congo.
>
> And we also desire as soon as possible to see the establishment of African fraternity through an agreement between all African nations. Nevertheless Katanga rejects the intrusion of any foreign ideology.

My reply of 8 August could have left him in no doubt of Ghana's position:

> We believe that Katanga is an integral part of the Congo of which we and other members of the United Nations have already recognised the independence.
>
> The Government of Ghana in the interests of African solidarity cannot therefore recognise the establishment of a so-called state of Katanga within the Republic of the Congo.
>
> I urge you strongly to refrain from any action which is likely to compromise the independence and territorial integrity of the Republic of the Congo.
>
> Regarding your idea of foreign ideology I do not understand what you mean. We know of one ideology only, African ideology.

Tshombe's cable of 8 August contained the feeblest of arguments to support his secessionist policy. 'The Government of Lumumba is in minority'; and 'The Parliament does not truly represent the people of the Congo.' How could he have thought such arguments worth the paper they were written on? Lumumba was the only Congolese political leader to achieve a clear majority in the Parliamentary elections preceding independence, and the Chamber consistently supported him. As for the point about Parliament not representing the people of the Congo, this was sheer nonsense and came strangely from one whose leadership in Katanga was based on foreign support and did not meet with the approval of a large part of the Katanga population.

I determined to try for the last time to make Tshombe see reason:

12 August 1960

In answer to your last telegram to me, I should like to make one final appeal to you to act with a sense of responsibility and in accordance with the interests of Africa which I know you also have at heart. The whole world knows that your pretended State has been set up with the support of foreign interests. Your activities are applauded in South Africa and the Rhodesias and are condemned by every other Independent African State. This at least should give you food for thought. Your whole administration depends upon Belgian officials who are fundamentally opposed to African Independence and who are merely using you as their tool.

They will discard you as soon as you have served their purpose.

No true African nationalist can have confidence in you while you continue to allow yourself to be used as such. Your name is now linked openly with foreign exploiters and oppressors of your own country. In fact you have assembled in your support the foremost advocates of imperialism and colonialism in Africa and the most determined opponents of African freedom. How can you, as an African, do this? I appeal to you with all sincerity to denounce those who are merely using you as a puppet and who have no more respect for you than they have for African freedom and independence. Your allegations of Communism against the government of the Republic of Congo show how far you are under the influence of South Africa who regards any movement for African Freedom as Communist. You have allowed the Belgians to control the news coming out of Katanga. Nevertheless it is clear that serious disorder is occurring in the Northern part of the Province of Katanga and that your policy is endangering the lives of Africans and Europeans alike. Let me once again appeal to you and Ngalula to consider the position into which you have placed yourselves and to work for the unity of the Congo and of Africa.

While messages were being exchanged between Tshombe and myself, urgent debates were taking place in the UN building in New York. Mr Lewandowski (Poland) at the 886th meeting of the Security Council held on 8/9 August said there was one basic issue to the problem of Katanga's resistance to the entry into the Province of UN troops: 'Were the Belgian troops to be withdrawn from Katanga, the whole question of local opposition would undoubtedly change, if not disappear entirely.' The American and British view was that the UN should not be drawn into a struggle between Lumumba and Tshombe; the issue was a domestic one. This view was strongly challenged by the Congolese delegate, who insisted that Belgian troops must be withdrawn. With painful monotony the Belgian delegate reiterated the old argument that Belgian troops were only in the Congo to protect the Belgian nationals. Both the Soviet and the Tunisian delegates said the UN should use force in Katanga if necessary. There was no reason why the Council's resolutions should not be applied in Katanga as in any other Province of the Congo.

Finally, on 9 August, a resolution sponsored by Tunisia and Ceylon was adopted recognising 'that the withdrawal of Belgian troops from the province of Katanga will be a positive contribution to and essential for the proper implementation of the Council resolutions'. The resolution continued,

The Security Council:

1 *Confirms* the authority given to the Secretary-General by the Security Council resolutions of 14 July and 22 July 1960 and requests him to continue to carry out the responsibility placed on him thereby;

2 *Calls upon* the Government of Belgium to withdraw immediately its troops from the Province of Katanga under speedy modalities determined by the Secretary-General and to assist in every possible way the implementation of the Council's resolutions;

3 *Declares* that the entry of the United Nations Force into the province of Katanga is necessary for the full implementation of this resolution;

4 *Reaffirms* that the United Nations Force in the Congo will not be a party to or in any way intervene in or be used to influence the outcome of any internal conflict, constitutional or otherwise;

5 *Calls upon* all Member States, in accordance with Articles 25 and 49 of the Charter of the United Nations, to accept and carry out the decisions of the Security Council and to afford mutual assistance in carrying out measures decided upon by the Council;

6 *Requests* the Secretary-General to implement this resolution and to report further to the Council as appropriate.

The resolution was adopted by 9 votes to none, with France and Italy abstaining.

3 Lumumba's Dilemma

WHILE members of the Security Council were discussing the new situation in the Congo resulting from Tshombe's threat to oppose by force the entry of UN forces into Katanga, Lumumba was ending his brief visit to America and various African countries. He was trying desperately to explain the true position in the Congo and the need for strong measures to end Katanga's secession. People seemed to have lost sight of the fact that it was his government which had invited UN intervention; yet the UN operation in the Congo (ONUC) did not appear to respect the wishes of that government. Furthermore, the Security Council had passed a resolution calling on Belgium to withdraw its forces; yet it was common knowledge that Belgian troops were still in the Congo in considerable strength, and were even being reinforced.

When I addressed the National Assembly in Accra on 8 August 1960 I spoke at length of the Congo struggle, saying that the Ghana Government wholeheartedly supported UN intervention in the Congo but that 'it came too late and is acting too slowly'. I went on:

Recent events in the Congo have shown that independent African States are capable and better equipped to deal with the great problems of Africa than are the powers outside the African continent. This does not mean that Africa will not need the disinterested and impartial aid of the United Nations and other powers working through the United Nations, or through the African States themselves. A situation, however, has been reached when African States are technically competent to tackle any problem arising on the African continent. I would not be so presumptuous as to put forward a Monroe Doctrine for Africa. I must say, however, that the

Great Powers of the world should realise that very often African questions can be settled by African States if there is no non-African intervention or interference.

Later in the same speech I warned against the dangers of balkanisation in Africa, and I had in mind Katanga's claim to independence when I said, 'The new colonialism creates client states, independent in name but in point of fact pawns of the colonial power that is supposed to have given them independence.' I ended by asking the support of members for a motion authorising the Government of Ghana to take such military action against Belgium as might be necessary:

The Government wishes to have this authority from Parliament in order to be able to inform the United Nations that Ghana will fight under UN leadership against Belgium in support of the Security Council resolution. However, if the United Nations are unable to implement the Security Council's resolution, Ghana would co-operate with the military forces of other independent African States to drive the Belgian aggressors from African soil.

This is a turning point in the history of Africa. If we allow the independence of the Congo to be compromised in any way by the imperialist and capitalist forces, we shall expose the sovereignty and independence of all Africa to grave risk. The struggle of the Congo is therefore our struggle. It is incumbent on us to take our stand by our brothers in the Congo in the full knowledge that only Africa can fight for its destiny. In this struggle we shall not reject the assistance and support of our friends, but we will yield to no enemy, however strong.

By a large majority, members voted the government the necessary powers to mobilise Ghana's armed forces and so approved my Congo policy. It was an historic day, not only for the important Assembly vote, but because it was the day on which two very significant documents were signed by Lumumba and myself. The first was a joint communiqué issued at the conclusion of talks we had during 7/8 August. I quote it in full:

Joint Communiqué issued in Accra on 8 August 1960 in connection with the visit to the Republic of Ghana by His Excellency Mr Patrice Lumumba, Prime Minister of Congo

On his return from a visit to the United States of America, His Excellency Mr Patrice Lumumba, Prime Minister of the Republic of Congo, made a brief stop in Accra from the 7th to the 8th

August 1960 at the invitation of Osagyefo Dr Kwame Nkrumah, President of the Republic of Ghana.

In the course of the discussions President Dr Kwame Nkrumah and Prime Minister Lumumba reaffirmed their determination to work in the closest possible association with the other Independent African States for the establishment of a Union of African States, with a view to liberating the whole continent of Africa from colonialism and imperialism.

The two Heads of Government:

(a) Condemned unreservedly the refusal of the Belgian Government to withdraw their troops from the Congo, contrary to the decision of the Security Council of the United Nations. They agreed, in conjunction with other Independent African States, that in the event of the United Nations failing to effect a total and unconditional withdrawal of Belgian troops from the Congo as a whole, they will establish a Combined High Command of military forces to bring about a speedy withdrawal of these foreign troops from the Congo. They will also enlist the support of any other Nation prepared to assist them in the achievement of the following objectives:

  (i) withdrawal of Belgian troops from Katanga and all other parts of the Republic of Congo;

  (ii) recognition of the sovereignty and territorial integrity of the Republic of Congo;

  (iii) total and complete evacuation of the military bases in Kitona and Kamina.

(b) They agreed to issue invitations to an African Summit Conference of the Independent African States to be held in Leopoldville from the 25th to the 30th August, 1960.

KWAME NKRUMAH
President of the
Republic of Ghana

PATRICE LUMUMBA
Prime Minister of the
Republic of Congo

The second was a secret agreement providing for the union of Ghana and the Congo, on the pattern of the Ghana-Guinea-Mali union.

Secret Agreement signed by Osagyefo Dr Kwame Nkrumah and his Excellency Mr Patrice Lumumba, Prime Minister of the Republic of Congo, at Accra on 8 August 1960

The President of the Republic of Ghana and the Prime Minister of the Republic of Congo have given serious thought to the idea of

African Unity and have decided to establish with the approval of the Governments and peoples of their respective States, among themselves a UNION OF AFRICAN STATES. The Union would have a Republican Constitution within a federal framework.

The Federal Government would be responsible for:

(a) Foreign Affairs
(b) Defence
(c) The issue of a Common Currency
(d) Economic Planning and Development

There would be no customs barriers between any parts of the Federation. There would be a Federal Parliament and a Federal Head of State. The Capital of the Union should be Leopoldville. Any State or Territory in Africa is free to join this Union. The above Union presupposes Ghana's abandonment of the Commonwealth.

Dated at Accra this 8th day of August 1960.

KWAME NKRUMAH
President of the
Republic of Ghana

PATRICE LUMUMBA
Prime Minister of the
Republic of the Congo

For obvious reasons it has not been possible to publish the terms of this agreement before. Now, some five years after Lumumba's cruel murder, I feel bound to make our views on African unity known. How different might have been the unhappy story in Rhodesia, not to mention South Africa, Angola and Mozambique, if the terms of the agreement had in fact been carried out and Ghana and the Congo had freely united. Progress towards an All-African Union Government would have been greatly accelerated.

On 10 August, after Tshombe had issued conditions under which he would allow UN entry into Katanga, I sent a note to our delegate at the United Nations, Mr Quaison-Sackey, informing him of the government's view of the Congo situation, and suggesting that a copy of the note should be sent to all members of the Security Council and to the delegates of independent African States. I pointed out that the Ghana Government had put its armed forces at the disposal of the UN in the Congo so that the mandate entrusted to it by the Security Council might be carried out. Should, however, the UN fail to carry out the instructions, Ghana would be justified in taking independent action in agreement with the Congolese Government and if necessary in concert with other African States. The note continued:

The view of the Government of Ghana is that United Nations forces are in the Republic of the Congo at the request of the lawfully constituted Government of that Republic, and Ghanaian forces were contributed to the United Nations contingent upon that understanding. In these circumstances it would be in the view of the Government of Ghana entirely inappropriate for the United Nations to have any dealings with any group of persons who base their authority to negotiate on a repudiation of the authority of the Congolese Government.

The Government of Ghana takes the view that in relation to internal matters in the Congolese Republic the only authority from whom the United Nations can obtain an authoritative view of the obligations existing under the Constitution of the Republic is the Government of the Republic which requested United Nations intervention.

It is the responsibility of the United Nations to restore order in the Congo. It would be the grossest breach of faith in the view of the Government of Ghana if, after this has been done with the consent of the Government of the Republic, the United Nations were to agree to any conditions under which any other rival and illegal grouping were allowed to retain their arms.

The so-called Government of Katanga was set up under the shadow of Belgian military occupation which in itself was contrary to the resolution of the Security Council. The puppet nature of this regime has been a subject of almost universal acknowledgment in the press of the world.

In the view of the Government of Ghana it would be entirely contrary to the mandate of the United Nations forces if a regime illegally originated in this way by the Belgian Government were allowed to continue against the wishes of the Central Government through the protection of the United Nations.

On 12 August the Secretary-General of the UN arrived in Katanga with a token UN force and agreed with Tshombe the terms under which UN troops should enter the Province. There began a bitter dispute between Hammarskjöld and Lumumba on the terms of the UN mandate, Lumumba maintaining that the UN should enter Katanga by force if the provincial government made conditions. As soon as I heard this on 17 August I instructed our Ambassador in Leopoldville 'to impress tactfully upon Lumumba and Kasavubu the importance and absolute necessity for them to co-operate with the United Nations in securing our objective in the Congo'. Two days later, after ugly incidents between Congolese troops and UN personnel, I wrote to Lumumba:

Accra
19 August 1960

Dear Patrice,

I have already sent you a personal message on the subject of the situation in the Congo and in particular Leopoldville.

The main object of this letter is to appeal to you now to keep the Force Publique under restraint. A situation such as the one Leopoldville has experienced for some days now, can only lead to complete unemployment and economic chaos. You are well aware that I support you in all your aspirations but these aspirations can never be achieved if the Congo returns to chaos. The first thing to do is to restore law and order, so that the people may resume a normal life and live without fear. Therefore the first thing we must do is to restore such law and order in the city of Leopoldville. This will be possible if you instruct the Force Publique and the Congolese police to co-operate effectively with the Ghana Army; and I am sure that law and order can be very quickly restored.

In your interests as well as in the interests of the Congolese people and of Africa as a whole, I entreat you to give us this co-operation. For my part I shall insist on white troops being withdrawn from the Congo as soon as possible. I shall support your political aspirations and shall try to ensure that the UN forces do not remain in the Congo longer than is necessary for them to restore confidence and stability.

I am absolutely certain that the Secretary-General will never allow the Belgians to re-establish themselves in the Congo, but if the situation remains chaotic, as at present in Leopoldville, there is a grave danger that the Congo which is dear to us may become a battlefield between East and West. This would be a disaster for all of us in Africa.

Yours very sincerely,
Kwame Nkrumah

Lumumba declared martial law and threatened to attack Katanga unless the UN enforced his rule there. There were still large numbers of Belgian troops in Katanga. On 18 August 1960 the Secretary-General had reported to the Security Council that there were approximately 8,600 Belgian troops in Katanga at the time of the UN Special Representative's visit on 4 August. Throughout the Congo struggle the Belgian Government repeatedly assured the UN that it was withdrawing its troops but nevertheless kept forces there, sometimes in the guise of 'technicians'. In a *note verbale* of 30 August 1960 to the representative of Belgium, the Secretary-General complained that Belgian troops were still in the Congo in strength and expressed his surprise 'at finding there is a marked difference between the information received from Brussels and the facts observed on the scene'.

During this time I was in close touch with Lumumba. In a letter to him dated 22 August I told him not to despair:

> The problem seems to me to be to convert the Congolese national army into an efficient fighting force within a very short space of time, to provide it with air and other forms of transport and such ammunition and weapons as may be necessary.
>
> I think this can be done by the use of a military mission from the African States and by the recruitment from abroad of a number of key technicians. Great care and tact will require to be used in selecting these outside military technicians. We must avoid involving the country in any way in a cold war situation and so provoke a supply of counter technicians to rebel forces.

With each day that passed the situation in the Congo grew more serious. It became clear that the Congo Government could neither command full political support nor maintain order in the country without external help. I repeatedly made it known that Ghanaian forces would be at the disposal of the United Nations so long as the UN acted in support of the Security Council resolutions. Nevertheless, my government decided to consult with other independent African States to prepare a joint plan for military assistance to the Congo should it be needed.

On the invitation of Lumumba, a Conference of Independent African States was held in Leopoldville from 25 to 30 August. At the suggestion of the Sudan it was held at foreign ministers' level. Lumumba addressed the conference on several occasions and the delegates had a chance to express their views.

Although the Conference did not achieve its purpose, it demonstrated clearly the need for unity in the defence of freedom in Africa. Further, it enabled the members to take back to their various governments first-hand knowledge of the situation in Leopoldville. They reported that a major constitutional crisis was imminent owing to the quarrel between Lumumba and Kasavubu.

4 The Breakdown of Lumumba's Government

IN the two weeks which followed the ending of the Leopoldville Conference the political situation in the Congo deteriorated rapidly. The main objective of ONUC, the expulsion of Belgian troops from the Republic of the Congo and the safeguarding of its territorial integrity and political independence, had not been achieved. Lumumba had complained (20 August) to the Secretary-General of his failure to consult the Congolese Government, 'Until now everything has been done as if the United Nations Command in the Congo wanted to take the place of the Government of the Republic.' There was growing tension between Lumumba and the Secretary-General on the one side, and Lumumba and Kasavubu on the other. A complete breakdown of government appeared probable, which might leave the way open for a seizure of power by any adventurer who could command the necessary support. A particularly dangerous development was the entry of the Army into politics.

In this situation it seemed to me that the Government of Lumumba, as the only legal government in the Congo, must be strongly supported. In a succession of messages I urged Lumumba to proceed with great tact and caution both in his relations with the Secretary-General and with his own Head of State, Kasavubu.

On 5 September 1960 came the broadcast announcement of Kasavubu that he was revoking the appointment of Lumumba as Prime Minister because he had betrayed his office and plunged the country into civil war. A new government under Joseph Ileo, President of the Senate, was to be set up. Later in the evening, Lumumba broadcast saying that Kasavubu had no constitutional power to revoke his appointment and that Kasavubu's appointment as Head of State was in turn revoked. He called on people, workers and the Army to rise.

As a result of the two broadcasts ONUC closed all major airports to any traffic other than that of the United Nations.

As Miss Hoskyns has pointed out in her book *The Congo Since Independence*, the executive assistant to the Secretary-General, Andrew Cordier, knew in advance of Kasavubu's plan to dismiss Lumumba, and it is likely that the information was sent to Hammarskjöld in New York. Miss Hoskyns states:

> No evidence has so far been produced to suggest that United Nations officials played a part in the shaping of Kasavubu's plans. But there is no doubt at all that senior ONUC officials knew several days before hand what Kasavubu intended and that most of them hoped fervently that he would succeed.[1]

I sent a telegram to Lumumba on 6 September 1960:

> I have learnt with grief of recent incidents in the Congo. In the name of African solidarity and in the interest of the peace and unity of the Congo and the welfare of the Congolese people I appeal to you to exercise restraint and not do anything which will endanger the territorial integrity and sovereignty of the Congo or open the doors to foreign domination. Above all you must not do anything to jeopardise the great gains you have already achieved in unity.

During the night of 5 September the Council of Ministers published a communiqué declaring Kasavubu deprived of his functions and accusing him of high treason. At 1.30 p.m. on the 6th, the UN, using Ghanaian forces, temporarily closed Leopoldville radio station.

This action was indefensible. It deprived Lumumba of the means to address the people while Kasavubu, broadcasting freely on Brazzaville radio, and Tshombe on Radio Elisabethville, were openly stirring up anti-Lumumbist feeling. How could such action of the United Nations possibly be justified when Lumumba was the lawful Prime Minister? It can only be assumed that Lumumba's enemies knew the strength of his personality and the danger of letting him appeal to the people. It is certain, had he been allowed to broadcast at that critical time, he would have rallied very powerful support. Similarly, the airport ban operated entirely in Kasavubu's favour and against Lumumba. Two key supporters of Lumumba, General Lundula and Cleophas Kamitatu, were unable to return to Leopoldville, while the Prime Minister Designate, Joseph Ileo, was permitted to travel to the Provinces to test the degree of support he could count on for his proposed government.

[1] C. Hoskyns, *The Congo Since Independence*, O.U.P., 1964, pp. 200–1.

Conor Cruise O'Brien in an article in *New Left Review*[1] wrote that Press correspondents in Leopoldville at the time were convinced that the UN were helping to oust Lumumba. He points out (p. 9) that Miss Hoskyns quotes the *Christian Science Monitor*, *The Times* and *Libre Belgique* to this effect. 'The last paper which admired neither Lumumba nor the United Nations stated that without the UN Lumumba would in a few hours have gained control.'

On 6 September 1960 the Chamber of Representatives met and by a vote of 60 to 19 revoked both dismissals. On 8 September the Senate also gave Lumumba a vote of confidence by 41 votes to 2 with 6 abstentions. There were also on that occasion 29 absentees.

Encouraged by the support given to him by the Congolese Parliament, Lumumba, in a speech at Camp Leopold on 9 September, announced that he was Chief of State and Supreme Commander of the National Army. The same day Kasavubu issued a declaration rejecting the votes of the Senate and the Chamber of Representatives on the ground that the decisions of the Chief of State were not subject to the approval of either House.

This disturbing news reached me as I was drafting a telegram to Quaison-Sackey in New York, telling him to make Ghana's position absolutely clear to the UN in view of the dangerous military situation in the Congo:

> The first resolution of the Security Council of the 14th July stated that the Secretary-General was authorised by the Security Council, 'to take the necessary steps, in consultation with the Government of the Republic of the Congo, to provide the Government with such Military Assistance, as may be necessary, until, through the efforts of the Congolese Government with the Technical Assistance of the United Nations, the National Security Forces may be able, in the opinion of the Government, to meet fully their tasks.'
>
> It is the view of the Ghana Government that this directive by the Security Council is the overriding directive since it was upon these terms that the Government of the Congo accepted the entry into the Republic of the United Nations forces. Further, it was on these terms that Ghana and other States agreed to contribute contingents.
>
> In the light of this, the policy you should put forward should be
> 1 That only one Congolese army can be recognised by the United Nations. Anyone who raises a private armed force and employs that armed force without the authority of the Central Government is a mutineer and must be treated as such and disarmed

[1] No. 31, May/June 1965.

without bloodshed if possible. This applies equally to small bands of mutineers who commit undisciplined acts and murder and loot contrary to the instructions of the Central Government and also to the so-called army of Katanga.

2 The political difference between Tshombe and the Central Government are no doubt internal matters in which the United Nations should not interfere.

3 It is impossible for the Security Council to complain if the Central Government seeks help from outside the African continent in order to be able to deal with Tshombe, particularly as all African States are unable to give direct military assistance since they are fully committed to the United Nations.

4 Nevertheless, such help from outside the African continent is highly dangerous and likely to lead to world conflict.

5 Therefore, the policy of the Security Council should be to follow the first resolution and to reorganise the military forces of the Central Government so that they can fulfil their tasks of ensuring that there is only one army in the Congo and that army is a disciplined one under the control of the Central Government.

6 In order to avoid bloodshed in Katanga through the disarming of the Katanga forces negotiations should be carried out so as to see that all Belgian military officers are removed and the weapons recently supplied by Belgium collected and taken into the United Nations control.

7 Subject to agreement on the above points all powers outside the African Continent should be prohibited from supplying directly munitions of war and aircraft to the Congo. You should not on any account, however, agree to this proposal unless the United Nations are prepared to assist in the organising and supplying of the Congolese army in accordance with the first resolutions of the Security Council.

On 11 September the President of the Chamber of Representatives and the Acting President of the Senate informed the UN that the votes of their separate bodies constituted a sovereign determination of renewal of confidence in the Government of Lumumba and an annulment of Kasavubu's ordinance. That night, however, the Prime Minister Designate, Joseph Ileo, announced the formation of his new government.

Lumumba had his back to the wall. Prevented from using his own radio station by Ghanaian troops under UN command, he sent me the following message:

I hasten to express to you my indignation regarding the aggressive and hostile attitude of Ghanaian soldiers towards me and my Government.

Yesterday, 10th September, I invited Messrs Kojo Botsio and Djin to inform them of the Government's decision to take possession of the National Broadcasting Station and also the aerodrome at Ndjili, Leopoldville. This decision was previously communicated to all the Ambassadors of the African Countries. I insisted that Honorable Botsio and the Ambassador should advise the Ghana troops not to interfere in the conflict between us and the United Nations authorities on the subject of the arbitrary seizure of our radio station and aerodromes.

At 4.30 p.m. today, 11th September, accompanied by my soldiers I personally went to take over the radio station. The Ghana troops, however, opposed my decision with hostility and went to the extent of seizing arms from my soldiers. The Ghana troops even wanted to shoot me and my soldiers.

To these incidents add also the hostile declaration of Gen Alexander[1] of your army against the Government of the Republic. All these acts committed by your soldiers are far from proving the friendship I wanted to maintain with you and your people. In the circumstances, I feel obliged to renounce the help of your troops in view of the fact that they are in a state of war against our Republic. Instead of helping us in our difficulties, your soldiers are openly siding with the enemy to fight us.

With my profound regret,

I am your good friend, etc.

The full story behind Lumumba's protest was contained in a letter from our Ambassador in Leopoldville, A. Y. K. Djin:

As you might have been informed by now, yesterday evening Mr Patrice Lumumba called the special delegation you sent to Leopoldville, comprising Hon Kojo Botsio, Mr N. A. Welbeck and myself, to his residence. There he informed us of his intention to take back the Ndjili Airport and the National Radio Station. He appealed to us to advise our soldiers not to resist his soldiers when they came to take over the Radio Station which was being guarded by our troops. Mr Lumumba further told us that he had had a similar discussion with the Sudanese and the UAR representatives with a view to taking over the Ndjili Airport and that the officers

---

[1] General Alexander was seconded to the Ghana Government in 1959 and appointed Chief of Defence Staff. I dismissed him in 1961.

concerned had received the necessary instructions concerning the operation.

Referring to the bold stand which Guinea had already taken in the matter, Mr Lumumba read from a local newspaper the report of a declaration alleged to have been made by Gen Alexander in London against the Congolese National Army and told us that the declaration was not pleasant. He warned that public feeling was turning against us and that reports had reached him from the representatives of the provincial government about the military manoeuvres of Ghana troops all over the town as if they were at war.

During our discussion, the UAR and Guinea delegations also arrived on the scene and the former was asked to join us in order to confirm his country's position with regard to the Airport Operation. The UAR representative told us that in view of the improper interference of the United Nations in the internal affairs of the country, they had received communication from President Nasser authorising their soldiers to withdraw when the Congolese arrived to take the Airport. The UAR representative also informed us that the Sudanese with whom their soldiers were guarding the Airport had also agreed to take similar action and that the United Nations Headquarters in Leopoldville had been informed accordingly in writing. He, therefore, urged us to advise our troops who were guarding the Radio Station to refrain from any action which might bring them into a clash with the Congolese National Army.

As the Prime Minister wanted immediate action to be taken in the matter, we left for the military camp where we had a long discussion with Col Ankrah. The latter would not readily support the action proposed by Mr Lumumba unless an order to that effect came from the Ghana Government. In order to check the veracity of the statements made by the UAR representative, we asked Col Ankrah to find out from the Sudanese Commander at the Airport whether it was true he had agreed to the action proposed or had been given any instructions concerning the Airport Operation. The result of this enquiry was that no such action had been agreed upon by the Sudanese Commander.

From Col Ankrah's house, we proceeded to Brig Otu's residence. In the absence of the latter, we informed Mr Patrice Lumumba by telephone that we could not get in touch with the most senior Ghanaian officer and implored him to postpone the operation he had proposed; this suggestion was however not well received by Mr Lumumba.

We left Brig Otu's place and then went straight to the United Nations Headquarters to see Mr Dayal, the personal representative of the Secretary-General of the United Nations. Asked whether he knew anything about the UAR's proposal to withdraw their troops from the Airport when the Congolese Army arrived there, Mr Dayal flatly denied having received any such notification. In the light of these investigations we found that we would be committing a *faux pas* if we instructed the Ghana Commanding Officer to give way to the Congolese National Army when the latter came to take over the Radio Station. Before leaving the UN Headquarters we tried to secure an appointment with Mr Lumumba but we were told that it was no longer necessary, since the Congolese no longer had any confidence in us. We were further told that the present stand taken by Ghana was nothing short of treachery. In the circumstances we had to return home without seeing Mr Lumumba to tell him the result of our investigations.

If you would allow me, Osagyefo, I would say that this is the culminating point of Gen Alexander's intrigue and subversive action which I have time and again pointed out and which was also confirmed by all the delegations which had paid a visit to the Congo. If you remember all that I told you during my last consultations with you, you will no doubt agree that although we were responsible for making possible the independence of the Congo, since the Country became free we have been a liability to Lumumba and the Congolese. Without doubt, it was due to Gen Alexander's actions that Mr Lumumba had to give notice to the United Nations to quit from the Congo.

At the moment the situation has so much deteriorated that if you still have interest in your main aim, I suggest that you (i) dismiss Gen Alexander, (ii) withdraw all white soldiers from the Congo, (iii) stop supporting the idea of disarming the Congolese Army, and (iv) give strong support to the 'status quo' as against the illegal government put up by UNO.

I at once replied to Lumumba's note:

My dear Patrice,
I entirely appreciate your point of view and understand the difficult position in which you find yourself *vis-à-vis* the Ghana troops in Leopoldville. I also find myself in an embarrassing and invidious position in respect of the way in which my Ghana troops are being used in the Congo, though I have been fighting like mad day and night on your behalf.

As you will see from the text of the note which I have a moment ago sent to the Secretary-General of the United Nations, and which I quote below for your information, I have already taken steps to deal with the situation. I entreat you to be patient and calm. Everything will end well provided neither you nor I take any precipitous step. If Ghana troops are to be placed completely at your disposal, then you and your Government must find some way to declare that in this struggle, Ghana and the Congo are one. Only thus would it be possible for my Ghana troops to operate legitimately with the Congolese forces.

The following is the text of my letter to Mr Hammarskjöld:

The position in the Congo at the moment places Ghana in a most embarrassing and invidious situation *vis-à-vis* the legitimate Government.

Ghana originally went to the Congo to aid the legitimate Lumumba Government which invited Ghana to assist Lumumba. When the United Nations went to the Congo on Lumumba's invitation, Ghana agreed to place her troops under United Nations command. The whole development since has perverted the real objective and seriously undermines Ghana's position in the eyes of the legitimate Government of the Congo Republic in that at present Ghana's troops are used almost exclusively as a cat's paw against Lumumba, preventing him from using his own radio station. At the same time Radio Brazzaville, which is controlled by France, a permanent member of the Security Council, is allowed to indulge in the most violent propaganda against the legitimate Lumumba Government. Radio Elisabethville, which is in effect under Belgian control, is also allowed to indulge in similar propaganda. Thus Ghana is used virtually to tie Lumumba's hands behind him while a permanent member of the Security Council is allowed to whip him. In the circumstances, therefore, if Lumumba is not allowed to use his own radio station at Leopoldville for keeping the Congolese populace informed of the critical situation and thus mobilising support for the legitimate Government of the Congo Republic of which he is head, Ghana would withdraw her troops forthwith from the United Nations Command and reserves the right to place her troops in the Congo Republic entirely at the disposal of the legitimate Lumumba Government of the Congo Republic.

The same day, on 12 September 1960, I sent a further note to Lumumba explaining in detail how I thought he ought to proceed:

The first point I would like to bring to your attention again is that considering the fact that you had to form a very wide Coalition Government, and considering the fact that you have the Tshombe problem, the Kalondji problem, the Kasavubu problem and other similar problems so far concealed now; and considering the fact that the colonialists and imperialists are doing their utmost to retrieve their lost ground in the Congo, you cannot afford, my Brother, to be harsh and uncompromising. Do not force Kasavubu out now. It will bring too much trouble especially in Leopoldville, when you want calm there now. Do not make an issue of his treachery now, or even of Tshombe's treachery. The time will come to deal with them. Let sleeping dogs lie. Leave these people alone now. In the same way, please, do not come out with any new Constitution now. It will jeopardise your position. It will give the whip to Tshombe and the separatists to stir up trouble again. Be 'as cool as a cucumber', establish the administration and consolidate your position before you take the next step. I would be the last person to advise you to compromise on any matter of principle; but the very critical situation in the Congo demands you adopting what I call 'tactical action'. That is, you should so adapt your methods, without sacrificing any principles, that you work even with your bitterest political enemies in order to give you time to consolidate your position—organisationally, i.e. governmental and party, both with regard to the Central Government as well as in the Provinces, before you take the next step.

Allied to this is what I have sent to tell you before and I must repeat with all emphasis here, namely, that you must not push the United Nations troops out until you have consolidated your position, and then you can ask them to leave. I know the difficulties you are having with the United Nations and we are not sparing them at all, as you can find from my enclosed note to the Security Council. But if the United Nations troops move out now, you will not be able to cope with the confusion that will ensue, fomented by the colonial powers, Belgian and other imperialists working with the reactionaries at home.

The third important point is that you must quickly establish your administration so that people may feel secure and get work to do. Immigration and Customs should also be established immediately at all sea and air ports. Fortunately, the United Nations is there with plenty of funds to help you and you must set up the organisation you announced at your Press Conference two days ago to make use of the aid offered. Get hold of the aid and control it. Whatever the political squabbles with your opponents, the hungry unemployed people will not continue to stand by and go hungry; they will soon act and will respond to whoever will be able, or even promise, to give them 'bread and games', as the ancient Romans put it.

My dear Patrice, the above are my three basic and urgent suggestions. The position is critical; if you act quickly on them, the position will be saved; if you delay, anything may happen. Please, pay heed to my suggestions and tackle the internal situation which you alone can remedy, provided you pay heed to my suggestions. As regards the external work, especially concerning the Security Council and UNO, leave that to me. You can be sure that on any issue, I shall mobilise the Afro-Asian bloc and other friendly nations to support you as in the case of the present attempt to dethrone you.

Now a few other suggestions:

Firstly, your Cabinet is too big but it will not be wise to cut it down at this time. In the meantime the best thing is to establish a sort of inner Cabinet, called for instance the Cabinet Committee, to deal with urgent issues. A good excuse for setting it up is the present emergency facing the country, when urgent decisions have to be taken quickly as in war time. I suggest the membership of this Committee be as follows:

CABINET COMMITTEE:

1 Prime Minister and Minister of Defence and Foreign Affairs	..	..	..	..	.. Chairman
2 Deputy Premier	..	..	..	..	Vice-Chairman
3 Minister of the Interior	..	..	..	..	Member
4 Minister of Local Government	..	..	..	Member
5 Minister for Technical Assistance	..	..	..	Member
6, 7, 8 Three other Ministers	..	..	..	..	Members

CABINET COMMITTEE

Purposes:
1 To deal with the emergency.
2 For political, military and airport matters.
3 The Katanga and Kasai questions.
4 Relations with the United Nations.
5 Technical Assistance—approval of policy and programme.
6 Any urgent business.

You will see that because of the emergency and your having a lot to do with the United Nations and the Security Council, etc., I have added Foreign Affairs to your portfolio. But look out for two trusted comrades, one to be Deputy Minister of Defence, and the other to be Deputy Minister of Foreign Affairs, both under you.

You may hold ordinary Cabinet meetings with all your Ministers once a week for ordinary Government Business; but the Inner Cabinet, i.e. The Cabinet Committee, should meet every day. You should however keep Cabinet informed of decisions taken and executed. Some important matters dealt with by the Cabinet Committee have to be referred to the whole Cabinet for approval in order to get the full backing of your Ministers.

Your Technical Assistance Committee may be composed as follows:

TECHNICAL ASSISTANCE COMMITTEE:

1 The Deputy Premier	.. ..	Chairman
2 Minister for Technical Assistance	.. ..	Member
3 Minister of Local Government	.. .. ..	Member
4 Minister of Establishment	.. .. ..	Member
5 Minister of Labour ..	.. ..	Member
6 Minister of Public Works ..	.. .. ..	Member
7 Minister of Industries	.. ..	Member
8 Minister of Mines and Natural Resources	..	Member
9 Minister of Communications	.. .. ..	Member

TECHNICAL ASSISTANCE COMMITTEE

Purpose

To co-operate with the United Nations and other agencies and countries for the speedy and effective use of any technical assistance offered.

The Committee is to have weekly joint meetings with United Nations representatives to plan programmes for the approval of Cabinet before execution.

The Minister for Technical Assistance, as the Chief Executive for this programme is to be given adequate authority for effective and speedy action within approved policies and programmes.

Now, Patrice, I come to the question of the Force Publique. I admire them for what they have done and I would not have them disarmed. But it needs to be officered properly and trained to suit your requirements.

I urge you not to force out the United Nations troops until you have reconditioned the Force Publique. Their provincial loyalties are too strong and groups of them are inclined to follow Ministers from their areas. At the moment, too, you have not got adequate rations, supplies, etc. Considering therefore what the imperialists are pumping into Katanga, considering also the Kalondji, Kasavubu and other menaces, Brother, it is absolutely unsafe to depend entirely on the Force Publique at this critical time.

It is imperative to have your officers trained without delay and so let me have your reply to my offer concerning the training of your officers here in my Military Academy.

Finally, a word from you on the radio calling on all Congolese to bury their differences and come together in the interest of the nation will have an electric effect in bringing the people together and thus establishing your own position and the peace necessary for the development of the Congo. Brother, mark my advice.

Whenever in doubt consult me. Brother, we have been in the game for some time now and we know how to handle the imperialists and the colonialists. The only colonialist or imperialist that I trust is a dead one. If you do not want to bring Congo into ruin, follow the advice I have given. Brother, have implicit faith in me; I shall not let you down. Your stand for United Congo and for African Unity commend you dearly to me. Your friend, Mr Djin, is there to help you in every way possible; you cannot have a better admirer and supporter than Djin. Trust him as you have done heretofore and he will serve you well.

Patrice, I have surveyed the position in the Congo very, very carefully. If you fail, you have only yourself to blame and it will be due to your unwillingness to face the facts of life or as the Germans call it, 'real politik'. Your failure will be a great blow to the African liberation movement, and you cannot afford to fail. Your policy 'to do away with your enemies now' will fail; you must adopt TACTICAL ACTION. Remember, the forces pitched against you are legion. But the odds are in your favour and you will succeed if only you handle the situation carefully and tactfully.

Yours affectionately, etc.

As no violence occurred when Ileo announced the formation of his new government, the UN reopened the radio station and the Minister of Information designated by Ileo broadcast a speech in which he said that Lumumba would be arrested and given a fair trial.

Lumumba was, in fact, arrested on 12 September on the order of the Army Chief of Staff but was later released in circumstances which are unclear. The first I heard of his arrest was when I received a cable from Djin:

> Lumumba arrested this afternoon by Congolese gendarmes on orders of Kasavubu and taken to an unknown place. Will report further.

Later the same day a further message was received from Leopold-ville:

> Lumumba released. Arrest reported earlier made by Congolese soldiers of the Opposition who posed as the Government Gendarmes. Broadcasting station, about which already written is the bone of contention between Lumumba and Ghana Army who are guarding the place. For refusing to allow Lumumba to use the broadcasting station even though ban equally affects Kasavubu and Bolikango, Lumumba has taken the matter so seriously that in a note of protest delivered to me this evening he gave an ultimatum for the Ghana Army to cease all activities in the Congo within one hour repeat one hour, that is from 2000 to 2100 GMT failing which he will be compelled to break off diplomatic relations with Ghana. I suggest for your serious consideration that for the meantime part of the Army officered by expatriates be withdrawn immediately as the present attitude of the officers is greatly detested by Lumumba and his Government. Lumumba regards Ghana forces as a liability to his Government. My suggestion therefore takes into account the possible adverse political repercussions of accepting complete withdrawal.

The next day, 13 September 1960, Djin reported that the prestige of Ghana 'had been run down to its lowest ebb by General Alexander's intrigues'. He went on:

> Mr Lumumba has time and again repeated that you are his inspirer and has got all sorts of names for doing so. . . . I was not flattering you when I told you that Mr Lumumba had a high regard for you, but he has now had a rude awakening. . . .
>
> My task is to make every effort to retrieve the ground lost . . . every effort should be made by both of us to make Mr Lumumba believe once more that we are sincere and that we are not a pawn of the imperialists as Radio Brazzaville and the Katanga Radio are portraying us.

The reason for the deterioration of relations between my government and Lumumba was, as before, the conduct of Ghanaian forces under UN command.

Lumumba sent the following message to me on 13 September:

I am sorry to inform you about the hostile attitude of the Ghana troops who actually hinder the movement of the Government. I would like to remind you of my letter which I sent about that subject two days ago.

Similar actions have been renewed yesterday, and I immediately got in touch with your Ambassador, Mr Djin. I asked him to order the withdrawal of Ghana troops who were surrounding the broadcasting station. The Government has decided to break off diplomatic relations with Ghana in case your Government refuses to withdraw its troops.

The action taken by Ghana troops will only lead to strengthening the position of the Imperialists.

Ghana troops are now being used against the legally constituted Government and in the interest of the opposition. We are highly disappointed. We had hoped to find effective support from Ghana and its troops.

My Government request that you instruct your troops as soon as you receive this message to stop all activities within the framework of the United Nations and act only with the Government of Lumumba. This is the position of the parliament.

We wish you would meet your delegation today to solve these issues in an urgent way and to strengthen our brotherly relations. I am impatiently awaiting your reply.

My respects, etc.

Lumumba did not then know of the energetic part played by the Ghanaian Ambassador in trying to secure his release when he was arrested by the Congolese gendarmerie. When he did eventually hear about it, his attitude towards Ghana instantly changed. I received a full account of the dramatic happenings of 12 September in a letter written by Djin on the 15th. I quote it in full:

Osagyefo,
Fresh incidents broke out on the 12th September, 1960, in Leopoldville, the capital of the Republic of Congo, after Sunday's incident which was reported in my last letter.

At about 4.30 p.m. on the same day, news of the arrest of Mr P. Lumumba flashed through the town. The news was reported to me by two important Congolese Ministers who also informed me that Lumumba's arrest was made by Congolese gendarmerie and that it occurred in his former residence on the Boulevard Albert.

Without losing a moment I commanded a part of my personal guard, seven in number, to proceed with me at once to the place of his arrest. As there was no vehicle available at that time—the Embassy van having been sent out—my guards and my informants marched on foot but about half a mile from my residence we met a car driven by Mr Kandolo, Secretary of the Cabinet, who was also coming to report the incident to me and to seek my assistance. Mr Kandolo conveyed my guard in his car to Mr Lumumba's residence and later returned for me and the rest of the party. When we got to the Residency I found that any effort on my part would be useless and would amount to locking the stable when the horse had fled. I therefore decided to go to our Embassy near by to discuss the matter with Mr Mamphey and Mr Seddoh and to decide what action we could take in the circumstances. On my way to the Embassy I was met by two Ministers of Mr Lumumba's Government: they were Mr Mgwamba, Minister of Justice, and Mr Grenfell who is well-known to you.

In a short meeting held in the Ghana Embassy with the two Ministers we discussed Mr Lumumba's arrest and planned for his release. The Ministers informed me that I was their only hope and that they looked up to me for help in their present difficulty. I informed them that if they could show me where Mr Lumumba had been taken to I would do all I could to have him released immediately. In the excitement of the moment we agreed that there was no time to delay and that it was the duty of everyone to go and investigate the whereabouts of Mr Lumumba. Before they departed I sent a word to Mr Cobbina of the Ghana Police to alert 50 policemen for duty at my request later on. At the same time I sent instructions for reinforcement of the Police guard at my residence. On second thoughts I decided to set to work immediately to find Mr Lumumba and I accordingly left the Embassy with the result that when Mr Cobbina called at the Embassy later on I was away.

I learnt later that a scanty number of Congolese soldiers was present during Mr Lumumba's arrest but they offered no resistance. News of Lumumba's arrest came as a shock to everybody and until the plot was carried out the public was not aware of it. I may add that prior to the arrest a Congolese informant came to my residence and informed me that Mr Bolikango had gone to speak in the Broadcasting House and that he went with a detachment of Congolese soldiers to guard the approaches of the Radio Station. This information was later found by me to be false, as I shall explain later.

3

I proceeded with the two Congolese Ministers to the Camp Leopold II to check on the information regarding Mr Lumumba's arrest and to find out whether he had been imprisoned at Makabi Camp about 10 miles away as alleged. On our way to the Camp Leopold II we met Brig Otu who was coming to my residence for discussion. He stopped and alighted from his car when he saw me; I therefore instructed my driver to take the Congolese Ministers to Col Ankrah's residence in the Camp and I proceeded to the Camp's headquarters with Brig Otu. At the Camp Headquarters I discussed with Brig Otu and Col Ankrah my plans for releasing Mr Lumumba. The two Commanders considered my plan inadvisable and stated that they could not lend hand to me in such an action until they had been released from UNO command. It is relevant to mention at this point that before seeing our two Commanders I had been assured by the Moroccan politician in Leopoldville that if some Ghanaian troops could be released to join forces with the Moroccans they would be prepared to take part in our effort to release Lumumba.

I knew that if Lumumba's arrest was found to be true all our efforts in Congo would be valueless for there was not one single politician among the Congolese people who had the same ideal and aim as Lumumba, and though my plans for his release might be considered by some to be desperate I was prepared to risk everything to achieve it, especially as I knew the psychology of the Congolese people and the morale of the Army. I knew I was not taking any risk. I was also sure of the success of my plan as the day follows the night.

Another point and that was the main reason why I thought this effort to release Lumumba was necessary was that I knew quite well that the success of my attempt to release him would turn the tables completely in our favour and would prove to Lumumba that we are without doubt his best friends in his hour of peril if we succeeded to save him or even if we fail in the attempt. Unfortunately I lost such a great opportunity of proving to Lumumba our sincerity and our support for him; because our Army reckoned more on the pride of their military discipline that what Ghana would gain from their enterprise.

As I was about to get into my car after the meeting with Ankrah and Otu the latter came to me and informed me that he had heard news of the release of Lumumba and that someone had informed him that he had seen from a window Lumumba pass by in a jeep escorted by his own troops. From the Camp I proceeded to Col

Ankrah's house where the Congolese Ministers were waiting for me. On my way to the house the news of Lumumba's release was confirmed by my driver and another driver who had offered to act as a guide to show us where Camp Makabi was.

In order not to disclose what had happened in my discussion with our commanders, I seized the opportunity offered by the drivers' confirmation of Lumumba's release and informed the Congolese Ministers that they had given me false news about Lumumba's arrest, as he had been seen about the Camp. Let me hasten to add that I believed as everybody did that Lumumba was in fact arrested but I wanted to take an opportunity to impress upon the Congolese Ministers Ghana's gallant action in planning to release Lumumba from his captors. I would also like to add that I regretted the attitude adopted by our Commanders and their continued lack of co-operation. If the Army had seen my political point of view which I had on many occasions attempted to explain to them and had supported my plan they would completely have retrieved by their gallant action all that Ghana had lost in Congo and would have shown to UNO and all and sundry that Ghana and its President were firmly behind Lumumba and his Government. Even they would not act in a mock way to make Ghana regain her hope. I was particularly anxious that UNO who had all along played the political game against Lumumba to know that Ghana stood firmly behind Lumumba, but once more our soldiers proved unco-operative and unreliable at the critical moment.

From the Camp I left with the Congolese Ministers to my residence where I told them to go and find out the truth about Lumumba's arrest and to let me know their findings in order to enable me to storm the Makabi Camp for Lumumba's release. The Ministers left in search of Lumumba and although I knew that the Ghana Army would not support my plan for Lumumba's release, I had to make this statement in order to win the confidence of the Congolese Ministers, and subsequent events proved my action to be correct.

Not long after their departure, Mr Lasiry, Chief of Protocol in the Lumumba Government, rang to say that the Prime Minister would like to see me in his former residence. Without the least delay, accompanied by Mr Seddoh and four guards I dashed to Mr Lumumba's house. On arrival there, we noticed that the entrance of the house was being heavily guarded by troops of the Armée Congolaise in battle dress. Outside, there was a number of military jeeps.

It was with difficulty that the guards allowed us in. After waiting

for some time in the lounge, the Prime Minister arrived and summoned us into his office where the Vice Prime Minister, Mr Gizenga
and the Secretary of State for the Ministry of Foreign Affairs (he
has since the troubles started been acting as Foreign Minister)
Mr Andre Mandi were waiting. That was about 7.20 p.m.

In a grave tone and looking very serious, Mr Patrice Lumumba
told me that he had called me to protest once more against the
hostile attitude of the Ghana troops who were guarding the Radio
Station against him. He said that he had sent a note of protest to
the President on the previous day's incident and was very indignant
that the same aggressiveness of the Ghanaian soldiers was repeated
that afternoon. Mr Lumumba continued that he did not see the
usefulness of the Ghana troops here and that no other African
troops would have behaved in the way they did.

The Prime Minister then narrated what had happened. After his
release he paraded through the streets of Leopoldville to let the
public know that he was not under arrest. He later went to the
Broadcasting Station to speak to the Nation, but the Ghanaian
troops on guard there would not allow him to enter. Some of the
soldiers, he added, even used abusive language against him. He
continued that if there was any thorn in their flesh, it was Ghana;
the latter, he said, was responsible for their failure to carry out the
operation to seize the Airport and the Radio Station. What was
most surprising was that the Ghanaian troops were now working
for the Opposition. He could not understand why Mr Bolikango
could be allowed to enter the Broadcasting House and he the Prime
Minister was refused entry.

Mr Lumumba further said that in his first note, addressed to the
President, he had decided to break diplomatic relations with Ghana
if the Government of Ghana would not withdraw its troops from
the Radio Station. He added that his Government had now
decided to give Ghana the last chance, and that within one hour,
all the Ghana troops in the Congo should cease their activities (the
time was then 8.15 p.m.). If this was not carried out, his country
would be compelled to sever diplomatic relations with Ghana.

The Vice Premier and the Secretary of State for Foreign Affairs
also spoke in the same vein and the latter handed a formal note of
protest to me. In a short statement, I told the Prime Minister that I
was sorry for the incident that had happened but that it was impossible to ask all the Ghana troops, about 3,000 of which were
operating in the Congo, to cease their activities within one hour
and that unless the relevant portion of the ultimatum was amended

the letter of protest was unacceptable to me, for I could not deliver the ultimatum; then I was told that what I should first do was to order the Ghanaian troops guarding the Radio Station to withdraw and the entire troops to be withdrawn later. The Prime Minister told me that he would be prepared to amend his letter only after the troops at the Radio Station had been withdrawn. I said I could not carry the letter without the amended request. However, I promised to do what I could in the matter; but before leaving the Prime Minister the latter informed me that if no action was taken to withdraw the troops from the Radio Station within the time stipulated the ultimatum would stand and that he would have it published in the papers the following day. I replied that he was free to do as he wished.

From the Prime Minister's residence I went straight to the Military Camp to look for Messrs Otu and Ankrah. In a short meeting again with our Army Officers I emphasised the gravity of the situation and the embarrassment which the Ghanaian troops stationed at the Radio Station was causing the Congolese Government. I informed them that one Mr Bolikango had been allowed to use the Radio Station but our Army had prevented Mr Lumumba from using the same medium to talk to his people. I further emphasised that it was necessary that the Ghana troops guarding the Radio Station be withdrawn and that I was going to see Gen Van Horn to see that it was done immediately.

In a short discussion which followed as to the propriety of withdrawing Ghana troops from operating under UN command, Col Ankrah informed me that it was not correct that Mr Bolikango had been allowed to broadcast. He also stated that Mr Kasavubu had wished to broadcast at 8 p.m. that evening but he also was prevented by the Ghanaian troops from doing so. Brig Otu then appealed to me not to take any hasty action and to wait for the decision of the Security Council which was meeting to discuss the matter that evening. However I decided to go ahead with my plans.

We left the two officers after 9 p.m. for the United Nations Headquarters. There we were told that both Gen Van Horn and Mr Dayal had gone out for dinner and it was therefore impossible to see them. We therefore went back to the Prime Minister's residence to report to him. On our arrival we were told that he was in a Cabinet meeting and that the Vice Premier would therefore receive us. Gen Lundula, Mr Grenfell, Secretary of State in the Lumumba Government and another senior officer of the Congolese

National Army were present. I informed Mr Gizenga that I went to see Gen Van Horn about the withdrawal of the Ghana troops from the Radio Station but the General was not available. Mr Dayal, Special Representative of the Secretary-General of the United Nations, was also not there. I therefore promised Mr Gizenga that to prove that I was sincere in my efforts to have the Ghana troops withdrawn I would be glad if one could accompany me to the United Nations Headquarters to check up and if my statement proved correct for them to leave the one on guard to telephone me at my residence. I made this request as I had reiterated to them that I had had no sleep for almost two days and that had had an effect on my health and had made me unable to keep vigil until the return of Dayal and Gen Van Horn. Mr Gizenga however told me that he did not see how they could act as scouts for me and that it was my responsibility to watch for the arrival of Messrs Van Horn and Dayal and to take the necessary action. He continued that they had told me the action they would like me to take and could do no more. I replied that in the circumstances I could not do otherwise than accept the letter of protest from the Government. I pointed out that from there I would go straight to bed and would not get up until the next morning. In short I could not comply with their wish.

I may mention that all this time the part I played during the arrest of Lumumba was unknown to Mr Gizenga and his Ministerial colleagues as well as Lumumba. Mr Lumumba and the other Ministers were informed of my action the next day by the two Ministers who accompanied me to the camp. I gathered from the remarkable change in Lumumba's attitude towards me and from the friendly smile on the faces of his Cabinet Ministers that the part I played for his release had gone home to Lumumba and his Cabinet Ministers who on the previous day had insulted me as treacherous. Indeed so great was the impression created by my action on the previous day that Mr Lumumba invited me to meet his Ministers and in their presence gave a short speech in which he re-affirmed his confidence in you and me. He regretted however that our system of continuing to rely on expatriates for appointment to senior posts had caused him considerable harm and embarrassment. He wished me however to forget the past and let by-gones be by-gones. Later he asked me and his Cabinet Ministers to drink over the unfortunate past and to forget it all.

On 13 September, a joint meeting of the Chamber of Representatives and Senate voted full powers to Lumumba by 88 votes to 5 with

3 abstentions. The next day, Kasavubu declared that the joint session was illegal and that he was, therefore, adjourning Parliament for one month. At 2.30 p.m. Lumumba spoke on the radio, and formally asked the United Nations to help his government in the pacification of the country.

But the most significant event of a crowded day was the evening broadcast of the Chief of Staff of the Army, Colonel Mobutu, in which he stated that he was 'neutralising' both Lumumba and Kasavubu and that the Armée Nationale Congolaise (ANC) was assuming power, by means of a peaceful revolution, until 30 December 1960. Later, he ordered the Communist embassies to leave the country, and announced that he was setting up a 'collège des universitaires' (College of University Students) to run the country. It was clear that an even stormier period in Congolese history was about to begin. In these circumstances the UN agreed to guard the houses of any politicians who asked for protection.

5 Ghana Attempts Mediation

MOBUTU's intervention was made possible by the money given to him by the UN to pay his troops. Financial records of the UN show that five million Congolese francs were paid out in September to soldiers in Leopoldville, and that the money was handed over on Saturday, 10 September—just four days before the coup—Mobutu being allowed to claim the credit for this payment in order to build up his prestige among the troops.

Mr Lewandowski of Poland, in his speech of 16 September 1960 at the 904th Meeting of the Security Council, said: 'There is something basically wrong in a situation where the United Nations operations in the Congo run counter to the wish of the people and the government of the country. . . . It would be a grave mistake if United Nations operations in that country should lead to the overthrow of the government which turned to the organisation for assistance in the hour of need.' This was my view, and the view of all those supporting the cause of African freedom, as we watched the position of the legitimate prime minister grow daily worse, while the UN force which he had invited to the Congo to help his government seemed unable or unwilling to carry out its mandate.

At the same meeting of the Security Council, which Quaison-Sackey was invited to attend, the Secretary-General read a telegram he had just received from Kasavubu in which he complained of UN interference in the domestic affairs of the Congo and the protection given to Lumumba by Ghanaian troops. Lumumba had, on 15 September, taken refuge in the Ghana Officers' Mess in the Army's camp at Leopoldville. There hard-pressed Ghanaian troops successfully held off riotous soldiers of the hostile Baluba tribe. He had eventually been escorted out of the camp after intervention by the

UN Special Representative. The same afternoon, Kasavubu and Ileo had asked the UN to arrest Lumumba, but the UN had refused.

Kasavubu was desperately trying to consolidate his own position. On 14 September he sent me the following message from Brazzaville:

(*Translation*)

Now that the Congolese question is before the Security Council for the fifth time, I wish to underline the willingness of my Government to maintain legality and freedom, to assist in close co-operation and confidence with the United Nations to maintain our national sovereignty for the progress of our country and prosperity of our people. We count on the solid support of African countries to disperse from our Republic foreign intrigues and interference. Faithful to the African cause, we wish to remain outside East-West conflict. After having eliminated foreign colonialist intervention we favour support of the United Nations and African solidarity but we are today menaced by new threatening interferences to provoke civil war in the heart of Africa. The revocation of ex-Lumumba Government was necessary to restore internal peace and freedom and to bring an end to massacre of the people. Revocation was perfectly legal by virtue of the prerogatives of Head of State according to the fundamental law. We ask African countries to support the efforts of the legal Government of Prime Minister Joseph Ileo in order to evict neo-colonialism, balkanisation and anarchy. Africa will be made by Africans with friendship and co-operation of the United Nations.

I replied the same day:

Thank you for your telegram of the 14th September.

From the start I foresaw these difficulties of the Congo and, as you yourself must know, through my Ambassador Djin, I was able to reconcile Lumumba and yourself as Prime Minister and President respectively. This was an excellent arrangement to enable the Congo to settle down and to consolidate your independence and sovereignty.

Your present conduct and action will aggravate the difficulties of the Congo Republic and play her into the hands of her enemies and open the door to the return of colonialism, balkanisation and anarchy.

You will note that every reactionary newspaper and politician has applauded your action while those individuals and journals supporting the cause of African freedom are consistent in condemnation of your action. One of the most serious aspects of what you have done is the breach of the unanimous agreement into which your Party entered with Brussels.

The Lumumba Government was formed with the consent of Parliament and it is your duty to stick together and uphold the Brussels agreement. I therefore appeal to you in the strongest terms to reconsider your position and reconcile with Lumumba so as to prevent disaster to your country.

I have confidence that you can do this in the supreme interest of the Congo Republic and of the African cause so dear to the hearts of all African patriots. The eyes of all the African States are set on you and Lumumba. African unity and solidarity can be jeopardised by any wrong step you take now.

I must make it quite clear that my Government and I support the Government of the Congo Republic set up after the General Election in accordance with the will of the people, with you as President and Lumumba as Prime Minister. I am sending a copy of this telegram to Mr Lumumba.

I trust that you will not allow any military adventurer to take advantage of your differences with Lumumba which can after all be easily resolved.

I had determined to do all in my power to bring about a reconciliation between Kasavubu and Lumumba and had instructed Djin accordingly. He wrote to me on 16 September giving an account of his efforts to mediate between the two men:

'On the 14th September I met Messrs Mhamet Boucetta, Moroccan Minister of Public Works, and Ahmed Sounesi, Director of Information, Moroccan Foreign Service, and Galep, UAR Ambassador, at the Stanley Hotel for discussion on the present situation. I may mention that prior to this meeting the Moroccan diplomats had seen me on many occasions for information and discussion on the present crises. I had gathered from their talks that they were anxious as I was for an improvement in the situation in Leopoldville. On the morning of the 15th instant they 'phoned me for an appointment but as I was busily engaged I could not give any definite time, so they called at my residence at a time when I was getting ready to go to Camp Leopold II. We agreed to meet later at the Stanley Hotel. During our meeting we discussed the possible way of easing the tension which had developed between Lumumba and Kasavubu. We all agreed on the necessity for taking prompt action, so we decided that we should go and see Kasavubu at once and inform him of our intentions. It is relevant to state here that during the meeting at the Stanley Hotel I made it known to my African colleagues at Stanley Hotel your fervent desire to see the differences between Lumumba and Kasavubu settled without delay. I also informed them of your plan in sending a delegation under Hon Botsio to Leopoldville to mediate between the two Congolese leaders. I explained that in spite of the failure of Mr Botsio's delegation of which I was a member you had not given up hope but had sent Mr Welbeck to pursue the mediation.

As Welbeck was still in Leopoldville I suggested and it was agreed that he should be asked to join us to see Kasavubu and Lumumba. When Mr Welbeck had been collected we proceeded to Kasavubu's residence. During our discussion with Kasavubu he stated that the latter had on several occasions acted without consulting him on matters of vital importance to the State. He cited the following examples. His (acceptance of the) gift of aeroplanes from Czechoslovakia, trucks and fourteen aeroplanes from Russia in addition to a number of war materials he had received from countries behind the Iron Curtain. He stated that Lumumba was erratic and had made several irresponsible press statements which had done much harm to the reputation of the country. Mr Kasavubu ended by saying that in view of the instances he had quoted he felt that he could no more co-operate with such a man and he doubted whether we could restrain him from repeating his rash and irresponsible actions. He added that I was responsible for bringing them together but he doubted whether I could restrain him from his impetuous actions.

I explained to Mr Kasavubu that I had always worked for the peace and independence of Congo and it was within that context that I brought the two leaders together. I drew attention to an occasion in Stanleyville where I restrained Lumumba. I also pointed out how on many occasions I interceded on behalf of the Belgians whom Mr Kasavubu claimed had been driven out of the Congo when they should have remained in the country. I referred to an occasion when drinking in Mr Kasavubu's house together with Mr Lumumba when I stated that Lumumba was like a strong horse and I likened Kasavubu to a rider and pointed out that it was essential that he Kasavubu should control the reins well in order to keep Lumumba in check. I remember Lumumba saying that he was indeed a strong horse. I intended my anecdotes to be a joke which was enjoyed by both of them but I meant it. I pointed out that in the face of all those warnings I did not see how I could be blamed.

Kasavubu confirmed what I had said and after further discussion he agreed to co-operate with Lumumba but said that we must not let Lumumba know that we had seen him, otherwise it would appear that he Kasavubu had asked for the intervention. We then went to confer with Lumumba, who readily agreed to a draft communiqué which we had cleared with Kasavubu.

Lumumba inserted two sentences and amended the last paragraph of the communiqué. This in my opinion indicates how alert he is with everything that is going on around him.

From Lumumba, we went back to Kasavubu with the amended version of our communiqué. We informed him that Lumumba had agreed to the communiqué and before the communiqué was typed we discussed it with Kasavubu and Cyril Adoula, Minister of Information for Leopoldville Province. Mr Adoula at first tried to put spokes in our wheels and I seized the opportunity to let him know that I had not forgotten him and that he was the man who assisted me to deliver Osagyefo's message to the two leaders during the time they were trying to form a Government. I praised his efforts during the early days and asked him to co-operate with us as he had done before in the early stages when I was mediating between Kasavubu and Lumumba.

Kasavubu read the text of the agreed communiqué and gave it to Adoula, who also signified his assent to the communiqué. Mr Kasavubu then stated that before he could sign the communiqué it was necessary that Lumumba should see the agreement. We therefore went back to Lumumba, who readily agreed to the communiqué. Then we returned to Kasavubu for his signature. We found that the door to his house was barred. We waited for several minutes, and although we could hear the noises made from spoons and forks in the room we were made to understand that he was away. We therefore decided to return home as we had not even taken our breakfast, the time being 2 p.m.

We resumed our effort of mediation at about 5 o'clock when we went to the yard of Kasavubu and were told that he was in discussion with four UNO men, so we were ushered to his hall by his Secretary who had received us on previous occasions. We waited for about two hours. Later on, the same Secretary who had admitted us into the hall came and informed our delegation that Mr Kasavubu was not in.

As we were leaving Kasavubu's residence we found in the car park a Mercedes car belonging to an important UNO representative in Leopoldville. We asked the driver of that car, who confirmed that his master was upstairs and that he was in discussion with Mr Kasavubu. Mr Mensah, my driver, a Ghanaian who had lived in Leopoldville for over ten years and spoke the local language very fluently, said to me when we were leaving Kasavubu's residence that, when the delegation was waiting in Kasavubu's hall, the President of Congo looked through the window and in the local language addressed his servants below not to mind 'the African communists in the hall'.

When the delegation had moved to a point about 500 yards away from Kasavubu's gate, we alighted from our cars and waited for about one and a half hours to see whether we could meet the UNO officer who was in consultation with Kasavubu. Nobody turned up but we saw a car driving up from Kasavubu's residence, but when those in the car saw us from afar they returned back. I have written all this in detail in order to enable you to know what is happening here and to assist you in forming your own opinion about the changing events in Leopoldville. I have deliberately refrained from commenting on the events so as not to give colour to the report of my own opinions or prejudices.

Although at times it seemed an almost impossible task to bring Lumumba and Kasavubu together, I saw this as the only hope for peace in the Congo. I continued to send messages to Lumumba urging him 'to use restraint in the present circumstances' and warning him that his position would be prejudiced 'by any action which might be construed as irresponsible'. I urged him to take advice from the ambassadors of the African states and not from others whose motives were suspect.

But before normal government could be restored it was essential to remove the threat of armed violence. How otherwise could political discussion take place in a calm atmosphere? I advised Lumumba to bring the Congolese Army under effective control with the help of the United Nations.

Lumumba either could not or would not patch up the quarrel with Kasavubu, who for his part was becoming daily more insistent that Lumumba should go. In a message dated 17 September 1960 Lumumba told me of his plans to move the seat of Parliament and the government to Stanleyville:

Mr President and dear Friend,
It is with very real pleasure that I received your several messages, and I thank you most heartily. I have taken into consideration all

the advice you have given me and have spoken about it with Mr Djin, the Ambassador.

Mr Djin and the Ambassadors of the United Arab Republic, Morocco and Tunisia have proposed reconciliation between President Kasavubu and myself. I have given my full assent to the proposal and the text of a joint declaration was drawn up. Mr Kasavubu does not wish for any reconciliation, and prefers to play the game of the imperialists against Africa. And so, as you will see, the fault is not mine.

Everything is being done to stifle the Republic of the Congo and subject it to the tutelage of the Western Powers. The Ambassador will give you a detailed report on the situation, and he will point out my good faith and Mr Kasavubu's ill will.

Parliament and the Government have just taken a decision to remove the seat of Parliament and the Government to Stanleyville. All the agitation that is at present going on is localised entirely in the town of Leopoldville. The whole country is behind the Government. The removal of the seat of the Government to Stanleyville will soon frustrate the imperialist plots, because it will be seen at once that Kasavubu is isolated and that the country is not in agreement with him. The Brussels Round Table Conference had already decided that the capital of the Republic of the Congo should be transferred to Luluaborg, but because of tribal wars between the Balubas and the Luluas, we decided to establish ourselves at Stanleyville, a very peaceful city.

The Congo-Ghana Union will be immediately achieved and I shall submit the plan for Parliament's approval. Kasavubu was the obstacle in the way of this Union. The Ghana Embassy should be transferred at once to Stanleyville.

Nevertheless, I should like to ask you to continue the struggle at the United Nations. You will have to send me military reinforcements at Stanleyville. Congo and Ghana must fight together until final victory is achieved.

It is my absolute desire that the Convention for a Ghana-Congo Union should be ratified without delay. In this way, we shall prove to the world as a whole that we are united by bonds of active solidarity. It is time that we perform a solemn act.

The United Nations, as a result of their mischievous action in the Congo, wished to sow the seeds of discord between the Congo and Ghana. The situation has just been clarified and our ties are now stronger than ever. Consequently there is no further disagreement between us.

You can rely on me, and I can on you. Today we are one, and our countries are one.

Fraternally yours, etc.

P.S. PARLIAMENT has given me full powers and I have the law behind me.

P.L.

In the Security Council (905th Meeting, 16 September 1960) Quaison-Sackey explained Ghana's interest in seeing a successful solution to the Congo problem:

> Ghana and all the independent African states fully support the struggles of the Congolese government and people to preserve their independence, unity and territorial integrity. The support is amply shown not only by the presence of our troops in the Congo under United Nations Command, but was clearly stated during the recent Conference of Independent African States held in Leopoldville.
>
> My Government was the first Government to be approached by the Congolese Government for direct military assistance; if we preferred to channel such assistance through the United Nations, it was because we fully supported the United Nations' effort to achieve peaceful solutions in the Congo.

He went on to say that the Ghana Government considered the United Nations should assist the Congolese Government to re-organise its security forces 'so that they could be used by it to restore law and order'. There should be no private armies; all forces in the Congo, except the ANC, should be disarmed, and this included the so-called Katangan army. 'The task of the United Nations will be frustrated so long as Mr Tshombe and others are allowed to have private armies at their disposal. It is equally important, however, that the Security Council should call upon all those who insist on supplying arms to these gentlemen to stop.'

Quaison-Sackey then gave details of the import of Belgian arms into the Congo and ended:

> I would sum up the views of my Government as follows: My Government considers that greater urgency and priority should be given to the task of helping the Central Government reorganise its military forces so that they may be able in the words of the Security Council resolution of 14 July 'to meet fully their tasks' including the maintenance of law and order in the whole of the Congo.
>
> Secondly, the private armies at the disposal of the secessionists, Mr Tshombe and Mr Kalondji, should be disarmed. The disarming

of these units would be greatly facilitated if the Belgian incubus, especially in Katanga, were entirely removed. The United Nations Command, with the explicit authorisation of the Security Council, should see to it that all Belgian military officers are removed and the weapons recently supplied by Belgium are collected and taken under United Nations control.

My Government believes that if these suggestions are followed it should be possible to re-establish law and order throughout the Congo. . . . But time is running short. The situation in the Congo takes on a new complexion every day. . . . In these circumstances, my Government proposes that there should be a United Nations mediation. We suggest that the Security Council should give consideration to the idea of offering to the Congo the services of a good offices committee of six, a committee under whose umbrella the various political persuasions in the Congo may hold *pourparlers* with a view to resolving their political difficulties in a just, peaceful and constitutional manner. . . . Such a committee might consist of the African and Asian members of the Advisory Committee in the Congo. My delegation will be prepared, with your permission, to elaborate our ideas on this suggestion to the Secretary-General if the Council sees fit to give it some consideration.

There followed a speech by Mr Caba (Guinea), who also complained of the non-withdrawal of Belgian troops in the Congo. He pointed out that they were still hanging on to the Kitona and Kamina bases. 'Today', he said, 'we hear little of the secession of the rich Province of Katanga, but the problem is still there'.

In his reply, M. de Thier (Belgium) admitted that there had been delays in the withdrawal of troops, but they were 'due to practical difficulties, such as lack of means of transport'. Referring to a recent shipment of Belgian arms, Thier said:

An investigation made by the Belgian Government regarding a delivery of arms from Belgium shows that this involved a small order of light weapons intended exclusively for the maintenance of internal order. This order was placed on behalf of the Force Publique of the Congo prior to independence, and its execution was due to the inadvertence of an ill-informed official. The Belgian Government immediately took all the steps necessary to stop any further consignment of arms to the Congo.

The explanation might have been more convincing if continuing Belgian military activities in the Congo had been less obvious. In his third Report to the Security Council the UN Secretary-General told of a formal protest to the Belgian Government requesting the immediate evacuation of troops still in the Congo. In the reply he received it was stated that transport difficulties had caused some delay but the evacuation would be completed as speedily as possible. That was at the end of August. In a telegram of 4 September 1960 to the Belgian Minister of Foreign Affairs, the Secretary-General said his representatives had informed him of the presence of 650 Belgian combat troops at Kitona base, and two gunboats at Banana. On 10 September the representative of Belgium stated that the men at Kitona were 'technicians and airfield guards'. They would leave, he said, as soon as they were relieved by United Nations troops.

In the meantime there was an exchange of communications, 5–10 September, between the Secretary-General and the Soviet delegation about the arrival of between eleven and fourteen Russian aircraft in the Congo. The Russians argued they had the right to assist, if asked to by the Congolese Government. In view of the build-up of military strength against him, Lumumba can hardly be blamed for seeking help. In a telegram dated 12 September he asked the UN for twenty aircraft, arms and ammunition 'to prevent the attacks being prepared at the instigation of certain Powers'.

After two months of United Nations intervention, the underlying causes of the Congo crisis remained virtually the same: they were the open or camouflaged presence of Belgian forces and the secessionist movements fostered by colonial interests. The point was put well by Mr Aboud (Morocco) at the 906th Meeting of the Security Council on 17 September when he said:

> Belgian aggression and the attempts to Balkanise the Congo are at the root of the evil. It is neither logical nor wise to concentrate on the details and to forget the whole, which constitutes the essence of the problem. . . . The independence of Katanga, if the worst comes to the worst, will not mean that Katanga is independent but that the Union Minière du Katanga is independent.

6 Tshombe and Katanga

TSHOMBE'S Government proclaimed the Independent State of Katanga on 11 July 1960, less than two weeks after the establishment of the Republic of the Congo. From that date, the problem of Katanga has been at the root of most of the Republic's difficulties. It was in Katanga that Patrice Lumumba was murdered. It was close to the Katanga border that Dag Hammarskjöld died, in a mysterious aircraft accident. All through the troubled early years of the Republic, time and again it was affairs in Katanga which prevented peaceful solutions.

Why is Katanga so important to the Congo? Why did it secede? Who is Moise Tshombe, and how did he manage to defy the strength of the United Nations and survive? Did he really represent the people of Katanga?

The Province of Katanga, in the southern part of the Congo, has immense mineral wealth. Its copper deposits alone are estimated at about 115 million tons. It is the world's largest producer of uranium and one of the world's biggest producers of cobalt. It produces zinc, coal, manganese, tin, lead, silver and cadmium. The manufacture of cement and the generation of electricity, both vital for a developing country, must also be noted.

For economic reasons, therefore, Katanga is essential to the Congo. It is also politically necessary to preserve the unity of the Republic. Africa already has too many small states which are politically weak and not economically viable. Further fragmentation would serve only the interests of the neo-colonialists who seek to maintain their hold on Africa.

Until the emergence of Tshombe on the political scene the question of secession had hardly been raised. To most, there was no doubt about the status of Katanga: it was a Province which formed an integral part of the Congo. With the formation of Tshombe's Party, Conakat (Confédération des Associations du Katanga) in July 1959, however, talk of secession grew. In January 1960, at the Round Table Conference in Brussels, Tshombe called for a loose federation for the Congo with a certain amount of provincial autonomy and close ties with Belgium. Later, in the elections which preceded the independence of the Congo, he again campaigned on a federalist and not a secessionist policy. Evidently he was either unsure of support for his secessionist views or he was merely awaiting the right moment to strike. His opportunity came with the mutiny of the Force Publique and the breakdown of law and order shortly after the establishment of the Republic.

Conakat had won only 8 of the 137 seats in the National Assembly in Leopoldville but it succeeded in gaining 25 of the 60 seats in the Katanga Provincial Assembly. Conakat's nearest rival was the Balu-bakat Party, led by Jason Sendwe, which obtained 23 seats. Tshombe was accordingly elected Provincial President and formed an exclusively Conakat administration. He began at once to negotiate with Lumumba over membership in a coalition government but negotiations broke down when he demanded more seats in the Cabinet than his strength in the National Assembly justified. It was then that he began to talk of secession.

The way in which Tshombe was able to form a Conakat Government in Katanga, when in fact he had not secured an overall majority in the elections, is worth examining.

Immediately after the elections, the anti-secessionist Cartel Katangais, of which the largest component was Sendwe's Balubakat Party, decided to boycott the Assembly because they held that the elections had been unfairly conducted by the Belgian administration. They thought by doing this that they could prevent Conakat from forming a government, since a two-thirds majority was legally necessary before a new government could be established. They underestimated the determination of Conakat and the Belgian Government. After Tshombe had threatened to appeal to Southern Rhodesia or the United Nations, the Belgian Parliament altered the Basic Law to enable him to form a government. As Conor Cruise O'Brien has pointed out, 'The point about the Loi Fondamentale is that it was worked out at a Round Table with the political leaders of the Congo as a whole. Now it was amended in a critically important way by the Belgian Parliament, without consulting any Africans except those of the "European-cemented Conakat.[1]"'

[1] C. C. O'Brien, *To Katanga and Back*, Hutchinson, 1962, p. 84.

There has never been any doubt that Conakat was formed by Europeans. It was openly supported by the Belgian Government and the Union Minière. A Belgian observer, Pierre Davister, went so far as to say that it was being 'clearly manipulated from the wings by Europeans' (*Katanga Enjeu du Monde*, p. 67). Among the Africans, it drew its main strength from the Lunda tribe, of which Tshombe's father-in-law was paramount chief.

It was this Conakat provincial government which on 11 July 1960, without consulting the people, proclaimed the independence of Katanga:

This Independence is total. None the less, conscious of the imperious necessity of an economic collaboration with Belgium, the government of Katanga, to which Belgium, in order to protect human lives, has just granted the assistance of its own troops, asks Belgium to join with Katanga in a close economic community.

It asks Belgium to contribute its technical, financial and military aid.

It asks Belgium to re-establish public order and security.

The Declaration of Independence clearly gave away the source of Tshombe's strength and the real concerns behind Katangan secession: Belgian support and foreign big-business interests. The Elisabethville correspondent of the (London) *Daily Telegraph* summed up the position neatly in his report published on 27 July:

M. Tshombe, the self-styled President, is today far more under the domination of Belgian officials than he was as an obscure politician before Congo independence. His regime depends entirely on Belgian arms, men and money. Without this, his government would in all probability be quickly pulled down from within and without. The outline of Belgium's emergency policy for Katanga is now discernible. It is to protect the great Belgian financial stake here and hold a political bridgehead in the hope of a Congolese union amenable to Belgium and the West.

Moise Kapenda Tshombe was born at Musamba in Katanga in November 1919. His family was rich, having made money out of commerce and being related to the royal house of the Lunda tribe. Educated at Methodist mission schools, Tshombe took an accountancy course by correspondence and then went into business himself. But he was not as successful as his relatives and was declared a bankrupt on three occasions. Between 1951 and 1953 he was a member of the Katangan Provincial Council and in July 1959 helped to found Conakat. He became President of Conakat and in that capacity went to Brussels in December 1959 to press for elections and a Round Table Conference.

Here was the man the Belgians were looking for; a man ambitious for personal power who could be used as a puppet to promote their interests. After the declaration of Katanga independence, Union Minière assured him of financial backing by making over to the Katanga Government all taxes legally payable to the Congolese Government in Leopoldville, while Belgian advisers and Belgian troops gave him the necessary administrative and military support.

All the time, however, the Belgian Government protested to the rest of the world that it was against Katangan secession. In other words, it was refusing publicly to recognise the new state, while at the same time it was encouraging it by underhand means in every way it could. On 17 July 1960 the Provincial Assembly, which contained only Conakat members, approved the Declaration of Independence and the Assembly became the National Assembly under the Constitution of the State of Katanga drafted by Professor Clemens of the University of Liège.

To read the day-by-day reports of diplomats, UN officials and newspaper correspondents is to be reminded constantly of the damaging effect of Belgian interference in Congolese affairs. In the Second Progress Report of Rajeshwar Dayal, the UN Special Representative, to the Secretary-General, 2 November 1960, the problem of Katanga is described at length. Reference is made to the persistent and methodical press campaign being conducted in Katanga against the United Nations. The hostile attitude 'may be ascribed in part to the influence of Belgian advisers in Katanga'. Dayal continued, 'There is clear evidence of the steady return in recent weeks of Belgians to the Congo and . . . of increasing Belgian participation in political and administrative activities. . . . Belgian military and para-military personnel as well as civilian personnel continue to be available to authorities in the Congo, notably in Katanga and South Kasai.' He mentioned a recruiting agency which had been set up in Brussels. 'The object of the agency seems to be to assist in re-establishing a civil service of Belgian nationality, principally at the policy level.' This had made the task of ONUC more difficult. 'United Nations documents and reports have frequently been withheld from the Congolese officials in the ministries and propaganda has been engineered regarding the supposed dangers of the emergence of United Nations trusteeship as a result of ONUC's mission.'

Dayal was referring not only to Katanga, where he described

Belgian influence as 'omnipresent', but also to other parts of the
Congo. 'In the so-called autonomous State of South Kasai there is
also a considerable Belgian presence. . . . There is no apparent
shortage of rifles. Moreover, arms from Katanga are brought in
through the Mwene-Ditu territory of the Kabinda district, reportedly
with the help of a Belgian businessman.' In another section of his
report, Dayal referred to a Belgian colonel 'who recently arrived
from Brazzaville'. This man 'acts as adviser to the Leopoldville
Ministry of National Defence, while a former Belgian warrant
officer serves as aide-de-camp to Colonel Mobutu, with the rank of
captain . . . in the outlying area of Thysville, where ANC armoured
cars are stationed, the number of Belgian military officers has
increased from one to five and they are presumably training ANC
personnel in the use of their equipment.' Dayal concluded:

> Belgian activities in recent weeks have increased the intransigence
> of the ANC Command as well as of the Katangese authorities,
> inhibited peaceful activity and therefore the possibility of an
> eventual return to constitutional government and the re-establish-
> ment of the unity and integrity of the country.

In a *Note Verbale* dated 8 October 1960 the Secretary-General
again asked the Belgian Government to withdraw all military, para-
military and civil personnel from the Congo, since he wanted all aid
to the Congo channelled through the United Nations. A copy of the
Note was sent to Tshombe. As might have been expected, Tshombe,
in a telegram to the Secretary-General dated 27 October 1960, denied
that the presence of the Belgians in Katanga was detrimental. 'Their
presence has been a factor making for peace and not disorder. It
should also be borne in mind that the Belgians are here at the express
request of the Katanga authorities and on their terms.'

It was in this situation that I addressed the Fifteenth General
Assembly of the United Nations in New York on 23 September and
devoted much of my speech to the situation in the Congo. After
tracing briefly the history of the Congo immediately before and since
independence, I spoke of the failure of the UN to distinguish between
legal and illegal authorities, which had led to the most 'ludicrous
results embarrassing both to the Ghanaian forces who were called
upon to carry them out and to the United Nations itself which was
exhibited in a ridiculous light. For instance, the very troops which
Ghana sent to help the legitimate Lumumba Government at the
request of Lumumba were employed by the United Nations in preventing Lumumba, the legitimate Prime Minister of the legal Govern-

ment of the Congo Republic, from performing the most obvious functions of his office—for instance, using his own radio station.' I continued:

Distinguished Delegates, these difficulties are in essence growing pains of the United Nations and it would be entirely wrong to blame either the Security Council or any senior officials of the United Nations for what has taken place. However, a new approach is clearly required. I believe that it is not difficult to devise methods by which the issue can be appropriately dealt with.

Let us get down to realities. The United Nations were invited to enter the Congo in a message from the Head of State Mr Kasavubu, and from the Prime Minister Mr Lumumba. Both these gentlemen were appointed to their respective offices in accordance with the will of the Congolese people expressed through election. Here then is the legal Government which should be supported and behind which the United Nations should throw its authority.

I am sure that the independent African States will agree with me that the problem in the Congo is an acute African problem which can be solved by Africans only. I have on more than one occasion suggested that the United Nations should delegate its functions in the Congo to the Independent African States, especially those African States whose contributions in men and material make the United Nations effort in the Congo possible. The forces of these African States should be under a unified African Command with responsibility to the Security Council under which the United Nations troops entered the Congo Republic.

I suggest that the General Assembly should make it absolutely clear that the United Nations contingents in the Congo Republic have an overriding responsibility to preserve law and order which can only be done by supporting, safeguarding and maintaining the legal and existing Parliamentary framework of the State.

I am sure, Mr President and distinguished Delegates, that no African State would lend support to any secessionist move in the Congo. The Congo is the heart of Africa and we shall do our utmost to prevent any injuries being inflicted upon it by imperialist and colonialist intrigue. The Congo, including Katanga and Kasai, is one and indivisible. Any other approach is mere wishful thinking, for not all the mineral wealth in that integral part of the Congo can create Katanga into a separate State.

I personally, and my Government, have done everything possible to assist and advise the leaders of the Congo to resolve their differences and place their country's and Africa's interests first. Both of them, President Kasavubu and Prime Minister Lumumba, speak the same language of peace and unity. Both of them are anxious to see stability achieved in their country. Both of them agree on reconciliation. What, then, prevents them from coming together? What has led to the fake Mobutu episode? I can assure distinguished Delegates that but for the intrigues of the colonialists a document of reconciliation which has been drafted in the presence of my Ambassador in Leopoldville and approved by both Mr Kasavubu and Mr Lumumba would have been signed by them. Imperialist intrigue, stark and naked, was desperately at work to prevent this being signed. The policy of divide and rule is still being practised energetically by the opponents of African independence and unity.

In these particular circumstances the Congo crisis should be handed over to the Independent African States for solution. I am sure that left to them an effective solution can be found. It is negative to believe, and (yet to) hesitate until the situation becomes irredeemable and develops into another Korea.

I would go further and suggest that all financial aid or technical assistance to the Congo Republic should be arranged only with the legitimate Government of the Congo Republic channelled through the United Nations and guaranteed and supervised by a Committee of the Independent African States appointed by the Security Council who should be accountable to the United Nations. . . .

. . . It is pertinent here to sound a strong note of warning, namely, that if some people are now thinking in terms of trusteeship over the Congo to carry out the exploitation of her resources and wealth, let those people forever discard that idea, for any such suggestion would be resisted. There can be no question of trusteeship in the Congo. The Congo is independent and sovereign. The colonialists and imperialists must remember this fact and remember it for all time. . . .

The following are the recommendations I made:

1 That the United Nations Command in the Congo should be changed forthwith and a firm strong command established with clear positive directions to support the legitimate Government with Kasavubu as President and Lumumba as Prime Minister, whose jurisdiction should be recognised throughout the whole Congo Republic. In other words, the present composition of the United Nations Command should be changed and the composi-

tion of the United Nations Force, its military command and administration altered so that it is drawn entirely from contingents of the forces of the independent African States now serving in the Congo.

2 That every support should be given to the Central Government, as the legitimate Government of the Congo, with the full support of the United Nations.

3 That all private armies, including the Belgian officered groups in Katanga, should be disarmed forthwith and the Congolese National Army be regrouped and reorganised for the purpose of training so that ultimately it can play its proper role as a national army of the Congo Republic until such time as the Central Government considers it possible to dispense with the services of the United Nations forces.

4 That this new Command of the United Nations forces should support the Central Government to restore law and order in the Congo in accordance with the first Resolutions of the Security Council in reliance on which Ghana and other African States placed their contingents under United Nations Command.

5 That the United Nations should guarantee the territorial integrity of the Republic of the Congo in accordance with the provisional constitution agreed at the time of independence.

6 That all financial aid and technical assistance to the Congo Republic should be arranged only with the legitimate Government of the Congo Republic and channelled through the United Nations and guaranteed and supervised by a Committee of Independent African States appointed by the Security Council, and (who should be) accountable to the United Nations.

A few days after my speech was made, news was received of fresh attempts by Kasavubu to strengthen his position at the expense of Lumumba by means of a Round Table Conference. A further stage in the struggle for power in the Congo was about to begin and behind it all were the meddlesome hands of foreign Powers and interests.

7 The Struggle for Power

THERE were many who thought Lumumba ought to have gone to New York to address the General Assembly of the United Nations. Lumumba himself wanted to go but was with difficulty persuaded to remain in the Congo. It was feared his absence might allow his enemies to triumph over him and even prevent his return from America. On 19 September I received the following message:

> The African States request Mr Lumumba at New York and Mr Lumumba requests Osagyefo to send Mr Lumumba a plane to Leopoldville to fetch Mr Lumumba to join Osagyefo at Accra so that he goes with him to New York.

In the meantime, the whole question of Lumumba's proposed visit to New York was discussed at a meeting in Leopoldville of the representatives of Morocco, Tunisia, United Arab Republic and Ghana, held in the residence of Ghana's ambassador. Lumumba sent an official delegation to the meeting comprising the Secretary of State for the Foreign Ministry, Mr A. Mandi and the Chief of Protocol, Mr Lasiry. Mandi told the representatives that Lumumba had spoken by telephone with his delegation in New York headed by Mr Kanza. He was glad to report that the representatives of all the independent African states in New York were doing everything to support the prime minister. They considered, however, that Lumumba should go to New York 'to defend the Congo position.' Mandi then went on to state that the Secretary-General had been approached about the possibility of making a plane available to Lumumba to enable him to travel to New York, 'but the Secretary-General had refused to offer any help'. Lumumba, he said, would welcome the advice of the representatives of the independent African states.

According to the official report of the meeting, our ambassador, A. Y. K. Djin, opened the discussion after the departure of the Congolese delegation:

Mr Djin told the meeting that if Lumumba left for New York it would be difficult to come back and that if that happened it would be very bad for all of them. He drew the attention of members to the Secretary-General's refusal to provide Mr Lumumba with a plane, since the Secretary-General would not like to guarantee his return. Mr Djin further said that even now there were plots to have Mr Lumumba arrested. In the circumstances, he concluded, they had to prevent the Prime Minister from leaving the country.

At this stage of the discussion, Mr Djin informed the members present that he had been requested by the President to accompany him to New York and suggested that it would be good if one or two of them could also join him in order to present the situation in the Congo. Mr Djin said he was telling members of his proposed visit to New York for their information only. He then suggested that a communiqué should be issued on the present Congo situation to enable the President to follow up. Mr Djin ended by saying, 'this is a momentous occasion which needs courage and immediate action'.

The next to speak was the representative of the UAR. He said he was also against the departure of Mr Lumumba for New York. He would not also like any of his colleagues to leave, since their presence here was necessary in order to keep their Governments fully informed in view of the rapidity with which events were happening here. The Guinean and Tunisian representatives also supported the view that it was not advisable for Mr Lumumba to leave the country at this moment. Replying to the statement made by the UAR representative, Mr Djin told the meeting that his departure from Leopoldville would not create a vacuum since Messrs Welbeck and Barden, both of whom are authorities on African affairs were being expected that day to relieve him. He further told members that he would only be away for about four to five days.

The Moroccan Minister told the meeting that they should not take a definite stand against the proposed visit of Lumumba to New York, in view of the importance of the problems to be discussed there. In his opinion, the Minister continued, Mr Lumumba's departure was conditioned by a number of facts. If Mr Kasavubu and Mr Lumumba patched up their differences and the situation became normal there would be no objection to Mr

Lumumba leaving the country. Mr Djin told the Minister that his statement was very diplomatic and added that knowing Mr Lumumba as a strong and determined person they should not deal with him softly. He continued that he admired the way the Minister spoke but considered that since 'we are in a war field' they had to be firm. Mr Djin further said if Mr Lumumba was told he could go when conditions became normal he would create one to enable him to leave the country. A member of the representatives present interrupted to say that Mr Lumumba could not travel since he had no plane.

The UAR representative also spoke against Mr Lumumba's proposal to leave for New York and asked what would be the position when something happened during his absence. Mr Djin suggested that the Moroccan Minister should give reason why Mr Lumumba should not leave the country and that there should be no diplomacy about it. Mr Djin further charged the Moroccan Minister to be the spokesman of the delegation when they went to see Mr Lumumba. He insisted the points discussed should be put down in writing.

The Guinea representative then spoke. In his opinion if they decided against Mr Lumumba's departure they should be able to provide a guarantee for doing so, e.g. holding brief for Mr Lumumba in the United Nations. He continued that if they agreed that Mr Lumumba should leave for New York they should provide certain guarantees while he was away. Mr Djin said he did not want Mr Lumumba to leave for New York and that Mr Kasavubu and Mr Mobutu were all against him. He added that they could not provide any guarantees and that UNO could not do so. Mr Djin further said he considered Kasavubu very evasive and nobody knew what he would do in the next minute. The Guinea representative thought that he was not well understood by Mr Djin and explained what he meant by providing guarantees for Mr Lumumba. Mr Djin, however, thought that if they had agreed that Mr Lumumba should not leave for New York the question of an alternative proposal did not arise.

The Moroccan representative told the meeting that the question at issue was straightforward. It was not advisable for Mr Lumumba to leave because his position was not consolidated. What concerned him was what he should do to consolidate his position to enable him to attend the forthcoming session of the General Assembly. He therefore asked whether they could not do anything to give effect to the declaration of Lumumba during the recent Pan-African Conference. The Guinea representative said he agreed with the Minister and added that since the Leopoldville Conference had a great importance their actions should be orientated on the resolutions adopted.

The Moroccan representative suggested that it would be good for them to support the efforts being made by the Parliamentary Commission to bring the two leaders together. At this stage the UAR representative suggested that the discussions should be postponed since Mr Lumumba might be waiting for them. Mr Djin, however, thought that it would be better to decide on something before seeing him, since Mr Lumumba would quickly win them over in view of the sympathy they had for him. He reiterated his point that the decision taken should be put down in writing.

At 12.45 a.m. the delegation of the representatives of African states called on the Prime Minister, who informed them a declaration would be signed at 4.00 p.m. by him and Kasavubu, ending the present differences between them. He further told members that the reports he had from New York showed that the public there were behind him. The Moroccan delegate thanked the Prime Minister for the good news and said that the members of his delegation fully supported their reconciliation move. Mr Lumumba then informed the delegates that he would like to leave one hour after the declaration had been signed in Parliament.

Possibly Kasavubu agreed to some kind of reconciliation with Lumumba so that the prime minister would leave the country and go to New York. In the light of later events, it seems likely that Kasavubu was insincere, since on 29 September he formally installed the College of University Students, known as the 'College of Commissioners', and shortly afterwards signed a decree defining its powers. He could not work closely with Mobutu and at the same time be genuinely reconciled to Lumumba.

On 30 September, Welbeck sent me the following message:

The new-fangled manoeuvre to overthrow Lumumba is a round table conference originated by Mobutu but which is now being convened and presided over by Kasavubu. This was confirmed in his speech at the installation of members of Mobutu's College of Commissioners. Foreign missions in Leopoldville invited to the ceremony except Ghana but representatives of Guinea, UAR and Morocco refused to attend ceremony as a result of decision taken at a meeting of Independent African States. Liberia and Tunisia however attended the ceremony.

Later, in a broadcast in Lingala on the Leopoldville radio Kasavubu stated that Ghana and Guinea were interfering in the internal affairs of the country. Earlier in the day a local paper *Courrier D'Afrique* had published copies of letters written by you to Lumumba and which were stolen from him. In an interview with Lumumba this morning he informed representatives of Ghana, UAR, Morocco and Guinea that Kasavubu is being offered assistance by the government Belgian-owned Air Congo to enable 'the soldiers and Kasavubu's supporters to travel about while Lumumba and his followers are being denied the same facilities'. Lumumba further stated that it is alleged that substantial sums of money have been paid to Kasavubu and Mobutu by UNO out of funds provided by UNO for technical assistance to Congo.

Discussions continued on the round table conference which was to be called to try and solve the political crisis. Lumumba made it known that he favoured the use of Parliament instead of a round table conference. His political opponents, however, were against this because they knew the Deputies would support Lumumba. Tshombe, for his part, suggested that the round table conference should meet outside the Congo. By the end of October it was generally agreed that the project had failed.

In the meantime, on 11 October an attempt was made by Mobutu to arrest Lumumba. Troops of the Congo National Army arrived at United Nations headquarters to ask if UN forces guarding Lumumba's house would facilitate his arrest. They were told that Lumumba enjoyed Parliamentary immunity and the UN could not comply. Mobutu then threatened an attack on ONUC if Lumumba was not handed over by a specified hour. The United Nations forces stood firm and the hour passed without incident. Mobutu, it seemed, had been checked. But for how long? Belgian 'technicians and advisers' were returning in large numbers to Leopoldville and Lumumba's position grew increasingly precarious.

On 1 October Welbeck informed me of the views of representatives of the independent African states in Leopoldville:

After having analysed the present political situation in the Republic of Congo the representatives of the African States in Leopoldville deplore all the manoeuvres which aim at stifling democracy and compromising the independence and unity of the Republic of Congo. They ask that a strong appeal be made to the UNO so that it guarantees the normal functioning of democratic institutions. In particular they ask that Parliament be immediately reopened without any conditions and that members of Parliament be allowed to perform their duties without let or hindrance or any sort of external pressure.

They consider that the mere object of a round table conference is to upset democracy and to neutralise Parliament in a country where popular representation is already guaranteed.

The UN Special Representative, Dayal, was no less concerned about the worsening political situation. In his second Progress Report he wrote, 'The various contenders for political power are still at a complete stalemate.' He went on:

In the last few weeks there has been increasing evidence of the return of Belgian nationals into many places of public life in the Congo. . . . Unfortunately, there has been a substantial incursion of those elements which appear in the councils of administration to exclude or obstruct the application of United Nations technical assistance and influence. Some Belgian nationals are believed to have been actively arming separatist Congolese forces and, in some cases, Belgian officers have directed and led such forces which, in certain areas, have been responsible for brutal and oppressive acts of violence. Advisers of Belgian nationality have been returning to governmental ministries both in Leopoldville and the province, partially through what seems to be an organised recruiting campaign in Belgium.

It was in this report that Dayal declared the UN could not recognise the College of Commissioners since it had no legal basis. He criticised Mobutu for the indiscipline of the ANC and the Belgians for not channelling their so-called 'aid' through the UN.

In the confused constitutional situation, with virtually three 'governments' in the Congo, the recall of Parliament seemed the right and obvious first step to reaching a solution to the crisis. But Lumumba's enemies were unlikely to agree to this without first making sure that they would obtain a favourable vote. Welbeck informed me of their manoeuvres in a telegram dated 6 October 1960:

At a meeting with Lumumba this morning he expressed to representatives of African States his concern about denial of freedom of movement to his supporters. He stated that while supporters of Kasavubu and Mobutu are granted free transport facilities members of Parliament known to be supporters of Lumumba are being prevented from leaving Leopoldville to visit even their dependents. As you are aware, the first strategy was the military coup d'état staged by Mobutu. The present move is to isolate the parliamentarians from meeting their constituents and to strangle them financially in order to make them vulnerable to corruption and as a result quite a number of parliamentarians have started denouncing Lumumba in anticipation of the opening of Parliament when the final blow will be struck by a vote of no-confidence in Lumumba by both Houses.

Leopoldville was full of rumours. It seemed that Lumumba's former Minister of Foreign Affairs, Justin Bomboko, was trying to form a new government which would initially be without a president or a prime minister. It was rumoured that Bomboko intended at a later date to name Kasavubu as President but to ignore Lumumba entirely. In the highly charged atmosphere of Leopoldville political circles almost anything could happen and it was dangerous to ignore any rumour.

Djin and Welbeck kept me fully informed. At the same time, I instructed them to continue their efforts to achieve a settlement by which the legitimate government of the Congo could function normally. Their efforts on Lumumba's behalf incurred the bitter hostility of Kasavubu. On 7 October I received a telegram signed by Kasavubu and Bomboko.

(*Translation*)

Mr President, we have the honour to inform you that the Government of the Republic of Congo at Leopoldville is forced to declare your Ambassador in the Congo, Mr A. Y. K. Djin, as well as Mr N. A. Welbeck, Minister, as 'Personae Non Gratae' (unwanted persons). In fact certain documents and information which have come to our knowledge have proved clearly that these diplomats have mixed themselves up in the internal affairs of the Congo in an inadmissible way. The same action is being taken against Mr Botsio, Minister of Agriculture of Ghana, whom in one of your personal letters to the ex-Prime Minister Lumumba you have presented as being one of your emissaries. Please accept Mr President the assurances of our highest esteem.

I at once made it clear that I could not recognise any document not emanating from the legal Government of the Congo. On 10 October 1960 I instructed the Foreign Office to reply:

A message has been received by the Ministry of Foreign Affairs purporting to have been signed by the President of the Congo Republic and addressed to the President of the Republic of Ghana.

President Nkrumah wishes it to be made clear, however, that he cannot treat as official any document not emanating from the legal Government of the Congo Republic.

President Nkrumah considers it particularly unfortunate that the message, if genuine, should have apparently been signed by some private individual, one Justin Bomboko, styling himself as Minister of Foreign Affairs. Accordingly I am asked to request you to impress on President Kasavubu first of all the necessity of all official documents being authenticated in accordance with the Constitution of the Congo Republic.

Secondly, the President has directed that it be emphasised to President Kasavubu the extremely undesirable international complications which are bound to arise if he attempts illegally to meddle in matters which are the prerogative of the legally appointed Government of the Congo Republic.

The President takes note of the remark attributed to President Kasavubu in which it is stated that documents and information have come to his knowledge which have clearly proved that the Ghana Mission has mixed itself in the internal affairs of the Congo in an inadmissible way. The President wishes it to be emphasised to President Kasavubu that the Government of Ghana first used its good offices in relation to the affairs of the Congo Republic in order to secure President Kasavubu's election as Head of State. Subsequently the President has communicated with President Kasavubu on a number of occasions in order to assist in the difficult and dangerous situation which existed in the Congo Republic. In order, however, that there can be no misapprehension of the part played by the Government of Ghana, it is the intention of the President to publish the entire correspondence which he has addressed to the President and the Prime Minister of the Congo Republic. In this regard, the President hopes that President Kasavubu would agree to the publication of his letters to President Nkrumah.

In a broadcast to the people of Ghana on Sunday, 9 October, I spoke of Ghana's efforts in the Congo and explained the government's policy. Ghanaian troops, I said, must not be impeded in the carrying out of their duties under the command of the United Nations, and they must under no circumstances be removed from Leopoldville. The Congolese Parliament must be allowed to function as the only legally constituted authority deriving its mandate from the Congolese people. There must be the immediate withdrawal of Belgian troops

4

still lingering in the Congo and surreptitiously rearming the Force Publique. Private radio stations sponsored by imperialist powers operating from Brazzaville should be eliminated. Financial assistance should be given to Lumumba and his government. Finally, the duly selected representatives of the legitimate Lumumba Government should be left free to take their seats at the United Nations.

The Ghanaian Embassy in Leopoldville remained open, in spite of Kasavubu's message declaring Djin, Welbeck and Botsio 'personae non gratae'. On 15 October Welbeck reported a Lumumbist demonstration in Leopoldville and added a note in code which contained, among other information, a warning about the moving of Ghanaian troops from Leopoldville:

> Yesterday morning 14 October there was a demonstration by a large crowd of Lumumba's supporters who paraded the streets starting from UN Headquarters to Lumumba's Residence. The demonstrators which included both men and women carried among others placards saying 'We support UN action in protecting Lumumba.' 'Long live the legitimate government of the people's choice.' The afternoon was all quiet, but in the evening there was an incident at the end of a Press conference which involved Mr Ndele, Vice-President of the so-called College of General Commissioners. A Ghanaian soldier on patrol was accused of not intervening and yet it has been proved that he was the saviour of the victim.

(In code)

> There was also news of the assassination of the Provincial Minister of Education from Kasai, Mr Joshua Mamboshie, by reactionary elements of Kalondji taking reprisals against Lumumba's supporters from Kasai. Up till now the MNC Lumumba youth have been on the offensive against the opposition faction, viz. Abako, Puna and MNC-Kalondji elements. Documents captured prove machinations and subversive activities of the resident and commercial firms. Records of aid from France to Abako have been discovered and plans for the Abako Youth Movement against the legitimate government have also been uncovered. Today it has been quiet at all fronts.

> The independent African States met as usual but failed in an attempt to visit Lumumba. Plans for the organisation of youth activities have started in full swing. Message about plot to assassinate Lumumba transmitted and latter warned accordingly. Despite protest to UN headquarters in N.Y. two advance guard units of the

Ghana Brigade are moving at 7 hours gmt on Sunday 16/10/60 for Kasai.

Awaiting instructions.

The following day, 16 October, Welbeck cabled again:

Contrary to your protest to UN against withdrawal of Ghana troops from Leo, fifty-one soldiers including officers which formed the advance guard units of the UN Forces left Leo this morning at 7.30 hours gmt by a DC4 Air Congo plane for Kasai under the command of Lt Col D. A. Hansen. A second batch of troops is expected to follow by boat toward the end of October and it is hoped that by November the whole operation will have been completed. Your immediate renewal of pressure on UN for cessation of present move is required, since Brigadier Michel says that up to date he had no instructions to the contrary. A large number of African and European traders dissatisfied with this move surrounded the Ghanaian troops as they were preparing on the eve of their departure trying to convince them not to leave.

The moving of Ghanaian forces from Leopoldville, in spite of the protest made to the UN headquarters in New York, further convinced me of the need for an African solution to the Congo's problems. Imperialist intrigue had already been largely responsible for the secession of Katanga, the breakdown of Lumumba's Government and the failure of mediation attempts to bring about a reconciliation between Lumumba and Kasavubu. Now it seemed the UN was not only failing to carry out its mandate in the Congo but was putting Lumumba in even graver personal danger by withdrawing, from the Congolese capital, Ghanaian troops which might be expected to defend him. A strange state of affairs, to say the least, with the legitimate prime minister virtually a prisoner in his own house and the UN forces, which he had invited into the Congo, allowing his enemies to operate freely against him.

8 The Final Betrayal

EARLY in November 1960 the struggle for power between Kasavubu and Lumumba turned strongly in favour of Kasavubu when he flew to America to address the UN General Assembly. There were then two Congolese delegations in New York, one accredited by Kasavubu and the other by Lumumba. The Credentials Committee, on 10 November, recommended the seating of the Kasavubu delegation and on the 22nd their recommendation was accepted by the General Assembly by 53 votes to 24 with 19 abstentions. Not surprisingly, Belgium, France, South Africa, the United Kingdom and the U.S.A. were among those who voted in favour of Kasavubu's delegation.

On 1 December I despatched a telegram to the heads of independent African states telling them of a cable I had sent to the Secretary-General about the seating of the Kasavubu delegation:

> I have the honour to forward herewith for Your Excellency's information a copy of my telegram to the United Nations Secretary-General in connection with the decision to seat the Congolese delegation led by M. Joseph Kasavubu:
>
> Consequent on the seating of the Congolese Delegation led by M. Joseph Kasavubu, I invite your attention to the following points:
>
> 1 The seating of the Congolese Delegation confirms the appointment of M. Kasavubu as Head of State and confirms recognition of the legitimate Lumumba Government and the legally constituted Congolese Parliament which so appointed him. The United Nations, therefore, by this decision, recognises the Government of M. Patrice Lumumba.
>
> 2 That in the light of this fact, the United Nations would not be

adhering to the instructions of the Security Council if it did not restore law and order in the Congo under the aegis of the Lumumba Government and its Parliament.

3 That in these circumstances, the United Nations should see to it that the legally constituted Parliament re-assembles and functions as the Parliament of the Congo Nation.

I should be grateful if the observations above would be brought to the notice of the Security Council. I am releasing a copy of this message to the Press.

By then it was clear that the situation in the Congo was causing the governments of independent African states to re-examine their policies with a view to taking some kind of concerted action. On 5 November, a Conciliation Commission, consisting of the representatives of the African and Asian countries with troops in the Congo, was established in New York. Four days later, President Sékou Touré of Guinea wrote to me:

(Translation)

We have the honour to bring to Your Excellency's notice that information has come to me giving a pretty gloomy picture of the present situation in the Congo, notably in Leopoldville, where the army of Mr Mobutu is carrying out a reign of terror against the defenceless civil population by day and night: tortures, assassinations, rape and deportations are being constantly perpetrated by these soldiers and by bandits disguised as military.

Mr Lumumba is held in his residence by seditious soldiers who forbid him visitors and obstruct his children leaving home for school.

Ministers and Parliamentarians are daily arrested, pillaged and molested. Eight children of the President of the Senate have been raped by the army on 23 October last. Loyal soldiers are dismissed, repatriated or exiled.

No intervention by the United Nations Organisation.

Without vigorous intervention by the Heads of African States, the situation will end by complete degradation followed by general panic, insecurity and neutralisation of the nationalists.

We feel that it is imperative that the Heads of African States review the extreme urgency of using their troops in the Congo where illegality reigns without precedence and we would like to know the opinion of Your Excellency on this point.

Please accept, Your Excellency, the assurances of my highest consideration.

I did not receive the letter until 21 November and I at once replied:

Thank you for your letter of 9 November, which I have only just received. I agree with you that some definite action must be taken by the Heads of African States in an endeavour to restore law and order in the Congo.

I have today written to President Nasser suggesting to him that the time has come to form an African High Command. I feel that those African States who wish to join should get together a few officers to form this Command. Whether the African High Command is stationed in Cairo, Accra or Conakry is, to my mind, immaterial but the important thing is that it must be so stationed that in the event of an emergency we can rush to Leopoldville and help to maintain law and order.

I consider, as you do, that the situation in the Congo is so serious that we must take a determined stand to establish law and order there and to restore the Government to the lawful prime minister, Lumumba.

I would like you to give my suggestion your urgent attention.

The idea of forming an African High Command was not new. I had urged this step before and was to do so many times more. It was my belief that such a Command was essential if the independent African states were to intervene effectively to save the Congo. Separately, they did not have the military strength to exercise any real weight in international politics; with a united force their views could not be ignored. However, it was to be some time before my suggestion aroused sufficient interest for action to be taken on it.

Welbeck, in the meantime, was having a very difficult time in Leopoldville where Congolese troops tried to expel him by force. I wrote to him on 21 November:

I have received your message of the 19th and what you have to report has been carefully studied.

I am writing to order you to remain at your post in Leopoldville. I am aware of the deterioration of the situation in Leopoldville but I expect you to rise to the occasion. The Ghana Government does not take notice of the expulsion order emanating from certain quarters in Leopoldville; nor does it recognise the so-called Mobutu Government which is usurping the powers of the legally appointed Government. President Kasavubu has no constitutional right or power to act in such matters alone without the explicit approval and authority of Mr Lumumba, Prime Minister of the legitimate

Government of the Republic of the Congo. The Mobutu gang propped by imperialist and colonialist powers, is clearly creating confusion in Leopoldville and the tacit connivance of these powers in the Congo makes it imperative that Ghana and other African states should be effectively represented in Leopoldville. To give in to these threats of expulsion is to accept defeat at the hands of imperialists and colonialists in the Congo.

You must know that our position namely, support for the Lumumba Government, has been consistent and must remain consistent. I ask you, therefore, to resist any temptation to concede in any way a *de facto* recognition of Mobutu and his cohorts by any action or conduct that may be construed as complying with any orders or requests from Mobutu.

In the circumstances, it is not necessary to authorise a stand-by plan in Leopoldville which may give the impression of weakness. I am demanding from the Secretary-General of the United Nations adequate protection for you and all Ghanaian personnel. I am also requesting United Nations to secure Mensah's release. He should be sent to Accra immediately.

I expect you to stand up to the situation. Report regularly on the situation to me. General Alexander and Mr Dei-Anang are coming to Leopoldville on my instructions.

There followed an attack on our Embassy in Leopoldville, during which several demonstrators were killed and Welbeck was persuaded to leave the Congo in order to avoid further bloodshed. The situation might never have arisen had Ghanaian troops not been moved from Leopoldville.

About a week after Welbeck's departure I cabled Kasavubu asking his consent to the appointment of a Ghanaian ambassador. He replied that Ghana must make amends for certain losses incurred in the Congo before approval could be given. I wrote to him on 6 December:

I regret that you have not seen fit to convey your *Agreement* in accordance with normal diplomatic practice, because you consider that my Government must first make restitution for certain losses incurred in the Congo as a condition for the granting of approval.

I am extremely surprised that you of all people should take such a stand against a sister African state which has done the Congo no wrong and has rather identified herself closely, by means of substantial material, political and moral support, with the aspirations of the Congolese people for their independence from the very beginning of their struggles and which at the time of your personal tribulation and arrest by the Belgians rendered you prompt assistance. This story is well known to you. I am the more surprised that you should have shown this strange attitude to Ghana, although you do not appear to be anxious about the imperialists and colonialists who are infiltrating back into the Congo in a determined effort to rob it of its legitimate freedom and independence and to enslave it economically.

You ask me in your letter to indemnify the victims or their relatives for the losses incurred during the attack on our Embassy in Leopoldville. This request is most unfortunate, for you must be aware that at the time when Mobutu's men surrounded Mr Welbeck in our Embassy I had already despatched my Chief of Defence Staff and a high official of my Government who were on their way to collect Mr Welbeck from the Embassy. You are also aware that a military siege upon diplomatic premises and personnel is, in any circumstances, contrary to international practice and without precedent in diplomatic relations.

I can only ask you therefore to apologise for this unwarrantable attack upon my representative, which caused the unfortunate loss of lives to which you have referred and I for my part shall be ready to express sympathy for this tragic loss of lives of our Congolese compatriots which need not have taken place if you had allowed wiser counsel to prevail.

The Ghanaian Embassy in Leopoldville was not the only one to close at this time. The United Arab Republic ambassador and his Embassy staff were also expelled from the Congo and President Nasser retaliated by breaking off diplomatic relations with Belgium. On 6 December I sent a message to President Nasser supporting the stand he had taken:

I am happy to learn from reports that you have broken diplomatic relations with Belgium following the expulsion of the United Arab Republic Ambassador and his Embassy staff from Leopoldville.

I am also happy that you have decided to seize all Belgian assets in the United Arab Republic.

It is now abundantly clear that the Belgians are fully responsible for the breakdown in the administration of the legal Government and Parliament of the Congo, of which Lumumba is the Prime Minister.

I write on my own behalf, and on behalf of the Government and people of Ghana, to express solidarity for the stand you have taken in this matter. It is only by such firm measures that we can impress on the imperialists and the colonialists and their avaricious agents that there is a new African who will no longer accept their persistent efforts to deprive him of his legitimate rights and aspirations.

As for the African stooges of colonialism who are content to become willing marionettes in the exploitation of their own country, one can only be sorry for them, for the trend of events in Africa indicates that their days are numbered. Their successes must therefore be regarded as short-lived and ephemeral.

As from today, Ghana has broken diplomatic relations with Belgium and the Belgian ambassador has been ordered to leave the country within 48 hours.

I trust that my last communication on the formation of an African High Command has now reached you and am awaiting an early reply.

The toughening of my attitude and the attitude of all those who supported African freedom at this time was due partly to the news received of the arrest and ill-treatment of Lumumba by Mobutu's men at Mweka in Kasai Province on 1 December. Lumumba's departure from Leopoldville and the failure of ONUC to supply transport and protection for him provide one of the most pathetic and at the same time disastrous episodes of the whole Congo tragedy.

Lumumba, closely guarded in his house in Leopoldville by Mobutu's men, was worried about the burial arrangements of his infant daughter. He and his wife wanted her buried in the family burial ground at Stanleyville. Lumumba telephoned UN headquarters in Leopoldville on 27 November to ask if an aircraft could be put at his disposal to take him to Stanleyville for the burial ceremony. The UN replied that they could not provide air transport as UN aircraft were only available for the transport and provisioning of UN troops and personnel. Lumumba gave no hint then that he might try to escape. But anyone knowing the man's impetuous nature and his contempt for personal danger might have guessed the outcome of the UN refusal to help.

That night Lumumba managed to leave his house secretly to begin the four days' drive to Stanleyville. It seems incredible that he was undetected by Mobutu's soldiers, but obviously they were totally unsuspecting when the car containing Lumumba drove away from the house. Even Lumumba's own colleagues, when told of the escape the following morning, could scarcely believe that he would be so foolhardy as to leave without taking any precautions.

Three days later he was arrested at Mweka, near Port Francqui. Ever since his escape, Mobutu's men had been in hot pursuit. They caught up with him after he had made an impromptu speech at a café where he had stopped for lunch. Typically, he could not resist speaking in public and revealing his whereabouts, even though he must have known he was taking terrible risks. The pursuing soldiers, hearing of his speech, easily tracked him down and arrested him. Press and radio reports indicated that at the time of his arrest he was brutally manhandled and struck with rifle butts by ANC soldiers. The reports were confirmed two days later when he was brought back to Leopoldville. Observers of the UN reported that he was 'without his glasses and wearing a soiled shirt; his hair was in disorder; he had a blood clot on his cheek and his hands were tied behind his back. He was roughly pushed into an ANC truck and driven off'.

The next day Lumumba was removed to Camp Hardy, near Thysville. According to the report of the UN Special Representative to the Secretary-General (5 December 1960), Lumumba's departure 'was witnessed by members of the international Press, who report that Mr Lumumba walked to the truck with considerable difficulty. He was in a dishevelled condition and his face showed signs of recent blows.' UN troops in Thysville said Lumumba was suffering from serious injuries. 'His head has been shaven and his hands remain tied. He is being kept in a cell under conditions reported to be inhuman in respect of health and hygiene'.

Both Dayal and the Secretary-General vigorously protested against the treatment of Lumumba. Dayal tried to get permission for a member of the International Red Cross to visit him, but without success. Kasavubu insisted that Lumumba was in good health and that his arrest was a purely domestic matter of no concern to the United Nations. In a note of 7 December 1960 to Hammarskjöld, Kasavubu charged Lumumba with five offences—usurpation of public power; assaults on individual freedom accompanied by physical torture; attacks against the security of the state; organisation of hostile bands for purposes of devastation, massacre and pillage; inciting soldiers to commit offences. He then drew the attention of the Secretary-General to the disorders in Stanleyville. He continued, 'I am somewhat surprised at the importance that a number of African-Asian and East European delegations attach to the arrest of Mr Lumumba. . . . Please regard this question, as I and the entire country do, as a domestic matter'.

So great was the concern of all of us who regarded Lumumba as the legitimate prime minister of the Republic of the Congo that a meeting of the Security Council was called on 7 December to consider the implications of his arrest. At the 915th Meeting held 8/9 December, Mr Aw of Mali read a telegram from President Modibo Keita expressing the same views as myself on the question of Lumumba's treatment:

> United Nations would be betraying its mission if it did not help Lumumba to restore authority to the Congolege Central Government and to enable Parliament to function. Central Government sole legal authority.

Mr Aw went on, 'Why should we recognise that Mobutu has any authority whatever?' He called for the immediate release of Lumumba, the re-convening of the Congolese Parliament and the sending of a mission of enquiry to make an accurate report.

The following day, at the 916th Meeting, a stronger speech was made by Dr Fawzi, representative of the United Arab Republic:

> Are we, in the United Nations, merely to adopt paper resolutions and express futile resentments if those resolutions are flouted and looked on with disdain? Are we to continue for ever to talk about helping the Congo, while imperialism helps itself to the Congo?... A new, more realistic and responsible approach by all of us to the present situation and eventually to other situations has become imperative. . . . To attain this objective it is evident that the obstacles in our way should be promptly removed. By far the biggest and worst of such obstacles is imperialism, recurrent, obstinate and dominating at present the whole Congo scene. No one here or elsewhere can doubt that, as long as there is any imperialist presence in the Congo, even under a different name there will continue to be dissension, 'stoogism' and the disruption of the very concept of Congolese independence and territorial integrity. No one can doubt either that, once imperialism disappears, stooges will too, the real leaders of the country will again be effectively at the forefront and unity and independence will both prevail and rapidly flourish.

He ended his speech with an appeal for Lumumba's release. Mr Wirjopranoto of Indonesia who followed him spoke also of the disastrous effects of the return of Belgian military and civilian personnel to the Congo. It was only due to them that Mobutu's growing ascendancy could be maintained.

On 10 December, at the 917th Meeting the Secretary-General explained some of the difficulties facing the UN in the Congo:

Lumumba was arrested under a warrant of arrest which is probably signed, certainly approved, by the Chief of State, who is also the head of a delegation to the United Nations. That is to say any action by force to liberate Mr Lumumba would, in fact, mean overriding by force the authority of the Chief of State. I think we are all aware what that means in legal terms in relation to a country. . . . The Armée Nationale Congolaise as it functions in Leopoldville under Colonel Mobutu is sanctioned by and under the authority of President Kasavubu, who in fact is regarded and regards himself constitutionally as the Commander in Chief. . . . It is again a question of an action which overrides the authority of the Chief of State in his own country.

After a speech by the Indian representative, Mr Krishna Menon, who also condemned the continued presence of Belgian forces in the Congo, Mr Boucetta of Morocco spoke. He said that a military regime had been established against the will of the Congolese people, 'the administration is in a process of collapse, the country's economy in ruins, chaos supervenes and the crisis is at its culminating point'. He continued:

I should like to tell you something that I saw with my own eyes. I was present at the last two meetings held by this (Congolese) Parliament—a Parliament like any other anywhere else in the world. I heard statements from the legitimate and legal Government of the Republic of the Congo—that is, from the Prime Minister, Mr Lumumba, and the Deputy Prime Minister, Mr Gizenga, and the Minister for Youth, Mr Mpolo. I heard members of Parliament supporting the Government; I also heard members of the opposition, speaking out freely and forcefully. Both sides gave their explanations and defended their points of view. And, after several hours of debate, a vote was taken. By an overwhelming majority, the Parliament gave the legitimate Government a vote of confidence and renewed its mandate. That is legality, that is constitutionalism, that is the valid and unchallenged expression of the will of the Congolese people.

The next morning, a hundred soldiers with helmets and submachine guns at the ready and an old tank with a rusty gun were stationed in front of the Parliament building. The elected representatives of the people were not allowed to enter to continue their deliberations and carry out their tasks. The curtain had fallen on legality.

The President of the Chamber and the Senate wrote to the

Secretary-General's Special Representative asking him to defend legality and allow constitutional matters to be dealt with in the normal way. What was the result? Whatever the pretext—that it was a domestic affair or something else—the fact remains that the Parliament has not met since that day. The members of Parliament were rounded up and hustled away, payment of their allowances was stopped and the voice of the people was stifled. That is what with bitterness and regret we saw.

We have always considered that the maintenance of order was more than a negative or defensive task. It also implies the preventing of all encroachments upon freedom. Peace and order have no meaning unless the country's institutions are functioning normally. Mr Kasavubu and Mr Mobutu have been protected. Why was not Parliament protected also? . . . The paralysis of the country's institutions is, in our opinion, one of the main factors in the chaos which is taking root in the Congo. . . . The United Nations has in the Congo more than 20,000 troops, over 3,000 of whom are from my own country. It also has hundreds of technical assistants there. It really cannot continue to claim that it has nothing to do with the situation.

Mr Boucetta's speech expressed the views of many other delegates at the United Nations. Time and again they pressed for the release of Lumumba, the recall of Parliament and the expulsion of the Belgians from the Congo. As Mr Lewandowski of Poland said, at the 918th Meeting of the Security Council on 12 December, 'It is inconceivable that thousands of United Nations soldiers should stand idle while the chief and members of the Government, on whose specific request the United Nations Force was sent to the Congo, are kept in prison like common law offenders'.

The reason given for UN non-interference was, of course, that it could not properly interfere in domestic affairs. Yet who was to determine the limits of what could legitimately be termed 'domestic affairs'? Tshombe, Mobutu and Kasavubu always claimed their actions were no concern of the UN since they were purely of an 'internal' nature. Katanga's secession was a 'domestic' affair, so was the dismissal and arrest of Lumumba, and so also was Mobutu's rule. If these kind of arguments were to be accepted then the whole purpose of UN intervention, which was to secure Belgian withdrawal so that the properly elected government of Lumumba could carry out its mandate, was likely to be defeated.

As time went on and the position in the Congo grew worse, people seemed to have lost sight of original objectives. They became used to tales of atrocities on both sides and accustomed to rapid changes in the political fortunes of Congolese leaders. At the time of Lumumba's arrest it had become possible for UN troops to stand by and watch the person who had asked for their help being manhandled by soldiers under the command of a man who had seized power and had not the slightest claim to represent the Congolese people. The point was put well by Touré Ismael of Guinea, 'We think that those who engineered the humiliating arrest of Mr Lumumba have humiliated not only this man and the Congolese people but Africa as a whole'.

On 7 December, in a lengthy note to Dag Hammarskjöld, I explained my views on the worsening situation in the Congo resulting from the arrest of Lumumba. I reminded him of the warning I gave on 21 July of the dangers of not bringing the Force Publique under proper control. It was this force, financed and directed by interested powers, which was now preventing the due process of parliamentary democracy and was imprisoning the prime minister and other members of the legitimate government. I went on:

Today, world public opinion has been confused by the agents of imperialism into accepting the thesis that the tragedy of the Congo is essentially a domestic dispute between rival leaders.

With sinister methodical efficiency, these agents proceeded to discredit certain members of the United Nations who have contributed forces to the Congo operations. Official and unofficial propaganda was aimed at the removal of Ghanaian and other forces and creating an anti-United Nations feeling so that at the moment any United Nations official is liable to be arrested, searched and subjected to other indignities. When it was decided to remove the Ghanaian forces from Leopoldville, I stated in my message to you through my Permanent Representative on October 17, that 'Quite apart from the political objections to the move at the present time there will undoubtedly be serious security repercussions in Leopoldville'.

This warning was reiterated in my telegram No. GN622 dated October 27. In this telegram I referred to various grave incidents which had occurred in Leopoldville, including the arrest of 176 supporters of Lumumba and the disarming and detention of soldiers known to support Lumumba. I stated that the civilian population, including foreign traders, were frightened because of the constant rumour that they would be attacked as soon as Ghanaian troops left Leopoldville. In the light of these incidents I informed you that I could not share your confidence that the disorders in Leopoldville were not in any way related to the projected move of Ghanaian troops.

You disagreed with me on important points in your telegram of October 31 but on November 20 I was forced by events to inform you that:

'Reports reaching me clearly indicate that the situation in Leopoldville is deteriorating since Ghanaian troops left Leopoldville. As you yourself may be aware, hundreds of Belgians are returning to the Congo daily and are indulging in intrigues of all kinds calculated to hamper United Nations operations in the Congo and to enable them to restore their influence and control in the Congo. There is sufficient evidence of reprehensible Belgian activities to discredit the United Nations troops and create disaffection amongst sections of the Congolese people against units serving under United Nations command in the Congo.

Since the removal of the Ghanaian troops from Leopoldville there has been, as I foresaw, ample evidence of acts of violence and lawlessness.

I have frequently advocated a strong and effective military command for the United Nations Forces in the Congo. The ineffectiveness of this command has been clearly demonstrated by the trend of events and by the fact that, in spite of the original intention to restore law and order in the Congo, the United Nations has slowly but surely lost the initiative in its task, and we see the United Nations Secretariat tamely acquiescing in this position. In Leopoldville, at least, the Organisation is now being dictated to and pushed around by Mobutu's band, which is actively maintained by the Belgians and other foreign agents, although it is itself incapable of controlling its own troops. I therefore urge most strongly that the military leadership of United Nations Forces be changed immediately and is taken over by commanders who have sufficient experience and judgment to re-establish dignity and confidence in the higher direction of the United Nations military affairs.

It can, of course, be argued that acts similar to those being committed at present by Mobutu's men were earlier committed by the old Force Publique.

As you are well aware, I have frequently urged that the influence of the so-called Congolese Army should be eliminated from politics and I did my best to persuade Lumumba to use restraint in this direction.

I would not object, nor I feel sure would my African colleagues, to a firm statement that United Nations command will ensure that the ANC is eliminated from the political argument. But to effect this now will require much greater firmness than has hitherto been shown by the United Nations military command in the Congo. Nor can I imagine that Premier Lumumba would now dispute the right of the United Nations to re-establish proper law and order. This could not be construed as interference with the internal affairs of the Congo; it has now been amply demonstrated that internal affairs cannot function at all under existing conditions.

I am also distressed by the fact that United Kingdom Royal Air Force aircraft flying in support of the Ghana contingent at present in Kasai have not been allowed to land at Leopoldville. Surely the whole authority and purpose of United Nations efforts to restore peace in the Congo cannot be allowed to suffer from the irresponsible acts of individuals. These aircraft are used solely for the support of the Ghana troops, which have done so much to restore peace in Kasai and there can be no possible excuse for obstructing their work. It is absurd that in circumstances such as this the United Nations command in the Congo should find itself incapable of eliminating unwarranted interference with aircraft carrying out their normal duties under the auspices of the United Nations.

The intrigue and activities of the colonialists and imperialists against the independence of a young African State are carried on with such effrontery and cynicism that those who want to see cannot be deceived. Mr Dayal's report came in time to give adequate warning to the dangers facing our young sister African State in the return of Belgians obsessed with revenge, spite and utter contempt for African aspirations. Unfortunately, powerful states came to the defence of their imperialist friends and statements were issued challenging the accuracy and objectivity of Mr Dayal's report. Needless to add that these very detractors were at one time so keen on saving the United Nations that they considered the slightest criticism of United Nations action in the Congo as treason.

Now we see the legal Prime Minister of the Congo in chains with the sovereign Parliament of his country surrounded by arms and men undoubtedly maintained by foreign interests.

Do you, Your Excellency, not see bitter irony in the fact that the Government and Parliament which invited the United Nations to assist with the restoration of law and order have been forced to the wall by the systematic use of violence before the very eyes of the United Nations High Command?

How can we, the small nations within the United Nations, maintain confidence in this Organisation when we witness situations which remind us so vividly today of the fate of the League of Nations? It seems quite clear that your own position as Secretary-General is seriously compromised and undermined by the apparent inability of your military representatives in the Congo to carry out faithfully and effectively the Resolution of the Security Council.

I have made these points in a genuine effort to call a serious warning against a situation which might lead to grave consequences for the future peace of the world. Timely action is therefore necessary. I, on my part, must confess that I am utterly dismayed at the prospect of the United Nations finding itself in opposition to the attitude and policies of the government which invited this Organisation to the Congo to give much needed assistance for the restoration of law and order. Can any one genuinely say that a so-called administration which attempts to function by means of violence and disregard for all the principles of international relations can be considered legal authority for the day-to-day running of the affairs of a newly independent state?

Now, Your Excellency, I would like to ask a few simple questions. How are the ANC being paid? Who is paying them? Where is the money coming from? Who supplied the Kalondjists with their arms?

The United Nations' claim that it is in the Congo to maintain law and order could at least make some meaning if the claim were established on the side of the legitimate government, but I am now appalledto see that a band of armed men which has prevented the functioning of the elected Parliament of the Congo is being loudly applauded from the roof tops of the Western world as an organisation which can be relied upon to bring about peace and security in a confused State. Your Excellency, the United Nations Organisation is the last bulwark of peace and the hope of the new Independent Sovereign States of Africa. I am therefore concerned that nothing should happen to disparage its efforts and reputation in the eyes of the world.

In the Congo today the United Nations is facing its first real challenge since its establishment and I am most anxious that you, as its Chief Agent, should have full opportunity to consolidate and reinforce its power and authority in accordance with the Security Council Resolutions on the Congo. This must be done effectively by the immediate and unconditional release of the legal Prime Minister, Mr Patrice Lumumba, the clearing out of the Belgian *saboteurs* of Congolese independence who have infiltrated back into the Congo and by eliminating the connivance of the colonialists seeking to perpetuate their control and domination in the Congo. Unless everything is done quickly to re-establish the political *status quo*, namely, the release forthwith of the legitimate Prime Minister with those members of his government now under arrest and the restoration of the normal processes of parliamentary democracy, there will be left a tragic mess in the Congo for which the United Nations cannot, I fear, escape responsibility.

I avail myself of this opportunity to renew to Your Excellency the assurances of my highest consideration.

I sent notes also to Adlai Stevenson, then American Ambassador to the United Nations and to President Kennedy and to Harold Macmillan, then Prime Minister of the United Kingdom, appealing to them to do all in their power to secure the release of Lumumba. In my letter to Adlai Stevenson I said:

As you are no doubt aware, to most of us in the independent African States Mr Lumumba represents the will of the Congolese people for freedom and independence and the majority of the people of Africa still regard him as the legal Prime Minister of the Congo. It will be a significant act of goodwill towards Africa if the new United States Administration as its first act in relation to Africa could assist with plans for securing the immediate release of Mr Patrice Lumumba. This would materially help to reinforce the confidence of the truly independent states of Africa in the United States and make a positive contribution to the maintenance of world peace and security.

We in Africa are very confident of the contribution that you can personally make in the United Nations to promote the courses likely to advance the welfare of the peoples of Africa because of your special interest in and knowledge of the peculiar problems which confront us in Africa today.

My letter to the American President and to the British Prime Minister I quote in full. First, the note to President Kennedy:

I am taking advantage of the happy occasion of the presentation of credentials of your new Ambassador to ask him to convey to you a personal note from myself.

I am venturing at the same time as I congratulate you most heartily on your assumption of your great and high office to write to you personally about matters which concern Africa and which I feel may have a decisive effect in the coming year on world affairs. I believe that I am the only head of a Government in Africa who has had the great advantage of education in the United States. This is a privilege which I shall always remember with the most sincere feelings and it is because I believe that through this education I understand to some extent how people in the United States react to world affairs that I am venturing to write to you explaining how we in Africa react to the policy of the Great Powers and particularly of that of the United States.

It has given me great hope and confidence for the promotion of better relations between Africa and the Western powers that you have chosen, among your Cabinet, advisers who, I believe, understand the fundamental problems of our continent and it is gratifying and reassuring to us that so many of those who will be assisting you in the conduct of the United States foreign policy have had personal experience of the African Continent and that we have been fortunate in having them here as our guests. On the other hand there is always a danger that any visitor however sympathetic may not be able to appreciate fully the problems with which we are faced.

I believe that there is no point in writing a personal letter such as this unless I speak frankly. I do not wish, however, to trouble you with complaints or with criticisms of a past administration for whose actions you were nowhere responsible and if I refer to these differences it is only to explain to you what are the problems as they exist at the moment and which both of us have to face if we are to secure a speedy improvement in our relations which have recently deteriorated. I would like, however, to start on the basis that there is complete kinship and that we look to the future and not the past in dealing with the present most serious situation on the African Continent.

I would like to put before you what I believe to be the future of all the truly independent African States. For a realistic approach to African policy it is necessary to realise that some States which are nominally independent have neither the finances, resources, or economic independence to pursue at this time a policy which clearly reflects the true aspirations of their peoples. We in Ghana and, I believe, in the other independent African States judge other countries not by words but by deeds. Every administration in the United States since its very birth has expressed itself as opposed to Colonialism and in favour of governments which represent the will of the people. What then are we to think when we find in the Congo the United States supporting a regime which is based on the denial of democracy and which only exists because international support if not from the United States itself at least from countries closely allied to the United States such as Belgium, maintain a military dictatorship of a brutal and ineffectual type under which the Congolese Parliament is not permitted to meet. The freely chosen Prime Minister of the country, actually appointed to that office by the King of Belgians himself, is now in prison under disgusting and degrading conditions in which his life is in danger and is held captive in a puppet state which is maintained by Belgian armed force and foreign financial interests in which I must say to you American interests have a considerable part. The inactivity of the United States in the face of this situation is impossible to reconcile with their long-professed opposition to colonialism and well-known avowal to the principles of democracy and law. We appreciate here and if I may say so in that so far as I can recall in the very first speech which you made in the United States Senate you advocated the policy of Algeria for the Algerians. I am certain that you are right in this course and I regret that you were unable at that time to persuade the United States Government to follow the courageous and realistic policy which you advocated. I am quite certain that you will approach the question of the Congo with the same courage and realism as you have shown on that occasion.

I believe that if the United States were to propose that the United Nations should be given sufficient authority by the Security Council to insist that the Parliament of the Congo was to be reconvened in conditions in which members could speak and vote completely freely it would convince all the African States that they stood for the course of popularly elected Government and were opposed to colonialism and imperialism.

The practical policy which I would like you to consider is the following:

(i) That the Security Council should be invited to make such changes as necessary in their Resolutions covering the Congo as would enable the contingents of the troops now in the Congo to ensure that the Parliament of the Congo should be reassembled.

(ii) That the United Nations should not recognise or have any dealings with any government which was not formed in accordance with the present constitution of the Congolese Republic.

In this connexion we had a most interesting discussion here with your brother, but I think that possibly the brief which he has received did not sufficiently explain either the constitutional, moral or legal position of the Government of the Congo. Mr Kasavubu is the Head of State in exactly the same way as the Queen of England is the Queen of Canada and I am quite certain that your brother would not have argued as he did in Accra that if the Queen of England owing to a difference of policy between England and Canada dismissed the Prime Minister of Canada that was in any way in accordance with moral law, justice or good sense. The government of Ghana lent its good offices during the whole period which preceded the enactment of the Constitution of the Congo and I think that I can say that my advisers in regard to this are better informed on the real basis of the Congo Constitution than, if I may say with respect, anyone outside Africa. Kasavubu's office was constructed on the model of that of the Belgian King. At the round table conference in Brussels it was most clearly laid down that in order to ensure the stability of the Government it should be set up during independence that the Prime Minister must not be dismissed unless he was defeated by an absolute majority in both Houses of Parliament or a two-thirds majority of both Houses sitting together. So important was this principle considered that there were long arguments at the round table conference as to whether the majority should be that of both Houses of Parliament or of the double membership and in the end a compromise was arrived at that a majority should have to be an absolute majority of both Houses or a two-thirds majority of members sitting and voting as two Houses sitting together. To this agreement Mr Kasavubu's party assented and this was a compromise accepted by every group, including Mr Tshombe. In the face of this agreement it is our view a smack on the face to take words of that context in the actual Constitution itself and make this a justification for international support and recognition of a military dictatorship.

(iii) It will be for Parliament to say whether they have withdrawn their confidence from Mr Lumumba's Government and wish to entrust their confidence to some other Government. Otherwise in accordance with the Constitution Mr Lumumba remains in office until his successor has been appointed in accordance with the Constitution—a formality which cannot take place until his successor receives a majority vote in both Houses of Parliament. In effect, whatever view is taken of the Constitution, Colonel Mobutu and those appointed by him cannot in any stretch of imagination be said to constitute a legal government and indeed to do Mr Kasavubu justice even he has no right to exercise any governing functions.

(iv) Once Parliament has freely endorsed either the Government which they previously freely appointed or a new Government freely chosen by them, then the full authority of the United Nations should be put behind that Government and an illegal and private army suppressed, all foreign intervention eliminated and 'foreign volunteers' and 'advisers' sent home.

(v) All advisers and volunteers which the Government of the Congo may require should be offered by the nations which wish to put them forward through the United Nations and should be employed in such positions as may be agreed between the United Nations and the Government of the Congo. This would not preclude Belgians who are genuinely needed in the Mission field, in medical, teaching and any other technical and administrative services returning to positions which they previously held. It would be necessary however, to prevent the continued supply of army and police officers and equipment from Belgium.

I am absolutely certain that if you were personally to intervene to secure the release of Mr Lumumba, this would be in fact significant and I would like to make as strong as possible a personal appeal to you to do this. Even if in the most unlikely event that appeal was not successful it would clearly demonstrate to the world the position of the United States in this matter. On the other hand the reputation of the United States could be irretrievably damaged in Africa if your powerful nation sits by and watches one of your close military allies—Belgium—which is after all dependent on the United States for its defence and to a considerable measure economic existence crumpling up democracy in Africa in flagrant disregard of the unanimous opinion and sentiment of all those African people who are free to express their views.

· · · · ·

I hope you will find it possible to reply to me with the same frankness as I have written to you. I shall certainly not be offended however frankly you express your own point of view but I dare hope that an exchange of correspondence such as this might lead to an agreed policy between the United States of America and independent States of Africa.

I hope you will not think it out of place in view of the fact that he has been such a good friend to Ghana and to Africa generally that I have written a personal note to Mr Adlai Stevenson, a copy of which I have given to your ambassador, Mr Russell.

Before concluding I once again congratulate you most warmly upon your election and wish you all success in the discharge of the high and onerous office to which you have been called at this time.

Secondly, my letter to Mr Harold Macmillan:

I wish to ask you again to consider the part that Great Britain should play as the premier country in the Commonwealth in helping to secure the immediate release of Prime Minister Lumumba, at least on humanitarian grounds.

It is most essential that I should impress upon you that what the Commonwealth does or fails to do in the Congo situation could very well weaken or strengthen the Commonwealth link. I know how much you personally appreciate this and I am confident that if your efforts were brought fully into play in the interests of a just and peaceful settlement in the Congo, we can all be sure of achieving a settlement acceptable to all sides. Mr Lumumba who is, in the view of not only Ghana but other Commonwealth Prime Ministers as well, the legitimate Prime Minister of the Congo, has been delivered into the hands of what we consider to be a government maintained and supported in the interests of Belgian colonialism. If he were to be murdered by his Belgian captors or so ill-treated that he were to die, this would have an effect upon the relations of Ghana with the Commonwealth and also with non-African powers whose extent it would be difficult to estimate.

The United Kingdom has always stood in theory for the principle of parliamentary government and I think I should say to you quite frankly that I find it hard to understand your attitude of passivity in the face of this challenge to parliamentary rule exhibited by Belgium in whose defence both my country and yours fought in the two World Wars. In my view the only solution to the present impasse in the Congo is to let Parliament function without further delay.

The United Kingdom is in a position to take a decisive step in this matter and if it does not do so, this failure will never be forgotten by the people of Africa.

9 The Casablanca Powers

LUMUMBA's arrest, and the failure of the United Nations to deal effectively with the Congo situation, led to the calling of a Conference at Casablanca from 3 to 7 January 1961. The Conference took place under the chairmanship of King Mohammed V of Morocco. Present were King Mohammed V of the Kingdom of Morocco; His Excellency Gamal Abdel Nasser, President of the United Arab Republic; Osagyefo Dr Kwame Nkrumah, President of the Republic of Ghana; His Excellency Ahmed Sekou Touré, President of the Republic of Guinea; His Excellency Modibo Keita, President of the Republic of Mali; His Excellency Ferhat Abbas, Prime Minister of the Provisional Government of the Republic of Algeria representing the provisional government of Algeria; His Excellency Abdelkader el Allam, Minister of Foreign Affairs, representing His Majesty King Idris I of the United Kingdom of Libya and His Excellency Alwin B. Perera, Ambassador Extraordinary and Plenipotentiary representing the Prime Minister of Ceylon.

The central problem for discussion was whether the African states, particularly Ghana, Guinea, Mali and the United Arab Republic, should withdraw their troops from the Congo. It was felt that the United Nations was clearly not going to take effective action and that our troops should no longer be made available to the United Nations Organisation.

I spoke strongly in favour of allowing African troops to remain in the Congo, pointing out that withdrawal would be tantamount to betrayal. But after much heated discussion it was finally agreed that troops of the Casablanca powers should be withdrawn unless the United Nations acted immediately in support of the Central Government of which Lumumba was Prime Minister. I, however, remained adamant. I felt that if Ghana withdrew her troops from the Congo, that would constitute a betrayal not only of the Congo but also of the African revolutionary cause. Eventually, the following declaration was issued:

The Conference at Casablanca:

1 *declares* the intention and determination of the respective Governments represented to withdraw their troops and other military personnel placed under the United Nations Operational Command in the Congo;

2 *reaffirms* their recognition of the elected Parliament and legally constituted Government of the Republic of the Congo which came into being on 30th of June, 1960;

3 *convinced* that the only justification for the presence of the United Nations troops in the Congo is:

(a) To answer the appeals of the legitimate Government of the Republic of the Congo at whose request the United Nations decided to create its Operational Command;

(b) To implement the decisions of the Security Council in respect of the situation in the Congo;

(c) To safeguard the unity and independence of the Republic of the Congo and preserve its territorial integrity;

4 *urges* the United Nations to act immediately to:

(a) Disarm and disband the lawless bands of Mobutu;

(b) Release from prison and detention all members of the Parliament and legitimate Government of the Republic of the Congo;

(c) Reconvene the Parliament of the Republic of the Congo;

(d) Eliminate from the Congo all Belgian and other foreign military and para-military personnel not belonging to the United Nations Operational Command whether operating as such or in disguise;

(e) Release to the legitimate Government of the Congo all civil and military airports, radio-stations and other establishments, now unlawfully withheld from that Government;

(f) Prevent the Belgians from using the United Nations Trust Territory of Ruanda-Urundi as a base to commit aggression, direct or indirect to launch armed attack against the Congolese Republic.

5 *decides* that if the purposes and principles which justified the presence of the United Nations Operational Command in the

Republic of the Congo are not realised and respected then the States here represented reserve the right to take appropriate action. (The implementation of Paragraph 1 of the Resolution on the Congo depends upon whether the United Nations fulfil the conditions laid down in Paragraph 4.)

Subsequent events in the Congo have strengthened my belief that the decision taken in January 1961 *not* to withdraw Ghanaian troops was the right one. Other problems were discussed, such as the Algerian struggle for independence, apartheid and the French testing of atomic bombs in the Sahara. But the most important result of the Conference was the publication of the African Charter of Casablanca. It was the expression of our belief in the need for African Unity. The text follows:

We, the Heads of African States, meeting in Casablanca from January 3rd to January 7th 1961, conscious of our responsibilities towards the African Continent, proclaim our determination to promote the triumph of liberty all over Africa and to achieve its unity;

affirm our will to preserve and consolidate our identity of views and unity of action in international affairs, to safeguard our hard-won independence, the sovereignty and territorial integrity of our States, to reinforce peace in the world by adopting a policy of non-alignment;

proclaim our determination to liberate the African territories still under foreign domination, by giving them aid and assistance, to liquidate colonialism and neo-colonialism and in all their forms, to discourage the maintenance of foreign troops and the establishment of bases which endanger the liberation of Africa and to strive equally to rid the African Continent of political and economic interventions and pressures;

proclaim the necessity for the Independent African States to direct their political, economic and social policies to the exploitation of the national wealth for the benefit of their peoples and to ensuring an equitable distribution of that wealth among all nationals;

affirm our will to intensify our efforts for the creation of an effective form of co-operation among the African States in the economic, social and cultural domains;

aiming at the consolidation of liberty in Africa and the building up of its unity and security, decide upon

1 The creation of an African Consultative Assembly, as soon as conditions permit, composed of representatives of every African State, having a permanent seat and holding periodical sessions.

2 The creation of the following four committees:

(a) *The African Political Committee,*
comprising Heads of States, or their duly accredited representatives, will meet periodically with a view to co-ordinating and unifying the general policy of the various African States;

(b) *The African Economic Committee,*
comprising the Ministers of Economic Affairs of the Independent African States, will meet periodically with a view to taking decisions with regard to African Economic Co-operation. One of the most urgent tasks of this Committee will be to establish postal and telecommunication links among the various African Capitals;

(c) *The African Cultural Committee,*
comprising the Ministers of Education of the Independent African States will meet periodically with a view to preserving and developing African culture and civilisation and intensifying African cultural co-operation and assistance;

(d) *A Joint African High Command,*
comprising the Chiefs of Staff of the Independent African States will meet periodically with a view to ensuring the common defence of Africa in case of aggression against any part of this Continent, and with a view to safeguarding the independence of the African States.

3 The creation of a Liaison Office for establishing effective co-operation among the different organisations mentioned above and particularly for the holding within three months of a meeting of experts charged with defining the practical procedure concerning the functioning of the organisations in question.

We, the Heads of African States, convened in Casablanca from the 3rd January to the 7th January 1961, reaffirm our faith in the Conferences of the Independent African States, held in Accra in 1958 and in Addis Ababa in 1960, and appeal to all Independent African States to associate themselves with our common action for the consolidation of liberty in Africa and the building up of its unity and security.

We solemnly reaffirm our unshakeable adherence to the United Nations Charter and to the Declaration of the Afro-Asian Conference held in Bandung, with the aim of promoting co-operation among all the peoples of the world and of consolidating international peace.

In my speech at the closing session of the conference on 7 January 1961, I emphasised the need for a *political* union of Africa:

What I fear worst of all is the fact that if we do not formulate plans for unity and take active steps to form a political union, we will soon be fighting and warring among ourselves, with imperialists and colonialists standing behind the screen and pulling vicious wires to make us cut each other's throat for the sake of their diabolical purposes in Africa. All over Africa artificial boundaries dividing brother from brother, sister from sister, have been erected by the colonisers. It is within the greater context of African Union that these artificial boundaries imposed by colonialism and imperialism will disappear.

At subsequent meetings of the Casablanca powers, further decisions were reached on the Congo, notably at the Accra Foreign Ministers Conference held in February 1961, and at the Conference of The Political Committee of the African Charter of Casablanca held in Cairo from 15 to 17 June 1962. In the final communiqué of that Conference, the member states reasserted their continued support for the unity and independence of the Congo. They urged the United Nations to double its effectiveness in order to attain these objectives and to implement its resolutions in this respect, 'to help in eliminating all foreign, profiteering elements in the Congo: to prevent any further foreign intervention and help to create an atmosphere in which the Congo will be able to realise its hopes for independence, integrity and the consolidation of its national economy.'

But this was all in the future. To return to the troubled months of December 1960 and January and February 1961, I still hoped then that it was not too late for the United Nations effort in the Congo to be made to succeed.

10 Gizenga's Government in Stanleyville

DURING the first two weeks of December 1960, several of the Asian and African governments which had supplied troops for the UN operation in the Congo decided to withdraw their contingents. They felt that ONUC had failed in its mission and their continued participation was no longer justified. Ceylon was among the first to announce its intention to withdraw. When I heard the news I at once (9 December) sent a telegram to the Prime Minister of Ceylon, Mrs Bandaranaike, urging her to reconsider the decision:

I understand that your government has decided to withdraw its contingent serving under the United Nations in the Congo. Although this is a matter for your government I most urgently appeal to you to reconsider your decision. It is imperative that the UN efforts in the Congo should not be paralysed by inadequate military support at a time when its authority is so seriously being thwarted by the self-styled Col Mobutu.

In these circumstances, I implore Your Excellency to reconsider your decision. As long as our troops continue to serve in the Congo, I am sure that our combined efforts would help to retrieve the situation.

I sent a similar message to Sékou Touré, on 14 December, after hearing from him that his government had also decided to withdraw its troops from the Congo:

I have received your message, and I am so grateful to you for informing me about your decision to withdraw your troops from the Congo. I still feel I must implore you to exercise patience in this regard and to allow your troops to remain in the Congo under United Nations Command. As I pointed out in my letter to the Ceylonese Prime Minister (a copy of which was sent for Your Excellency's information), entreating her to reconsider her decision to withdraw the Ceylonese troops from the Congo, the decision to withdraw troops from the Congo is a matter for the individual governments concerned; yet permit me to appeal most earnestly to you to reconsider your decision.

I am vigorously pursuing the idea of creating an African High Command and I must express to Your Excellency and the Government of Guinea my deep appreciation of your support.

In my considered opinion, however, it is imperative that we secure the support of at least some of the African states who have sent large contingents to the Congo. If we do not secure the support of some of these states beforehand, we may be faced with a situation in which we will find some of the African troops still serving under the United Nations in the Congo and most probably collaborating with the imperialists in the Congo.

While His Imperial Majesty Haile Selassie was here I took the opportunity to discuss my proposal for the creation of an African High Command with him and I am pleased to inform you that his reaction was favourable and encouraging. Since then, however, my attention has been drawn to a joint communiqué which was issued in Monrovia by His Imperial Majesty and President Tubman in which they have suggested the convening of a 'summit meeting' of Heads of African States to consider my proposal. Events are moving so fast in Africa and the situation in the Congo is deteriorating so rapidly that if we do not act now and spend time on sophisticated niceties of procedure, we may be overtaken by events. I am requesting some of the independent African states to give immediate consideration to my proposal in the light of the present dangerous situation in the Congo. I am still waiting for the views of our friend President Nasser who is reported to have reacted favourably to the idea.

If the African states who have troops in the Congo pull out individually now without first ensuring that there is an organisation capable of offering help promptly and effectively to the Congolese people the resulting confusion and anarchy in the vacuum thus created may give the imperialists and the colonialist a welcome subterfuge for direct military intervention. Should that happen it would be a serious setback for the cause of African independence and unity which you and I have so much at heart.

Although I, too, was disappointed at the obvious failure of ONUC, I considered it essential to continue supporting the UN effort in the Congo. Withdrawal would only play into the hands of Lumumba's enemies. Furthermore, there was encouragement in the struggle against Mobutu and Tshombe, in the establishment of a rival government in Stanleyville. This had been set up by Antoine Gizenga, a well-known supporter of Lumumba and a passionate African nationalist. He announced the new government on 12 December in a statement declaring that Stanleyville and not Leopoldville was now the seat of the central government of the Congo.

The thirty-five-year-old Gizenga was an experienced politician. In April 1959, when the Parti Solidaire Africain (PSA) was formed, he was elected President. He joined Kasavubu's ABAKO Cartel in December 1959 and led the PSA delegation to the Round Table Conference at Brussels in January the following year. In the May 1960 elections PSA won 13 seats out of the 137 in the central Parliament, and Gizenga became Deputy Premier of the Republic. He sided openly with Lumumba in the conflict with Kasavubu which followed independence, and later, fearing attack by Mobutu, fled from Leopoldville to set up a strongly Lumumbist provincial government in Stanleyville.

Although labelled a Communist by those who sought to discredit him, Gizenga was, and remains, a staunch African nationalist and a socialist. He collected around him in Stanleyville those who supported the legal government of the Congo. In serving this cause, Gizenga was also helping in the Pan-African struggle against neo-colonialism.

The Ghana Government officially recognised the Stanleyville Government on 15 February 1961. But in the meantime, I renewed my efforts to gain support for the release of Lumumba and the re-convening of the Congolese Parliament, so that the Congolese people themselves could decide how their country should be governed. Until these objectives were achieved it was essential for UN troops to remain in the Congo. I wrote explaining these views to the British Prime Minister, Mr Harold Macmillan, on 14 December 1960 in reply to two notes received from him concerning the Congo situation. After referring to the actions of 'concerns and interests of British origin' which 'because of the particular axes they grind in the Congo, use all their exertions to cause confusion and foment subversion', I came to the subject of Lumumba's arrest:

Premier Lumumba is in chains at the hands of a band of men who have no constitutional or legal *locus standi*. He is considered to have ceased to be Prime Minister on an announcement made merely by President Kasavubu. Who ratified this decision? Neither the elected Parliament nor the people as a whole had been consulted. On the other hand, Premier Lumumba's demand for a referendum under the auspices of the United Nations shows, at least, that he is prepared to bow to the voice of the Congolese people as the proper arbiters in the present most inflammable situation in the Congo.

If President Kasavubu's unilateral and unratified dismissal of Premier Lumumba works without the authority of its government, surely the unilateral dismissal of President Kasavubu by Premier Lumumba should also find acceptability. All the world knows, however, that the forces of the Belgian imperialists have been ranged on the side of President Kasavubu, who is pleased to enjoy the boisterous and violent protection of the self-styled Colonel Mobutu, so long as he is willing to acquiesce in the excesses of this self-appointed military leader.

Now, Mr Prime Minister, let me make clear to you the stand my Government has taken in the unfortunate Congo crisis. We adhere most rigidly to the principle that in these matters it is essential to allow the people themselves to decide in an atmosphere of *complete* freedom and security who their leaders should be. This can only be assured in the context of free and unfettered parliamentary elections.

In our view, until some kind of recognised and genuine effort has been made to secure the verdict of the people, we cannot withdraw our support to Premier Lumumba and his Government, without betraying the important principle of self-determination.

There is another point which weighs very heavily with us in these considerations, and it is this: that we cannot withdraw recognition from Premier Lumumba without at the same time undermining the authority of President Kasavubu, since under the Loi Fondamentale the two of them are inseparably linked to each other. In our view the fact that the Loi Fondamentale is in the nature of a provisional arrangement is immaterial, and we shall continue to stand by this constitutional arrangement until an adequate substitute generally acceptable to the Congolese people has been provided.

Furthermore, on grounds of temperament, we consider that the formula for the appointment of Lumumba as Prime Minister and Kasavubu as President was a most fortunate one. It will in this connection be remembered that this arrangement was made possible by the magnanimous concessions agreed to by Mr Lumumba in the interests of national harmony, since Mr Kasavubu did not secure enough votes during the elections to qualify him for his most important office in the new Government.

The combination was also fortunate because, on grounds of temperament, the two Congolese personages were admirably complementary to each other. They also represented fairly substantial tribal groups in a country in which tribal divisions are still very rigid.

This formula which, incidentally, Ghana helped to evolve and for which my Government earned the special commendation and gratitude of the Belgian Government, would have worked quite successfully but for the tragic intervention of imperialists who saw in Premier Lumumba everything they detested and feared as most unlikely to contribute to their plans for retaining their political and economic stranglehold on the Congo—Mr Lumumba's passionate sense of nationalism, his independent spirit, his fiery desire to eradicate all forms of foreign interference from his country's affairs and, perhaps, his youthful temerity. Even after the Belgians had loudly declared to the world that they had set the Congolese people free to determine their own destiny they were still anxiously looking for docile and willing lieutenants in their despicable struggle for domination and control in the Congo.

Evidence of this intention is clearly provided by the rapidity with which the Belgians have infiltrated back into the Congo. I am sure your Government's representative in Leopoldville keeps you fully briefed on this. The Congolese Ministry of Finance is apparently dominated by Belgians and Colonel Mobutu has a substantial number of Belgians on his military staff. Mr Prime Minister, if the Belgium authorities were really sincere in their protestations of good faith, would they not prevent their Army Officers from returning to the Congo at the present time? It is now quite clear that the Belgians now working on President Kasavubu's staff are determined to obstruct and paralyse the United Nations effort in the Congo.

I consider that you hold a special position in the present Congo crisis as a prominent member of the NATO Powers. Could you not, as such, bring pressure to bear on your NATO ally Belgium to stop arming Mr Tshombe and Mr Kalondji? The United Nations can play its role most effectively by stopping the supply of further arms to opposing factions. If need be, India, Pakistan and Malaya could produce more troops and this would be a magnificent Commonwealth effort.

5

Mr Prime Minister, you who are so remote from the scene of events and we who are so intimately affected by the consequences of these developments can hardly have a common point of view on such vital issues as those at stake in the Congo. Your detachment can admittedly contribute to impartial reasoning and analysis, but that very detachment is bound to cause you to exclude from your examination of events various extraneous circumstances which necessarily complicate the issues involved.

Permit me to reflect that this is why you in the Western European countries find it hard to believe that Belgium can possibly be actively engaged behind the scenes, doing everything in her power to make the elected Government ineffective and even the presence of the United Nations in the Congo an almost shameful farce.

What is happening in the Congo today is truly a world problem because the intervention of the United Nations at the request of the legitimate Government brings us all, who are members of the United Nations within the orbit of this grave danger, and the least miscalculation or unwise step would set the whole world ablaze again in a conflagration many times greater than what all of us have been through.

But it is also essentially an African problem which, because of our proximity with the Congo, leads us to suffer consequences more directly and more intimately than anyone living thousands of miles away. For this reason we are more qualified to provide a faithful assessment of the trend of events and can see dangers which must escape our most intimate friends and associates.

I am accordingly constrained to sound a warning that unless everything is done to eliminate interference in the Congo problem, we are in grave danger of making a farce of the United Nations by its failure to grapple with the problem effectively and courageously.

I have stated my views in considerable detail, because I wish to impress upon you that in our attitude to the Congo problem, we have been motivated by an earnest and sincere desire to see that the foundations of orderly progress and government are firmly laid in Africa where sovereignty and independence are subjected to serious and often unjustified pressures.

You will by now have seen the text of my communication to Mr Hammarskjöld which contains my views on Mr Hammarskjöld's handling of the Congo situation. The United Nations is mankind's last bulwark for peace, and it is the responsibility of all of us to see that its authority is maintained at all costs.

We cannot afford to see this great Organisation pushed around by the forces of anarchy, violence, vested interests and colonialism.

I have discussed these matters frankly and with the utmost sincerity, because nothing less than this is useful or beneficial.

On 20 December, an economic blockade was instituted by the Leopoldville Government against Orientale Province. Five days later, soldiers from Stanleyville arrested the provincial president of Kivu Province and assumed control. In an attempt to reoccupy Kivu, Mobutu sent troops to Bukavu, using the airport in Ruanda-Urundi. This caused international indignation, but no effective steps were taken to ensure that similar use of Ruanda-Urundi was not made again.

In this situation, I once more urged the establishment of an African High Command in a message to President Nasser dated 30 December 1960. After thanking him for a telegram I received from him in which he gave the draft of a joint statement calling for the release of Lumumba and the recalling of the Congolese Parliament, I continued:

I agree with you entirely that the Colonial countries are conspiring against Congolese independence and territorial integrity and that, in the pursuit of their wicked designs, they are now openly using the United Nations and its flag.

I also agree that the situation is so critical that we should not stand still or idle now. It is my view that we should not allow this disgraceful exhibition of Colonialism to gather force and momentum in Africa to destroy our hard-won independence. I consider therefore that the initiative must be taken energetically by the Independent African States so as to enable us to nip in the bud the kind of evil being perpetrated by the Colonialists, Imperialists and their Agents in the Congo. It is only when we in Africa who are immediately affected by these problems initiate action by adopting concrete measures to deal with them that we can justifiably call upon our brothers in the Asian countries to come to our aid.

It is for this reason that I have made proposals to Your Excellency and to the other Heads of the Independent African States for the establishment of an African High Command with military planning Headquarters in a suitable location in Africa. I quote below the text of the telegram which was despatched on 26 November. This contains proposals which appear to be in complete accord with your own views on the matter:

In the light of the trend of events in the Congo, I am addressing an urgent request to all the Independent African States to consider as a matter of the highest priority the establishment of an African High Command with its military planning Headquarters in a suitable location in Africa. The resources of this Command would be supplied by the Independent African States. This Command should operate independently or be placed at the disposal of the United Nations. In providing aid for any African country which may find itself in the circumstances that we now find in the Congo.

In view of the urgency of this proposal I am submitting it personally to President Abdul Nasser of the United Arab Republic, Emperor Haile Selassie of Ethiopia, President William Tubman of Liberia, President Sékou Touré of Guinea, President Habib Bourguiba of Tunisia, President Aboud of Sudan, King Mohammed V of Morocco, King Idris of Lybia and President Modibo Keita of Mali for their serious and early consideration. I am releasing a copy of this message to the Press.

The matter is now so urgent that I think our two Governments should begin immediately to concert measures for setting up the nucleus of this African High Command. I sincerely believe that other Independent African States will eventually come to appreciate the necessity for establishing such an organisation in the wider interests of our security and safety in Africa.

If my proposals are acceptable, I will appreciate it if you would send your military experts to Accra for joint planning, but should this not be possible I shall be prepared to send a team of my military experts to Cairo for the same purpose.

As you are aware, His Imperial Majesty Emperor Haile Selassie of Ethiopia is now in Accra with me on a State Visit. I am discussing this matter with him, and I know that I have your full support in the measures I have outlined. It is most essential that we should stand together, for our cause is just.

I was particularly concerned about the urgent need to provide food and medical supplies for the Stanleyville Government. At the same time, it was proving difficult to keep the Ghanaian forces in Kasai adequately provisioned. On 22 December I wrote to His Excellency General Ibrahim Aboud, President of the Supreme Council of the Armed Forces of the Republic of the Sudan, about the use of Khartoum airport by Ghana Government planes:

Some days ago I had discussion with your Ambassador in Ghana concerning the necessity to secure refuelling and staging rights in Khartoum for Ghana Government planes proceeding to the Congo from Accra. The reasons why we have found it necessary to approach you with this request are as follows:

1(a) The maintenance of the Ghana Brigade in Kasai depends upon a twice weekly maintenance flight from Accra to Luluabourg. At present these flights rely on refuelling facilities at Ndjili Airport, Leopoldville. These facilities are constantly interrupted by the Congolese Security officer at the airport, a Mr Pongo, who sometimes even gives instructions to prevent aircraft from landing in spite of prior clearance obtained from the United Nations Command in Leopoldville.

(b) There have been appeals from Mr Gizenga at Stanleyville for food and medical supplies. These appeals cannot be complied with unless staging facilities exist at Khartoum.

2 The Government of Ghana would not object if the aircraft involved were subjected to search at Khartoum airport. The aircraft would, however, be those of Ghana Airways—for flights to Stanleyville or British Royal Air Force—for flights to Luluabourg.

3 I have today sent you a separate communication by cablegram concerning the proposal for setting up an African Command, and I enclose a copy of this for your urgent consideration.

4 I should welcome Your Excellency's earliest attention to these matters as the situation in the Congo has now become extremely critical.

On 23 December I left for Conakry to discuss the Congo situation with Presidents Sékou Touré and Modibo Keita. We agreed that urgent positive measures were required by the African states and it was in this mood that we accepted the invitation of King Mohammed V of Morocco to attend a conference of African states early in January 1961.[1] In a letter dated 12 January 1961 I sent the Secretary-General the declaration concerning the Congo situation issued by the Casablanca powers. On the same day the Security Council resumed discussion of the Congo at the 924th Meeting. While the Soviet representative condemned the Belgian supplying of Mobutu's forces and the use made by Belgians of Ruanda-Urundi, the United Kingdom delegate argued that there had been no Belgian aggression, 'No blame attached to the Belgian Government'. Two days later, the Security Council rejected a resolution condemning the Belgians for having allowed Congolese troops to pass through Ruanda-Urundi. In Elisabethville, several people thought to be supporters of Lumumba were arrested, and tension increased both in the Katangan capital and in Leopoldville as rumours spread of a possible coup in favour of Lumumba.

[1] *The Casablanca Conference.* See pp. 104–9.

Kasavubu was clearly nervous. In a letter to the Secretary-General of 14 January 1961, he requested the recall of the UN Special Representative, Dayal, 'whose irresponsibility and partiality have shocked all sectors of Congolese opinion', and asked for help to suppress 'the rebel bands of Gizenga and Lundula'. The Secretary-General refused to recall Dayal. Then came the very grave news that Lumumba and his colleagues Okito and Mpolo had been transferred from Thysville to a prison in Katanga. This could mean only one thing. That they were considered too dangerous. Even in prison, Lumumba was capable of arousing great enthusiasm for his cause and his opponents were determined to prevent him from becoming the centre of opposition manoeuvres. The choice of Katanga showed clearly to all but the deliberately blind that the intention was to kill him.

11 The Murder of Lumumba

LUMUMBA and his two companions were flown to Elisabethville in circumstances which shocked even the Belgian pilot and his crew. According to the pilot's evidence the three prisoners had been roped together and were beaten continuously throughout the flight. The crew were so sickened at the sight of the savage punishment inflicted on the prisoners that they shut themselves up in the front cabin. I can think of a more courageous reaction, though doubtless they considered it no part of their business to interfere. At Elisabethville airport, eye-witnesses reported that the prisoners showed obvious signs of ill-treatment and they were further manhandled by troops and police as they were pushed quickly into a waiting jeep.

Where they went, and what precisely happened that first evening, has yet to be conclusively proved but on the evidence available it seems certain that they were driven to a house on the outskirts of Elisabethville, where in the presence of Tshombe and Munongo and possibly others they were cruelly murdered. In giving evidence to the UN Commission, Tshombe admitted that he saw the prisoners on the night of their arrival (17 January), and that they were 'in a sad state'. What he did not reveal, and for obvious reasons, was that he had actually agreed that Lumumba should be sent to Elisabethville. All along, he maintained that he knew nothing about the transfer of the prisoners until they were about to land. He had repeatedly refused, so he said, Kasavubu's requests to have the prisoners in Katanga. In an interview with a correspondent of the Belgian weekly magazine *Pourquoi Pas* some three years after Lumumba's death, Tshombe went so far as to fabricate a completely false story about the whole affair. It was published under the title 'Tshombe Tells us how Lumumba

Died'. For the benefit of those who did not read this article and because I have proof of its dishonesty, I must quote part of it.

After explaining at length to the correspondent that he knew of Kasavubu's wish to get rid of Lumumba, and that he, Tshombe, had always insisted that Lumumba was of more use to his enemies alive, he went on to describe the events of 17 January 1961, which began with a telephone call at 5 p.m. Tshombe, according to his own account, was looking at a film entitled 'Liberty' put on by one of the Moral Rearmament teams. President Kasavubu was at the other end of the telephone line. I quote now from *Pourquoi Pas:*

'My dear Tshombe,' said the Head of the Congolese State, 'I am sending you three packets. You must not refuse to accept them.'

'Three packets? What's in them?'

'You will see. They are on a plane, and will be coming to you.'

Kasavubu had no idea that he had spoken so timely a word. He had no sooner hung up than the aerodrome announced the arrival of an Air Congo plane. This was indeed unexpected because, since the proclamation of Katanga's independence, Air Congo planes had stopped landing at Elisabethville.

As Minister of the Interior, Godefroid Munongo asked for precise details. It was a DC4 requesting permission to land. And so Munongo decided to go straight to the airport.

At this point I interrupted Mr Tshombe.

'Did you know then', I asked, 'who was in the aircraft?'

'No.'

'You hadn't the least idea?'

'No.'

Tshombe went on to explain to the correspondent that the aircraft landed at Elisabethville because the plane was running out of fuel. The pilot had intended to land at Bakwanga, but after flying over the city for some time, Ferdinand Kazadi, who was in charge of the three prisoners, forced him to go instead to Elisabethville. Kazadi had heard that Ghanaian troops under UNO were at Bakwanga airport, and had probably been ordered to take Lumumba, Okito and Mpolo under their protection.

According to Tshombe, the aircraft, a DC4, was allowed to land on condition that it would leave again as soon as it had refuelled. But after refuelling, the pilot refused to take off until the following morning because flight regulations in force in the Congo forbade internal night flights. When Munongo, who was at the airport, pressed him to leave, he became angry and told him that the Congolese could dispose of the 'strange cargo' themselves. He did not want to have anything to do with that kind of freight.

Tshombe then described in great detail the terrible condition the prisoners were in on their arrival at Elisabethville airport. He said that they had suffered such cruel beatings on the journey that they could hardly stand when they were bundled out of the aircraft and into a waiting jeep. Gagged and bound back to back, they were repeatedly struck by Mobutu's soldiers with the butt end of their rifles. As Lumumba lay full length on the floor of the jeep, ANC soldiers jumped on his body. The prisoners, more dead than alive, were then driven to an empty house in the 'Babana district'.

At this point of the interview the *Pourquoi Pas* correspondent asked Tshombe whether he personally saw the prisoners in the house to which they were transferred. Tshombe answered, 'No.' Yet earlier, when the UN delegate, Berendsen, questioned Tshombe about Lumumba's death, he had said that he was there and saw their wretched condition. Tshombe explained to the correspondent that he had deliberately told Berendsen a lie because he had wanted to present their case in a strong light, and Berendsen was more likely to believe him than any of the other witnesses.

Not satisfied with this explanation, the correspondent asked Tshombe how, if he was not present in the house that night, he could be sure that Munongo was speaking the truth and that no crime was committed. Tshombe replied that he had obtained his information from Pius Sapwe, Chief of Police in Elisabethville. Sapwe had never lied to him, and he was certain that his account of what happened was true. According to Sapwe, a medical examination showed that the three prisoners were already dying when they were taken into the house. Lumumba had an internal haemorrhage, a perforated stomach and broken ribs. Okito had a fractured skull, and Mpolo was unconscious.

Admitting that he was in a panic when he heard the news of their condition, Tshombe went on to describe how he called a Cabinet meeting in the middle of the night and spoke by telephone to Kasavubu. 'If they die,' said Kasavubu, 'bury them and let's hear no more of it whatsoever.' As the Cabinet meeting continued, news was received that the three prisoners had died.

Concluding the interview, the correspondent asked Tshombe about a conversation supposed to have taken place between Munongo and Lumumba in the house where Lumumba died. Tshombe denied that any conversation had taken place:

'No one spoke to Lumumba. In fact he was unconscious.'
'Are you absolutely certain?'
'Yes.'
'And yet it is said that the prisoners were not really in a bad way when they got to Elisabethville.'
'So many things have been said as well as written. I have told you the truth.'
'On your honour?'
'On my honour!'

Tshombe must have been very pleased at the result of the interview with Peter Davister of *Pourquoi Pas*. The article sounded convincing enough—every detail had been cleverly devised to build up a plausible explanation of Lumumba's death. Tshombe had had three years in which to fabricate his case. He wrote to me on 31 January 1964 from Madrid:

Your Excellency,
I have the honour to inform you that I always took great care to avoid being in any way responsible for the tragic death of H. E. Mr Patrice Lumumba, Prime Minister of the Congolese Government.

I think that the time has come to throw full light on the matter, and I can no longer continue to allow myself to be regarded by Africans and indeed the world at large, as guilty of that crime.

A pamphlet will soon come out in connection with Mr Lumumba's death, those responsible for the crime will be denounced, and evidence will be supplied. I have just seen in the Belgian weekly *Why Not* a press interview regarding the same matter, and I take the liberty of sending you a copy for your information.

Please accept, Your Excellency, the expression of my high esteem.

MOISE TSHOMBE

Tshombe's declaration of his innocence rested on one important point, his so-called reluctance to have Lumumba sent to Katanga and his ignorance of their journey until they were about to land at Elisabethville. This point has now been exposed for what it is worth in a note dated 15 January 1961, from Tshombe to Bomboko, in which Tshombe not only agreed to the transfer of Lumumba but asked for information about his arrival:

ETAT DU KATANGA

Cabinet du Président

S.R. 20/36/T.N.

Elisabethville, le 15 janvier 1961

Monsieur BOMBOKO,
Président des Commissaires Généraux,
LEOPOLDVILLE.

Monsieur le Président ,

    Suite au message que nous venons de recevoir, nous marquons notre accord de transférer immédiatement le communiste LUMUMBA à ELISABETHVILLE.

    Cette opération doit se faire secrètement: pourriez-vous nous aviser de son arrivée dans le plus bref délai?

    Veuillez croire, Monsieur le Président, à l'expression de mes sentiments les meilleurs.

Moïse TSHOMBE,
Président du Katanga.

Tshombe's letter to Bomboko

ETAT DU KATANGA   Elisabethville
Cabinet du Président   le 15 janvier 1961
S.R. 20/36/T.N.   Monsieur Bomboko
                                   Président des Commissaires
                                   Généraux Léopoldville

Monsieur le Président,

Suite au message que nous venons de recevoir, nous marquons notre accord de transférer immédiatement le communiste Lumumba à Elisabethville.

Cette opération doit se faire secrètement: pourriez-vous nous aviser de son arrivée dans le plus bref delai?

Veuillez croire, Monseur le Président, à l'expression de mes sentiments les meilleurs.[1]

MOISE TSHOMBE
Président du Katanga

This note, which reveals without any shadow of doubt Tshombe's involvement in Lumumba's death, reached me anonymously through Dar-es-Salaam. It appears, photographed, on page 123. It came with the following letter addressed to *All Friends of the Congo* from a body called the League of the Congolese Resurrection:

(*Translation*)

Dear Brothers,

Not long ago Tshombe called many press conferences at Madrid, despatched letters and gave interviews with the sole aim of recovering his reputation soiled with the blood of our honourable Patrice Lumumba.

It is clear that Tshombe was not the only one involved but also his imperialist masters who needed a man of this type to help them plunder the Congolese people.

Tshombe has been and still remains nothing but an assassin. The attached copy of his letter to Bomboko is an indisputable proof of his direct participation in the organisation of Lumumba's assassination.

No support for Tshombe, the murderer of Congolese patriots!

Long live free, independent and prosperous Congo!

In view of Tshombe's note to Bomboko which establishes his guilt,

[1] 'Mr President, following the message just received, we advise you of our agreement to transfer the Communist Lumumba immediately to Elisabethville. This must be done secretly: can you let us know of his arrival with the minimum of delay? With kindest regards, etc.'

it seems practically certain that the UN commissioners who subsequently enquired into Lumumba's death, were right in concluding that he and his companions were killed, probably in the presence of Tshombe, Munongo and Kibwe on the same night that they arrived in Elisabethville.

From the day of their arrival, rumours of their death began to circulate, but it was not until 10 February that the Katangan Government put out the ridiculous story of the escape of the prisoners, followed a few days later by the announcement that they had been killed by angry villagers. This news was given at a press conference held by Munongo, the Katangan Minister of the Interior, known to be one of Lumumba's most bitter enemies. In a statement, according to eye-witnesses 'savouring of personal spite', Munongo said, 'I know that some people will say we murdered him. My answer to that is: Prove it!'

At the United Nations Headquarters in New York delegates expressed the shock and disgust felt by their governments and people at the foul crime which had been committed. Mr Zorin placed the blame entirely on the shoulders of the Secretary-General, 'After all that has happened in the Congo and Katanga, one can no longer have any confidence in the Secretary-General or his staff.' The UAR delegate referred to Lumumba as 'the most respected and the most representative leader of the Congolese people', and said that he personified African nationalism. Other delegates spoke in much the same way; some emphasising the failure of the UN, some the interference of foreign interests but all deploring the killing of a man whose only crime was his patriotism and his refusal to compromise his beliefs.

The Secretary-General replied to the attacks made on him at the 935th Meeting of the Security Council on 15 February 1961:

Mr Lumumba escaped in a way unknown to the United Nations and travelled east. . . . He was arrested out in the country without any possibility for the United Nations to stop this action, as it was not in control of the situation. This may be the point to remind the members of the simple fact that a force of, at its maximum, 20,000 men spread over a country not far from five times the size of France, is not in a position to check what is going on everywhere in the country or in a position to protect individuals of whom the whereabouts are unknown.

I did not make any special efforts for our own representatives to see Mr Lumumba while at Katanga, as at that stage the United

Nations Conciliation Commission for the Congo and its members had solicited a promise from Mr Kasavubu to see him and were going to do so when they visited Katanga. When Mr Tshombe refused the contact with Mr Lumumba, I protested to Mr Kasavubu. For more than two weeks the Conciliation Commission made several representations to Mr Kasavubu with a view to arranging a visit to Mr Lumumba; they did not succeed in arranging his co-operation.

The inadequacy of UN action, the failure to provide Lumumba with transport when he asked for it in connection with his daughter's burial and then the feeble acceptance of a promise by Kasavubu that he would visit Lumumba in prison, makes it clear that the Secretary-General and his advisers cannot escape blame. As the UAR delegate, Mr Loufti, said on 17 February, 'It is ironical that the United Nations, which went to the Congo at Mr Lumumba's invitation, has been helpless to prevent his death.' Loufti then went on to announce that his government had decided to withdraw its troops from the Congo.

Although the UN had already come in for much bitter criticism for its actions in the Congo, the murder of Lumumba seemed to bring things to a head. Both the Secretary-General and the UN as a whole were to blame to some extent for the unsatisfactory handling of the Congo situation and Mr Wizegoonawardena of Ceylon received full support for his suggestion made at the 937th Meeting (16 February) for a full investigation into Lumumba's death.

A Commission of Investigation was established consisting of members from Burma, Ethiopia, Mexico and Togo. Justice U Aung Khine of Burma was elected chairman. The Commission met for the first time on 11 May 1961, in New York. After 16 meetings it left for Europe, where it visited London and Brussels before settling down in Geneva to hear witnesses. There it encountered many difficulties and delays and members pressed to be allowed to visit the Congo where on the spot enquiries could be made. This was obviously a necessity if they were to get at the truth, but their requests were repeatedly refused. Officials of the UN in the Congo were against the Commission's visit because of the delicate political situation. They wanted a postponement until after the new government had been formed.

The new government under Cyrille Adoula was formed and approved by the Congolese Parliament on 2 August 1961. The Commissioners then asked Adoula for permission to visit the Congo. He replied that the Congolese would, in due course, conduct their own investigation.

In the meantime, members of the Commission, by means of interviews and interrogations, were building up information which was to enable them to reach certain conclusions. Significantly, Tshombe was actually in Geneva for a time while the Commission was sitting but he did not acknowledge receipt of a letter from the Commissioners asking him to appear before them. However, if Tshombe was unwilling to co-operate, others were keen to testify and the Commissioners listened to several different accounts of Lumumba's death. According to one witness, Okito was killed by the gendarmerie at 9 p.m. and half an hour later Mpolo was brought along and shown his companion's dead body in a large pit. He had knelt down to pray and had been killed in that position. His body fell into the pit. A quarter of an hour later, Lumumba was brought there and killed by a Belgian captain. Another witness told the Commission that Munongo had stabbed Lumumba himself, and, as he lay on the ground, a Belgian mercenary ended his suffering by shooting him in the head. Yet another witness said that a Belgian officer, Colonel Huyghe, shot Lumumba.

The Commissioners carefully sifted all the evidence. They quickly disposed of the elaborate escape story told by Munongo. It did not hold water in any detail. The prisoners could not have made a hole in the thick wall of their prison; they could not have overcome fifteen guards, or started a conveniently placed car with wire. No disciplinary action was taken against the guards who allowed the 'escape'. Furthermore, the Katangan Government refused to allow the Commission to visit the scene of the escape or to surrender the bodies to the Commission for examination. Obviously the whole story was false and all who heard Munongo at the press conference when he told of the escape and death of the prisoners left convinced that he was lying.

The Commission formally concluded that the weight of evidence was strongly against the official version of the Katangan Government that the three were killed by tribesmen. It accepted that they were killed in a villa near Elisabethville on 17 January 1961 in the presence of high officials, namely Tshombe, Munongo and Kibwe and that 'the escape story was staged'. A great deal of suspicion was cast on Colonel Huyghe, a Belgian mercenary, as being the actual murderer. The Commission concluded by stating that Kasavubu and Tshombe should not escape responsibility for the murder, and that there should be further investigation. It was probably due to the Commission's report that Tshombe made no attempt to stick to the original escape story when he later, in 1963, told the *Pourquois Pas* correspondent his new version of the tragedy. Having allowed a completely false story to be put out by the Katangan Government in February 1961 he fabricated an even unlikelier one two years later, and apparently expected people to believe it.

Although the UN Commission recommended further investigation and said that Kasavubu and Tshombe could not escape responsibility for the murder, no further action has been taken. In 1963 I drew the attention of the Secretary-General to this state of affairs, but as has so often happened in the past, political considerations led to the matter being shelved once again. A crime of this magnitude must be solved to the satisfaction of all and those responsible brought to justice. With each year that passes the difficulties of getting the necessary evidence increase. Vital witnesses may die, and there may be further excuses made for postponement.

In his last letter, written to his wife from Camp Hardy, Lumumba made his own appeal to posterity. It was shortly before his death, and he was then only thirty-six years old:

My dear wife,

I am writing these words not knowing whether they will reach you, when they will reach you, and whether I shall still be alive when you read them. All through my struggle for the independence of my country, I have never doubted for a single instant the final triumph of the sacred cause to which my companions and I have devoted all our lives. But what we wished for our country, its right to an honourable life, to unstained dignity, to independence without restrictions, was never desired by the Belgian imperialists and the Western allies, who found direct and indirect support, both deliberate and unintentional, amongst certain high officials of the United Nations, that organisation in which we placed all our trust when we called on its assistance.

They have corrupted some of our compatriots and bribed others. They have helped to distort the truth and bring our independence into dishonour. How could I speak otherwise? Dead or alive, free or in prison by order of the imperialists, it is not myself who counts. It is the Congo, it is our poor people for whom independence has been transformed into a cage from whose confines the outside world looks on us, sometimes with kindly sympathy, but at other times with joy and pleasure.

But my faith will remain unshakeable. I know and I feel in my heart that sooner or later my people will rid themselves of all their enemies, both internal and external, and that they will rise as one man to say No to the degradation and shame of colonialism, and regain their dignity in the clear light of the sun.

We are not alone. Africa, Asia and the free liberated people from all corners of the world will always be found at the side of the millions of Congolese who will not abandon the struggle until the day when there are no longer any colonialists and their mercenaries in our country. As to my children, whom I leave and whom I may never see again, I should like them to be told that it is for them, as it is for every Congolese, to accomplish the sacred task of reconstructing our independence and our sovereignty: for without justice there is no dignity, and without independence there are no free men.

Neither brutality, nor cruelty nor torture will ever bring me to ask for mercy, for I prefer to die with my head unbowed, my faith unshakeable and with profound trust in the destiny of my country, rather than live under subjection and disregarding sacred principles. History will one day have its say, but it will not be the history that is taught in Brussels, but the history which will be taught in the countries freed from Imperialism and its puppets. Africa will write her own history, and to the north and south of the Sahara it will be a glorious and dignified history.

Do not weep for me, my dear wife. I know that my country, which is suffering so much, will know how to defend its independence and its liberty.

Long live the Congo! Long live Africa!

PATRICE

On 14 February 1961, the day after the announcement by the Katangan Government of the death of Lumumba, I broadcast to the Ghanaian people:

Somewhere in Katanga in the Congo—where and when we do not know—three of our brother freedom fighters have been done to death.

There have been killed Patrice Lumumba, the Prime Minister of the Republic of the Congo, Maurice Mpolo, the Minister in his Government who was elected from Katanga Province, and Joseph Okito, the Vice-President of the Congolese Senate.

About their end many things are uncertain, but one fact is crystal clear. They have been killed because the United Nations, whom Patrice Lumumba himself as Prime Minister had invited to the Congo to preserve law and order, not only failed to maintain that law and order, but also denied to the lawful Government of the Congo all other means of self-protection.

History records many occasions when rulers of states have been assassinated. The murder of Patrice Lumumba and of his two colleagues, however, is unique in that it is the first time in history that the legal ruler of a country has been done to death with the open connivance of a world organisation in whom that ruler put his trust.

These are the facts. Patrice Lumumba was appointed Prime Minister by the departing Belgian authorities because he was the leader of the Parliamentary Party with the largest representation and was the only Member of Parliament who could obtain a majority in both the Senate and the Chamber. Kasavubu was subsequently elected the ceremonial Head of the State, but it was clearly agreed and understood that he should have no more authority or power than has the King of the Belgians in Belgium. This fact, clearly written into the Constitution of the Congo, has been deliberately ignored and distorted by those who have sought for their own ends to give some appearance of legality to the military usurpers and the agents of colonial rule who have illegally seized power in some parts of the Congo.

Shortly after independence the Congolese army mutinied. Patrice Lumumba and his colleagues had to secure outside support from somewhere if they were to preserve the legal structure of the State.

In the interests of world peace and in order to prevent the cold war being brought into Africa, Patrice Lumumba invited the United Nations to preserve law and order. The United Nations insisted that they should have the sole mandate to do this and that the legal Government of the Congo should not obtain that military assistance which would have otherwise been forthcoming from many other friendly African States.

However, instead of preserving law and order the United Nations declared itself neutral between law and disorder and refused to lend any assistance whatsoever to the legal Government in suppressing the mutineers who had set themselves up in power in Katanga and South Kasai.

When, in order to move its troops against the rebels, the Government of the Congo obtained some civilian aircraft and civilian motor vehicles from the Soviet Union, the colonialist Powers at the United Nations raised a howl of rage while, at the same time, maintaining a discreet silence over the build-up of Belgian arms and actual Belgian military forces in the service of the rebels.

With a total disregard of the Constitution, which expressly provided that the President could not dismiss the Prime Minister unless there had been a vote of 'no confidence' in the Parliament, Kasavubu illegally tried to remove Patrice Lumumba from office and to substitute another Government. When Lumumba wished to broadcast to the people, explaining what had happened, the United Nations in the so-called interest of law and order prevented him by force from speaking.

They did not, however, use the same force to prevent the mutineers of the Congolese Army from seizing power in Leopoldville and installing a completely illegal Government.

Despite the fact that one of the most important reasons for United Nations action was supposedly to see that all Belgian forces were removed, the United Nations sat by while the so-called Katanga Government, which is entirely Belgian-controlled, imported aircraft and arms from Belgium and from other countries, such as South Africa, which have a vested interest in the suppression of African freedom. The United Nations connived at the setting up, in fact, of an independent Katanga State, though this is contrary to the Security Council's own resolutions.

Finally, the United Nations, which could exert its authority to prevent Patrice Lumumba from broadcasting, was, so it pleaded, quite unable to prevent his arrest by mutineers or his transfer, through the use of airfields under United Nations control, into the hands of the Belgian-dominated Government of Katanga.

The United Nations is, on behalf of all its members, in control of the finances of the Congo. It is now two months ago since I personally wrote to Mr Hammarskjöld to ask him where the money came from which is being used to pay the soldiers in Mobutu's illegal army. I am still awaiting an answer. One thing is certain, however, this money does not come from the revenue of the Congo. It is supplied from outside by those who wish to restore colonialism in practice by maintaining in office a puppet regime entirely financially dependent upon them.

The time has come to speak plainly. The danger in the Congo is not so much the possibility of a civil war between Africans but rather a colonialist war in which the colonial and imperialist powers hide behind African puppet regimes.

At this very moment Northern Katanga is being laid waste by military units under command of a regular officer of the Belgian army, Colonel Crèvecœur, armed with the most modern weapons, supplied by Belgium.

Recruiting offices have been opened in South Africa, in France and elsewhere, and wages of over £400 a month are being offered to former German fascist officers and to former collaborators of Hitler and Mussolini in other countries in order to persuade them to enlist in an unholy war against the African people. Where, I ask again, does the money come from to pay these big salaries and to buy all of this modern and expensive armament which is now being deployed against unarmed peasants and villagers?

The rulers of the United States, of the United Kingdom, of France and of the other Powers who are militarily allied with Belgium, must answer these questions.

Why did they express so loudly their indignation when the Soviet Union placed at the disposal of the legal Government of the Congo civilian aircraft and civilian vehicles? Why are they so silent when their ally, Belgium, openly supplied military aircraft and armoured vehicles to the rebels? Why is it that no single Member of the North Atlantic Treaty Organisation has on any occasion addressed to Belgium any public rebuke for the flagrant breaches of the Security Council Resolution in which Belgium is every day indulging? Alas, the architects of this murder are many.

In Ghana, we realise the great financial stakes which some Great Powers have in the Union Minière and other industrial and commercial undertakings in the Congo.

I would, however, ask these Powers these questions: Do they really believe that ultimately they can safeguard their investments and their interests in the Congo by conniving at a brutal and savage colonialist war?

Do they realise that they are sacrificing African lives to continue in Africa the cold war at the very time when all powers, both great and small, should be concentrating on the abolition of colonialism and the establishment of world peace?

Patrice Lumumba, Maurice Mpolo and Joseph Okito have died because they put their faith in the United Nations and because they refused to allow themselves to be used as stooges or puppets for external interests.

There is still time for those who have supported this cruel colonialist war in the Congo to change their policy, but time is running out. The cynical planning of the murder of Patrice Lumumba and his colleagues is a final lesson for us all. We cannot ignore the fact that this crime shows every evidence of the most careful preparation and timing. First there came the handing over of Patrice Lumumba and others to the Belgian-controlled authorities in Katanga.

Next there came the contemptuous refusal of these same authorities to allow the United Nations' Conciliation Committee any access to the prisoners. From this came the final proof that the

United Nations would not effectively intervene to save the life of the Prime Minister or his colleagues. This was followed by the formation of the so-called new Kasavubu Government and the warning by Belgium to Belgian nationals to leave those parts of the Congo controlled by the legal Government.

Finally came the story so reminiscent of Fascist technique—the false account of an attempt to escape and the death of the prisoners following upon it.

What are the next steps in this plan? The information before me now is that the Kasavubu-Mobutu group has planned an offensive against Orientale Province in an attempt to secure a quick military victory before the Security Council can deal with the matter. My information is that this plan has been made with the full knowledge of the French and Belgian Governments and has their full support. Let me issue a most serious warning. Any such action, unless immediately denounced by the other members of the Security Council, will have a profound effect on African relations with the Great Powers.

Our dear brothers Patrice Lumumba, Maurice Mpolo and Joseph Okito are dead, and I ask you all to join with me in mourning the loss which the whole African continent has sustained through their cruel murder. But their spirit is not dead, nor are the things for which they stood: African freedom, the unity and independence of Africa and the final complete destruction of colonialism and imperialism. The colonialists and imperialists have killed them, but what they cannot do, is to kill the ideals which we still preach, and for which they sacrificed their lives. In the Africa of the future their names will live for ever more.

12 Call for a New United Nations Command

ON the announcement of Lumumba's death on 13 February 1961, the Security Council met immediately to discuss the new situation. There was grave danger of civil war spreading throughout the Congo, the colonialists playing their usual game of letting Congolese fight Congolese. It seemed to me that steps had to be taken at once to set up a new United Nations Command. On 18 February, I cabled Hammarskjöld:

It is now time that a new and serious approach be made to the present ineffective efforts of the United Nations in the Congo if the United Nations is to be saved and the future peace of Africa assured. As I indicated at the beginning of the operations in the Congo, the problem must be tackled in two phases; first the military problem and second the political one. Unless the military problem can be solved first there can be no lasting political solution.

I would like to come to New York to give my views on both phases because I am certain that from now on the initiative must come from the African countries with military support from the Asian bloc. All initiative or aid from the big or Nato powers should cease. The flow of arms and equipment into the Congo provides conditions which could lead to a civil war of the Spanish type, with grave consequences throughout the world. All Belgian military, paramilitary and other personnel serving the various factions should be expelled from the Congo at once. All non-African military personnel not specifically required to work under the United Nations Command must leave the Congo. The situation is so serious that in my view the interpretation of the Security Council mandate, namely, non-interference in the internal affairs of the Congo is no longer tenable.

The plan which I envisage for dealing with the present situation is as follows:

(a) A new United Nations Command should be established in the Congo;

(b) This command must be African and should take over complete responsibility for law and order in the Congo;

(c) All Congolese armed units should be disarmed; this disarming will involve their return to barracks and the surrender of their weapons to the new United Nations Command.

(d) The disarming and hand-over should be voluntary and should lead to the reorganisation and re-training of the Congolese national army; but if certain factions will not co-operate force must be used;

(e) All non-African personnel serving in the Congolese army must be expelled immediately;

(f) Once the military situation has been brought under control on these lines all political prisoners must be released by the new United Nations Command, and the new Command should then convene Parliament under its auspices;

(g) All foreign diplomatic missions and representatives should immediately leave the Congo for the time being in order to give this new United Nations Command a fair chance and to eliminate the cold war from the Congo.

In view of the importance of this matter I propose that you should circulate this communication to members of the Security Council, and I am releasing the contents of this telegram to the Press at 1800 hours GMT.

Awaiting your reply earliest.

In the meantime, on 14 February, the UAR recognised the Stanleyville Government and the next day Guinea, East Germany and Yugoslavia followed suit. Then came the announcement, on 20 February, that six prominent Lumumbist supporters had been executed in South Kasai. The news of this latest tragedy reached us in Accra while the foreign ministers of Ghana, Algeria, Mali, Morocco and the UAR were meeting within the framework of the Casablanca Charter to discuss the deteriorating situation in the Congo. I had called the conference in the hope that some kind of united policy might be agreed upon, and I was not disappointed. As a result of meetings on 20 and 22 February, the following resolution was adopted:

Assembled in an Extraordinary Conference in Accra on the 20/2/61 and the 22/2/61 within the framework of the Casablanca Charter, and on the initiative of President Kwame Nkrumah, the Foreign Ministers of the Algerian Republic, of the Republic of Ghana, of the Republic of Mali, of the Kingdom of Morocco and of the United Arab Republic:

Concerned over the deterioration of the situation in the Congo, following the assassination of the late Prime Minister, Patrice Lumumba, and of several members of his Government and the Congolese Parliament,

seriously concerned over the spread of civil war in the Congo,

take note of and condemn the failure of the United Nations to defend the independence, unity and the territorial integrity of the Congo and to find a solution compatible with the interests of the Congolese people,

fully aware of the particularly dangerous consequences of this failure on the general process of decolonisation and on the forces engaged in the struggle for African liberation,

consider that the United Nations, through its inactivity and its ineffectiveness, and the imperialist powers through their criminal acts, are responsible for the deterioration of the situation in the Congo,

vigorously denounce the vile assassination of the late Prime Minister, Patrice Lumumba, and his associates,

call for immediate action against the perpetrators of this assassination,

denounce all military and repressive measures directed against the Congolese people,

declare their determination, within the framework of the decisions taken at the Casablanca Conference, to take every appropriate and immediate step capable of ensuring the security of the civil population and of safeguarding the independence, unity and territorial integrity of the Congo,

reaffirm their recognition of the Central Government headed by Antoine Gizenga and renew their entire confidence in this Government,

request the States which have not yet done so to take steps to exchange missions with this Government,

recommend that the following measures be taken to prevent civil war in the Congo:

1(a) Reconstituting on new basis and reinforcing the United Nations representation, command and forces in the Congo with a view to the setting up of an African Command and providing this with new, clearly defined and adequate authority which should include the assumption of full responsibility for keeping law and order in all parts of the Congo.

(b) The complete and immediate stopping, by the United Nations forces, of all mobilisations in any part of the Congo.

(c) The immediate expulsion from the Congo of all Belgians, and of all other foreign military or para-military units and personnel or technicians not belonging to the United Nations.

(d) Neutralisation and disarming of all military and para-military forces, units and personnel in the Congo which do not belong to the United Nations pending reorganisation and training of the ANC.

(e) Eliminating foreign intervention, stopping the flow of arms, personnel, and money, from outside, except through agreed United Nations processes.

(f) Control and inspection of foreign companies and banks, commercial and trade organisations.

2 Setting up a highly qualified and neutral Commission which would be appointed by the General Assembly and entrusted with the duty of investigating urgently and thoroughly and reporting on the course of events in the Congo since its independence, events which culminated in the deplorable and treacherous killing of the Congo's late Prime Minister and leader, Patrice Lumumba, and his associates—such report to aim at establishing facts and assessing responsibility so as to contribute substantially to the enabling of the General Assembly and eventually of the Security Council, to take all necessary steps so that all those who are directly, or indirectly responsible for the killing of the late Prime Minister and his associates may be brought to justice.

3 The setting up in the Secretariat of the United Nations, with the approval of the General Assembly, a highly qualified neutral and independent board for the Congo, which would issue regular and special reports to be submitted to the General Assembly and the Security Council.

4 Setting up in the Congo a highly qualified and neutral Commission to be appointed by the General Assembly and entrusted with the supervision of and reporting on the implementation of the General Assembly and the Security Council resolutions relating to the Congo and aiming at safeguarding its independence, unity and territorial integrity and the elimination of all foreign intervention in its internal affairs.

5 The freeing of all political prisoners and guaranteeing of the freedom of the people.

6 The reconvening of the Parliament.

7 Reaffirming the recognition of the Gizenga Government as the legitimate Government of the Congo.

8 Any United Nations assistance to the Congo or action in it should be based on the initial or subsequent request by the legitimate Government of the Congo.

9 All foreign diplomatic missions and representatives should immediately leave the Congo for the time being in order to give this new United Nations Command a fair chance and to eliminate the cold war from the Congo.

Through the Ghana Mission, the Security Council was urged to take measures to halt the invasion by Colonel Mobutu's army of Orientale and other pro-Lumumba provinces. This was the subject of a resolution adopted by the Conference on 20 February. Finally, the Conference issued a statement demanding the immediate and unconditional release of all political prisoners and called upon all peace-loving peoples throughout the world to express their abhorrence and indignation at the barbarous plan 'hatched by the imperialists and their agents with a view to assassinate all pro-Lumumba members of Parliament so that when Parliament reconvenes, the stooges of the imperialists may be assured of an automatic majority'.

Violence was increasing in the Congo and on 21 February it was announced that fifteen political prisoners had been executed in Stanleyville. At the same time, reports came of the ill treatment of UN personnel in Leopoldville. This was the direct result of deteriorating relations between the United Nations and the Congolese Government. Kasavubu informed the Secretary-General that he intended to co-operate with the ONUC authorities 'to the extent that the latter themselves respect the Congolese authorities and Congolese sovereignty'. He was protesting against the setting up of protected areas in various parts of the Congo where political refugees could shelter. But the underlying cause of Kasavubu's anger was the resolution adopted by the Security Council on 21 February 1961.

The resolution, proposed by Ceylon, Liberia and the United Arab Republic, was adopted by 9 votes to none with two abstentions (France and Russia). It urged the United Nations to take immediate steps to prevent civil war in the Congo and to use force if necessary in the last resort. It called for the immediate withdrawal and evacuation from the Congo of all Belgian and other foreign military and para-military personnel and political advisers not under the UN command, and asked all states to take steps to prevent the departure of such personnel for the Congo from their territories and for the denial of transit and other facilities to them. In addition, the resolution contained the demand for an immediate and impartial investigation into the deaths of Patrice Lumumba and his colleagues so that the perpetrators of these crimes could be punished. It ended by urging the convening of Parliament 'and the taking of necessary protective measures in that connection' and the reorganising of the Congolese army with a view to eliminating any possibility of its interference in the political life of the Congo.

At once, negotiations began between the UN and the Belgian and Katangan Governments about the removal of mercenaries serving in Katanga. Shortly afterwards, Prime Minister Ileo, Kalondji of South Kasai, and Tshombe signed a military alliance against Communism; and it was announced that a Round Table Conference would be held in Tananarive in Madagascar on 3 March to consider a new constitution for the Congo. The Conference in fact opened on 8 March, and closed a few days later when agreement was reached on a constitution embodying a confederation of sovereign states under the presidency of Joseph Kasavubu. Significantly, the Conference contained no representatives from the Lumumbists in Stanleyville and Kivu and Gizenga denounced the settlement, which would have 'balkanised' the Congo and strengthened Tshombe.

It was against this background of growing disunity and violence that I flew to New York to address the resumed session of the 15th General Assembly of the United Nations. By then, the prestige of the United Nations in the Congo was at a very low ebb. Fighting had broken out between Congolese and Sudanese troops of the UN at several points in the Lower Congo and the Sudanese had been forced to withdraw from the port of Matadi, with the result that the UN had temporarily lost control over its incoming supplies.

I was determined to do all in my power to convince the delegates of the necessity for quick and effective action to remedy the situation and to preserve peace not only in the Congo but throughout Africa and the world. It was a sad and solemn occasion, that first meeting of the General Assembly since the murder of Lumumba and I began my speech on Tuesday 7 March by saying that his death was unique in that it was the first time that a ruler of a country had been killed in the very presence of the United Nations forces whom he himself had invited to his country to restore law and order. I went on to deplore the action of the UN in recognising the government of Kasavubu

and Mobutu, which did not even claim to speak for the whole
country:

> Even as I speak, the lives of soldiers of the United Nations contin-
> gents are threatened by the undisciplined mutineers enlisted by
> Kasavubu and Mobutu.
>
> The significance of the Congo situation is that it gives the United
> Nations an opportunity to reassert its authority. If speedy and
> effective action is taken now in the Congo, the United Nations will
> have that prestige and moral backing which it must have if it is to
> tackle other even graver world problems. I have in mind the problems
> bound to arise over Angola, Mozambique, the Union of South
> Africa, Rwanda-Urundi, South-West Africa, Algeria, the Rhode-
> sias and any other African colonial territories. These are all poten-
> tial problems of the United Nations and the United Nations must
> work out now the machinery which can be used to solve such
> problems should the necessity arise.

It was impossible, I said, to deny that there had been hesitation,
vacillation, inconsistency and weakness in the United Nations' handling of the Congo crisis. As a result, the moral authority of the United
Nations had been dangerously weakened, the dangers of a world war
had increased and even the office of the Secretary-General had been
called in question. It was for the non-committed nations of the world
to work out, within the framework of the United Nations, practical
plans to solve the crisis. These plans would have to be devised and
executed largely by the independent states of Africa and the Asian
countries. I continued:

> It is with these considerations in mind that I put my proposals
> before you. They are:
> *First* a new and strengthened United Nations civil and military
> Command should be established in the Congo;
> *Second* this Command, and the contingents under it, must be
> primarily African and should take over complete responsibility for
> law and order in the Congo;
> *Third* all Congolese armed units should be disarmed; this dis-
> arming will involve their return to barracks and the surrender of
> their weapons to the new United Nations Command;
> *Fourth* the disarming and handing-over should be voluntary and
> should lead to the reorganisation and retraining of the Congolese
> National Army; but if certain factions will not co-operate, force
> must be used;

Fifth all non-African personnel serving in the Congolese Army must be expelled immediately;

Sixth the United Nations Command should control the major air and sea ports in the Congo so that the flow of arms and equipment to warring factions may be stopped and adequate support for United Nations troops be guaranteed;

Seventh all foreign diplomatic missions and representatives should immediately leave the Congo for the time being in order to give this new United Nations Command a fair chance and to eliminate the cold war from the Congo;

Eighth once the military situation has been brought under control on these lines, all political prisoners must be released by the new United Nations Command and the new Command should then convene Parliament under its auspices; those responsible for the murder of Patrice Lumumba and his close associates should then be brought to justice.

It is self-evident that the first task of the United Nations is to allow the Congolese people to be ruled by a government of their own choice. The Congolese constitution provides a means by which such a government can be chosen and we support the Gizenga Government because it was chosen by this means and was the government that invited the United Nations to the Congo.

The duty of the United Nations is not to force on the Congolese people this or that government because the other states of the world think that any particular government would be a suitable one for the Congo. This is colonialism. I therefore do not understand the emphasis which a number of powers lay on recognising this or that government. Ultimately, it must be the Congolese people who choose their government and not the United Nations. What the United Nations must do is to see that the Congolese people have the opportunity to choose the government which they want.

I proposed that the United Nations should supervise a new general election. What was needed was a solution acceptable to the Congolese people. The United Nations had become mesmerised by the problems of the cold war and every solution to the Congo problem had therefore been worked out in terms of cold war politics, while the interests of the Congolese people had often been forgotten. I told delegates that the Government of Ghana had, from the very earliest moment, taken the view that the cold war must be kept out of the Congo but that if United Nations policy was limited to that negative objective it would fail. The cold war could, in fact, only be kept out of the Congo if the country became a strong and independent state not dependent on any of the Great Power blocs.

I then turned to the question of the Mobutu regime and the way in which the United Nations had collaborated with Mobutu's so-called College of Commissioners: 'Interested only in the narrow question of setting some sort of administration in motion, the United Nations officials never considered what that administration was or whether its aims were in any way consistent with the purposes for which the United Nations went to the Congo.' Similarly, the government of Joseph Ileo was based on no shred of legality, 'He is the very man who delivered an ultimatum to the United Nations and whose troops have attacked the United Nations forces.' Both Mobutu and Ileo were being supported by the Force Publique, a colonialist organisation steeped in a tradition of brutality and organised for the purpose of suppressing liberty. This Force had to be disarmed, preferably by African contingents in the new United Nations Command.

Let me now indicate how I envisage the working of the re-organised Command. It would, of course, be subject to the general direction of the Security Council and of the United Nations General Assembly. It would not function unless it was entrusted with a positive direction to establish law and order. As I have said, its first task would be to neutralise the Force Publique everywhere. It is only when the military situation has been brought under control that the Congolese Parliament can meet in an atmosphere of security. Until Parliament met it would be the duty of the United Nations Command to keep order in the Congo and to prevent tribal or political clashes which might involve loss of life. This Command will not interfere with existing organs of government and, in particular, will respect the Provincial Administrations in so far as they are functioning within the Constitution. Where Provincial Councils, as in the case of Katanga, have usurped powers not accorded to them by the Constitution, the United Nations should give the necessary mandate to restore the constitutional position.

Considerable increase in the existing United Nations force will be necessary. My government's calculation is that now a force of some twenty-seven battalions will be needed together with supporting air strength and with other appropriate services to bring the Congo to order. This is a very large increase over and above the existing United Nations force in the Congo. I am certain, however, that if the United Nations adopts a realistic policy based upon the points I am putting forward, then these troops will be readily forthcoming: I suggest that they should come in the main from Africa and Asia.

Mr President, Distinguished Delegates, let me now deal with the remaining points in my proposals. My third point was that all non-African personnel serving with the Congolese Army should be expelled immediately from the Congo.

The presence of 'volunteers' or officers and other ranks seconded by foreign powers is bound to lead to suspicion of intervention by one or other of the protagonists in the cold war and, therefore, to counter-intervention from the other side. My proposal under this head applies particularly to the Belgian forces in Katanga. Every Press account of incidents in that area shows that Tshombe's troops are invariably commanded by Belgian officers. Tshombe has admitted that the Commander of Patrice Lumumba's guard was a Belgian and even the doctor who certified his death was of Belgian nationality and apparently a Belgian official. Visitors to Elisabethville report that all military executive functions are in the hands of Belgian nationals.

It is useless to rely on the Belgian Government's 'invitation' to their 'volunteers' to return, particularly as the so-called volunteers are under no penalty if they refuse their Government's invitation.

The Belgian troops must all be expelled whether they call themselves volunteers or not. In regard to Belgian civil technicians, there can be no objection to teachers, doctors and the like carrying on with their work. However, Belgians controlling the banks and monetary policy of the Congo must be expelled if the Congolese people are to be in a position to assert an independent monetary policy of their own.

After giving figures of arms and equipment supplied by Belgium to the Katangan Government, I came to the last of my proposals, namely, the release of all political prisoners, the reconvening of the Congolese Parliament, the holding of a general election under United Nations supervision and the re-assertion of the territorial integrity of the State as provided in the resolution of the Security Council:

This last point is most important. For sixty years the sweat and blood of the Congolese people have been invested in the Province of Katanga. The development of Katanga has been paid for, not primarily by the people living in the Province, but by the whole population of the Congo. Katanga represents the Congolese people's greatest investment. Without it they would be condemned to a life of misery and poverty. If Katanga is joined to the Congo, however, the prospects of industrial development are unlimited. Potentially the Congo could produce the cheapest electrical power in the world. It has been calculated that if a dam were built at Inga on the lower Congo, it could produce eight times the power at present generated by the Grand Coulee Dam in the United States. The mineral wealth of Katanga, instead of being exported as it is at present, could be processed in the Congo itself more cheaply than it is now being processed abroad. In fact it would be possible to establish in the heart of Africa a great industrial centre.

I would like the financial groups who are encouraging Tshombe and the Belgians in their separatist policy in Katanga to take heed that such a policy is dangerous. There is still time for them to save their investments but time is running short and ultimately the world will not tolerate any financial group, however powerful, defying the United Nations. The question of the exact position of Katanga within the Congo must be decided by the Congolese people as a whole. It is their wealth and their endeavours over the last sixty years which have built up Katanga into what it is today and they should therefore be entitled to a decisive say in its future.

Mr President and Distinguished Delegates, we all wish for peace, not only in the Congo but throughout Africa and throughout the world. Those countries which have contributed contingents to the United Nations Command did so to bring peace, not to foster a great power struggle. It is only by facing the realities of the situation in the Congo that the United Nations can end the Congo crisis. I hope that I speak for all Africa—and I certainly speak for the Casablanca Powers—when I say that we can save the Congo, given the support of the uncommitted countries. Give us the mandate and the resources to do so.

The debate on the Congo resulted in the adoption of three resolutions on 15 April. The first one, sponsored by Burma, Ceylon, Ethiopia, Ghana, Guinea, India, Indonesia, Iraq, Libya, Mali, Morocco, Nepal, Saudi Arabia, Sudan, United Arab Republic and Yugoslavia, called upon the Belgian Government to comply with the resolutions of the Security Council urging the immediate withdrawal from the Congo of Belgian and other foreign military and para-military personnel and advisers not under the UN Command. This resolution was adopted by 61 votes to 5 with 33 abstentions. Among the five who voted against the resolution were Belgium, Portugal and South Africa.

The second resolution called on the Congolese to solve their problems by peaceful means and instructed the Secretary-General to take effective measures 'to prevent the introduction of arms, military equipment and supplies into the Congo, except in conformity with the resolutions of the United Nations'. The release of all members of Parliament, members of Provincial Assemblies and all other political leaders under detention was urged, together with the summoning of Parliament 'without delay'. Finally, it was decided to appoint a Commission of Constitution of seven members, to be chosen by the President of the General Assembly to help the Congolese leaders to achieve reconciliation and to end the political crisis. This time, the resolution was adopted by 60 votes to 16 with 23 abstentions.

The third resolution, sponsored by Ceylon, Ghana, India and Morocco, provided for the establishment of a Commission of Investigation consisting of Justice U Aung Khine (Burma), Mr Teschome Hailemariam (Ethiopia), Mr Salvador Martinez de Alva (Mexico) and Mr Ayite d'Almeida (Togo) to enquire into the circumstances of Lumumba's death. The resolution was adopted by 45 votes to 3 with 49 abstentions. Portugal, Spain and Congo (Leopoldville) voted against; and among those who abstained were France, South Africa, U.S.S.R., United Kingdom and the United States.

13 The April Resolutions and the Arrest of Tshombe

SHORTLY after returning from New York I received a report from Mr Ako Adjei, Minister of Foreign Affairs, of his conversation with Adlai Stevenson, U.S. Ambassador to the United Nations, about the eight points made in my speech to the General Assembly. He stated that the American Ambassador assured him of his support in bringing into effect any proposal to disarm, regroup and retrain the Congolese army but that he did not commit himself on other proposals. I therefore sent Adlai Stevenson the following note, elaborating on some of the reasons for putting forward the eight points. I hoped that he might then find it possible to give his support:

I think you will agree that the situation in the Congo cannot be allowed to continue to develop as it is doing at the present time. It appears to me that the whole country is gradually reverting into a series of small, separate states on the tribal system and the whole economy is coming to a halt. No solution is possible unless the Gizenga Government is a party to such a solution. If things continue as they are doing, the position of the United Nations Forces and technicians in the country will become quite impossible, and their withdrawal inevitable before very long. Should this happen, the country will be left in a state of anarchy, open to the inevitable intervention by the Great Powers. My aim throughout, as you are no doubt aware, has been to isolate this area from the cold war. If by hesitation and vacillation in the United Nations, New York, the withdrawal of United Nations Forces from the Congo became inevitable, and the situation deteriorates in the manner I have outlined above, I cannot see that the West in the long term will have anything to gain. Inevitably, and in my view rightly, the United Nations and the West will be blamed for the situation that develops and the majority of the Congolese will look elsewhere for help in solving their problems. I therefore believe it is in the interest of the United States themselves that constructive progress is made in solving the Congo problem. I would now like to say a little about each of my eight points.

'A new and strengthened United Nations civil and military command should be established in the Congo.' There is no doubt that the military command of United Nations Forces in the Congo has been discredited by the manner in which operations have been conducted to date. The position which was allowed in the Port of Matadi is the most recent example. If the contingents under the command of United Nations Military Headquarters at Leopoldville are to have confidence in their Commanders, reorganisation within this Headquarters is essential. The same applies on the civil side, where far too few Africans have been utilised to help the civil authorities. If you have an organisation largely dominated by representatives of the NATO Powers, their actions, however impartial, are bound to be suspect. This is certainly the position at present on the civil side of the United Nations organisation in the Congo.

'This Command and the contingents under it must be primarily African and should take over responsibility for law and order in the Congo.' The word 'primarily' was inserted intentionally by me because I realise fully that the young Armies of Africa cannot produce all the trained officers required to staff complicated Headquarters of this nature. I do, however, contend that if you are to expect countries like Morocco and the United Arab Republic to contribute contingents, they must be adequately represented on the staff of United Nations Headquarters. I want a United Nations Military Headquarters in the Congo that is suspect to neither faction. At present the fact that representatives of western powers hold positions on the headquarters is bound to cause suspicion, and here again I feel that much greater African representation is required, eliminating staff officers drawn from NATO powers. I have just received a request to produce additional staff officers for the Headquarters which may show that this point of mine is being taken into account, but I shall be interested to know what proportion of the military staff in Leopoldville is intended to be African and will ask my Foreign Minister to find out. As regards the latter portion of my second proposal that United Nations should assume complete responsibility for law and order. This of course will apply when the Congolese armed forces have been brought under control in the manner outlined in my third and fourth points. I understand that you are in agreement with my third and fourth points. I therefore do not need to elaborate on them, except to say that I have offered to help in planning the reorganisation and retraining of the Congolese national army and through Quaison-Sackey have outlined the various phases as I see them. It is surely no use accepting these points unless planning to put them into effect is started at once.

'All non-African personnel serving in all factions of the Congolese army must be expelled immediately.' As you yourself must know, these people are irresponsible adventurers. One only has to examine the situation now existing in Kalondji's so-called army to realise that these adventurers are commanding a band of thugs over which they have no control. My contingent in the Congo is in daily contact with these people who have in the last few days kidnapped three of my soldiers who were taking a so-called Kalondji Brigadier to hospital. To date no trace of these men has been found and efforts by various Belgians employed by Kalondji to find them has been unavailing. The incident serves to illustrate the lack of control that Kalondji's hired soldiers have over their armed bands. Quite apart from this, if you condone people like Tshombe accepting foreign mercenaries to help lead his forces, how can you condemn Gizenga if he avails himself of military advisers and leadership from countries like Czechoslovakia and Russia?

'United Nations Command should control the major sea- and air-ports in the Congo so that the supply of arms and equipment to the Congo may be stopped and adequate support to the United Nations Forces be guaranteed.' No army can function efficiently unless their communications are guaranteed. The uselessness of relying on the good faith of persons like Mobutu is clearly illustrated by the recent actions at Matadi, and it is only by strict control of Luluabourg Airport that I have been able to maintain the Ghana contingent in Kasai. Should I lose control of this Airport, I would feel forced to withdraw my contingent from the Congo for military reasons alone. Even so, British Royal Air Force aircraft supporting the Ghana contingent, which have to refuel at Ndjili Airport, have in the past been subject to constant interference by Kasavubu's officials. I cannot see how you can expect countries to contribute contingents unless one is certain that these contingents can be adequately supported. Quite apart from this, it is of little avail to disarm and bring the warring factions under control if more arms can be flown into the various airports.

'That all foreign diplomatic missions and representatives should immediately leave the Congo for the time being in order to give this United Nations Command a fair chance and to eliminate the cold war from the Congo.' I myself cannot see why western countries are so opposed to this proposal. The West continually reiterates its support for the United Nations efforts and yet there have been many examples of foreign diplomats trying to interfere with decisions, both of the civilian heads at United Nations Headquarters in Leopoldville, and of military commands. Since the Russian Embassy has withdrawn from Leopoldville, that country can justly claim that it has not contributed to the present chaos. On the other hand by continuous backing for Mobutu and his stooges on the spot, the representatives of a country like the United Kingdom have placed themselves in a position where they are justly suspected of having prejudiced the success of the United Nations efforts. Surely the West cannot expect a solution to the Congo problem which is 100% favourable to them? If it does, all I can say is that their representatives in Leopoldville are being completely unrealistic. What I wish to obtain is a result which is favourable to the Congolese people as a whole and to Africa, ignoring the selfish interests of either the East or West. The task of a strengthened United Nations Command will be greatly hampered so long as people like Kasavubu are daily advised by the representatives of the western countries. If such intrigues continue in Leopoldville you can hardly blame the Eastern Powers if they do the same thing in Stanleyville, thus accentuating the East and West struggle in the Congo.

'Once the military situation has been brought under control on these lines, all political prisoners must be released by the United Nations Command and the new Command should then convene Parliament under its auspices. Those responsible for the murder of Patrice Lumumba should then be brought to justice.' I find it difficult to understand how you cannot support this eighth point as it was elaborated in my speech on 18 March. One can hardly have a fair political solution if many of the main political leaders are in gaol. Nor can you produce a political solution unless Parliament is eventually reconvened. Is it possible to argue that those responsible for the murder of Patrice Lumumba should not be brought to justice? I hope that the above will help you clarify some of the reasons why I put forward these eight points which I think are both realistic and practicable, provided that United Nations receives adequate military support in the Congo.

In his letter, Mr Ako Adjei mentions your fear that if the United

Nations gave too much responsibility to the African States, especially Ghana, United Arab Republic, Morocco, Guinea and Mali, there is no doubt that these Casablanca African Powers would automatically use the situation to support Gizenga. On this I would like to make the following comments.

If as a result of the action taken through my eighth point, a central Government favourable to Gizenga emerges, it will only be because it is the wish of the Congolese people, always provided that foreign diplomats are kept out of the country until Parliament has been reassembled and new elections held. Does the West wish to impose upon these people a Government which is not of their choice? If so, I have no sympathy for these aspirations.

Further, if a central government of the Gizenga Party does emerge, I can only say it will be proof that the actions of the West and the United Nations in the Congo have been so suspect that the Congolese people wish for another solution. On the other hand, if after re-convening of Parliament and later elections Gizenga's Party is in the minority, it will also be the wish of the Congolese people freely expressed. I am sure you know that although I have consistently backed Lumumba politically, my military contingent serving under United Nations has throughout adopted a completely neutral attitude, obeying implicitly the United Nations Command in Leopoldville. I think I can say the same for the contingents drawn from Morocco and Mali. Nor have I had any information that leads me to believe that the United Arab Republic and Guinean contingents as a whole acted in any way favourably to the Lumumba Government, although I would concede that the actions of certain individuals were suspect. The exclusion of diplomatic representatives would guard against such a repetition. I have a feeling that all African States are anxious for an early solution to the Congo problem and that provided they have adequate representation on both the military and civil side at the headquarters in Leopoldville, they will be prepared to continue to act in a strictly neutral manner in their military activities. The last thing any of the Casablanca African powers wish for is for their contingents to become directly involved in a Congo civil war. You should also remember that other African contingents from countries such as Nigeria, Sudan and Ethiopia, together with a large Indian contribution will be part of the United Nations Command. They, too, will have their representatives upon the reorganised military and civil headquarters. It is hardly conceivable that African countries will take military action in the Congo which will lead to clashes between their contingents. President Sékou Touré of Guinea and President Modibo Keita of Mali are visiting me this weekend. I will discuss this point with them and communicate with you further on this matter.

In conclusion, I think the stage is long past when the West can afford to suspect the motives of the African States in their desire to save the Congo from complete anarchy and intervention by foreign powers. On the contrary. If the actions of the United Nations in the Congo continues to be as ineffective as it has been in the past, most Afro-Asian countries can but reach the conclusion that the West does not wish for a solution, merely because it fears that such a solution would not be favourable to the West. The result will of course be a failure of the United Nations operations in the Congo because African support is withdrawn.

Then, if as I fear, the result would be intervention by Russia and NATO Powers, sympathies throughout Africa are bound to lie with the former.

The new Kennedy Government in America which took office in January 1961 seemed to be more sensitive to Afro-Asian opinion than the previous administration. This was shown both in the support given to the Security Council resolution of 21 February calling for the removal of all mercenaries and political advisers from the Congo and in the stiffening of the American attitude towards Tshombe and the State of Katanga.

There began a noticeable deterioration in UN relations with Tshombe and an improvement in relations between the UN and Kasavubu. The authorities in Leopoldville began to go back on the Tananarive settlement and sent Cleophas Kamitatu, President of the Leopoldville provincial government, to establish official contact with Gizenga in Stanleyville. Kasavubu had never been happy about the Tananarive Conference and had only attended it after much hesitation.

On 15 April the UN General Assembly adopted three resolutions on the Congo. The first of them, sponsored by 16 states, including Ghana, called on the Belgian Government to accept its responsibilities as a member of the UN and to comply fully and promptly with the will of the Security Council and General Assembly in securing the withdrawal of all foreign soldiers, para-military personnel and political advisers from the Congo. Belgium, Portugal, Nepal, South Africa and Uruguay voted against this resolution, and among the 33 abstainers were the United Kingdom and the United States. The second resolution reaffirmed the resolution of 21 February; called upon the

Congolese authorities to solve their differences by peaceful means and urged the release of all members of Parliament and the convening of a new Parliament 'without delay'. In addition, the UN resolved to appoint a Commission of Conciliation of seven members to be chosen by the President of the General Assembly to assist the Congolese leaders to achieve reconciliation. This resolution was adopted by 60 votes to 16 with 23 abstentions. The third resolution, sponsored by Ceylon, Ghana, India and Morocco, provided for the setting up of a Commission of Investigation into the circumstances of the death of Lumumba.

Two days after these three resolutions were passed, Kasavubu signed an agreement with the UN accepting the resolution of 21 February and agreeing to co-operate in the removal of mercenaries and foreign advisers from the Congo. This action, which was aimed principally against Katanga, followed the conclusion of an agreement between Tshombe and the Government of Congo (Brazzaville) in which Tshombe promised to give the Republic economic aid.

Kasavubu's agreement to support the UN in taking a stronger line in Katanga came only about five weeks after the Tananarive Conference in which he had virtually acquiesced in the secession of Katanga. His change of policy reflected the Afro-Asian and American goal of a united Congo and when the Second Round Table Conference opened in Coquilhatville on 24 April, Tshombe demanded a repudiation of the agreement with the United Nations. Kasavubu and his associates refused, with the result that Tshombe walked out of the conference and was arrested at the airport (26 April). He remained a prisoner in Leopoldville until 22 June during which time the state of Katanga was governed by a 'College' consisting of the Vice-President Jean-Baptiste Kibwe, the Minister for Education, Joseph Kiwele and the Minister for the Interior, Godefroid Munongo.

In the meantime, all pro-Gizenga countries except Ghana had withdrawn their contingents from the Congo. I felt it was important at this stage to support the UN effort while at the same time to continue quietly and effectively to help the legitimate Government of the Congo in Stanleyville. I had by then received the report of Captain Hassan, a member of the Ghanaian mission to Stanleyville, which left Accra on 23 February and which met Gizenga and his Cabinet on 6 March. According to Hassan's report, among the important matters discussed and decisions taken were:

(a) Direct means of communication between Osagyefo and Antoine Gizenga.

(b) Non-withdrawal of Ghanaian troops from the Congo and the possibility of providing underground support and supply of material aid to the forces of Lundula.

(c) Immediate supply of munitions.

(d) Technical assistance from the Independent African States, especially from Ghana, to assist in maintaining vital public services.

(e) Effective continuous radio propaganda by Independent African States in order to help popularise the Stanleyville Government.

On 21 March I received a note from Pierre Mulele, who was the Minister of Education and Fine Arts in the Cabinet of Lumumba and who considered himself the sole person to assume leadership in trying to halt the sad course of events which followed the illegal dismissal of Lumumba as head of government. He described the tragic situation in his country and asked for help. I replied:

Thank you for your letter of March 21 about the unfortunate situation in your country which is so dear to my heart. I am glad to note that you are aware of the efforts we are making at this end to foil the machinations of the imperialists in your country.

I am also aware that the resolutions of the General Assembly and the Security Council are seldom applied promptly and often they are not faithfully applied. However, in the present circumstances, we have to make the best of that Organisation while we quietly continue with effective measures to help the legitimate Government of the Congo.

It is most unfortunate that the Government of the Sudan have not found it possible to allow the free passage of supplies to the legitimate Government of the Congo at Stanleyville. I am continuing my efforts to establish firm communication lines with your Government and my special Envoy has informed His Excellency M. Gizenga about the result so far. As soon as I find it possible to do so, I will sent a permanent Envoy to Stanleyville who will then be in a position to co-ordinate our efforts. There is still some hope that with the connivance of friendly elements I can ensure the passage of food, medicine, arms and fuel to Stanleyville.

Meanwhile, in view of the intrigues of the imperialists and their agents, I think it is necessary to re-examine our identity of views on the Congo and the other essential problems facing Africa. I there·fore attach copies of correspondence between the late M. Patrice Lumumba and myself so that your Government may examine the correspondence and let me know whether they agree with the ideas contained in them. It is necessary to ensure this identity of views so that we may be fortified by the knowledge that we are striving after the same goal and so that we may better be able to withstand the political intrigues of our enemies.

Mulele was then in Cairo. He had gone there in December 1960 after becoming disillusioned in Gizenga whom he described as 'incapable of withstanding the onslaughts of the neo-colonial forces'. In Cairo he kept in close touch with the Chinese Embassy, and eventually, in 1962, he left Egypt and travelled to Paris, Prague, Moscow and Peking, where he underwent a course of training in guerrilla warfare. In the summer of 1963 he trained the ALN (National Liberation Army) in Congo (Brazzaville) before penetrating Leopoldville and Kwilu Province. He proved to be a most effective guerrilla leader and for a time his forces threatened Leopoldville itself. Before he could achieve any decisive result he was reported killed by his own followers when intervening in a petty dispute about the division of spoils. Proof of his death, however, has not been given and there is good reason to believe that he is still alive.

But to return to the sequence of events in April 1961. It was in that month that I sent notes to various African and Asian Governments calling on them to give further assistance to the UN Command in the Congo. I also wrote to Hammarskjöld informing him of my action:

I have reason to believe that my appeal to the Governments concerned will evoke their sympathy and will result in their willingness to provide additional troops for the United Nations operations in the Congo.

You will also remember that I made a proposal to the United Nations General Assembly when I addressed it on 8 March 1961 that there should be a joint African Command which should be charged with responsibility for the operations in the Congo with support from the Asian and other uncommitted countries. I realise that there may be practical difficulties in putting this into effect immediately, but I think that it would help to foster keener interest in the United Nations operations in the Congo if at this stage it became possible to appoint an African as a Deputy to the Commander of the United Nations Forces in the Congo. I am aware that the Commander has a Deputy already, but I wonder, if from the point of view of the African countries which have troops in the Congo, it would not have a positive psychological effect to have a second Deputy appointed from any African country from which you are able to select an officer for duties in this capacity.

I have not raised this question with the other African countries but I know that if it is at all possible to consider it favourably you will be willing to give it the attention it deserves.

I may also add that the African and Asian countries will be encouraged to send more troops to the Congo or increase the size of their contingents if strenuous efforts are made to implement the latest resolution of the Security Council. In this regard I think every effort should be made to reconvene the Congolese Parliament to meet in an atmosphere free from foreign interference and intrigue. In my view it is futile to talk about the Congolese deciding their own future unless they are positively helped to meet to find a solution within their own constitutional framework. Attempts to find a solution outside Parliament will only prolong chaos and suffering and no true believer in democracy can welcome dictation by usurpers even if benevolent and wise.

Discussions and plans for the calling of Parliament were to occupy the attention of politicians and diplomats for the next three months, against a background of continuing unrest.

14 The Port Francqui Tragedy

FROM the point of view of the people of Ghana, one of the most tragic episodes of the Congo struggle occurred on 28 April 1961, when 'A' Company of the 2nd Ghana Regiment was brutally attacked by Mobutu's troops at Port Francqui. The trouble started on Wednesday, 26 April, when the new Minister of the Interior of the provincial government visited Port Francqui unannounced, in order to try to come to some agreement over the fighting which had taken place extensively in the area. The ANC who guarded the airport knew nothing of his visit and threatened to shoot him as a spy. As a result he was taken under UN protection to a small hotel in Port Francqui, part of which was being used as an officer's mess. The ANC followed him to the hotel, where a long discussion took place between the Company Commander, Captain Ralph, the Minister of the Interior, and two NCOs of the ANC. The NCOs asked for the Minister's credentials. They wanted to know why he had UN protection and the reason for the UN troops occupying part of the hotel.

It was decided that a conference should be held the next day to discuss these matters. The discussion between Captain Ralph, the Minister and the ANC was held behind closed doors, so one can only guess what happened but at the end of it the Minister said he no longer needed UN protection and the UN escort was dismissed.

Captain Ralph, however, was far from satisfied. He had been manhandled during the secret discussion and had subsequently ordered a stand-to.

The following day, 27 April, Captain Ralph had trouble with the ANC when he tried to find out what had happened to the Congolese minister. There was no ANC officer in Port Francqui at the time and tempers were rising. The Ghanaian troops, who were scattered throughout the town in small groups, soon found themselves suddenly surrounded by overwhelming numbers of ANC soldiers who disarmed them without a shot being fired. Two of the three British officers and three Swedish movement control officers were taken away to the ANC camp and beaten.

On 28 April, a relief force from Mweka, a village some 50 miles to the south, arrived outside Port Francqui and was ambushed. The sound of the firing greatly excited the ANC in Port Francqui. As a result, they herded the unarmed Ghanaians into various houses and began to open fire on them. The defenceless men scattered as best they could but suffered severe casualties.

Major-General H. T. Alexander, in his report to me of the massacre, blamed the military inexperience of McKeown and his predecessor Van Horn. 'The whole conception of how to conduct military operations in the Congo has, as you know, in my opinion been incorrect.' This had led to the troops under UN command not taking adequate military precautions while at the same time it had tried to impress on the undisciplined 'rabble armies' that they were friends with whom the UN wished to co-operate. Alexander went on to say that the UN had ignored the fundamental military principle of concentration:

> With the limited forces at UN Command they could not hope to be strong everywhere. I recommended as far back as February that the place where the United Nations needed to be strong was in Kasai, where all factions clashed. Even if this meant giving up areas such as Orientale and Equateur Provinces, it should have been done in the interests of the security and proper military handling of the troops entrusted to the United Nations Command. If you remember, we in fact sent a signal on 24 February, drawing the attention of the United Nations Command to the precarious situation into which our contingent had been put. I attach the reply. It should be noted that it is dated 28 February and is virtually a snub, telling me personally to mind my own business. Since that date no action whatsoever has been taken to reinforce the Ghana contingent in Kasai. As you know, I both saw and sent signals to McKeown when I visited Kasai last to exactly the same effect, with no result so far.

Alexander went on to mention the inexperience of officers, both British and Ghanaian, in dealing with the peculiar conditions which prevailed in Kasai and their too rigid adherence to the United Nations instruction that they should use all possible means of persuasion before opening fire. 'Argument from strength is the only answer with the Congolese armed man, since, sad to say, this is what the Belgians have taught him to understand.'

The Commander of the Ghana contingent, Colonel Ankrah, had been trying to control his area with the equivalent of $2\frac{1}{2}$ battalions and an armoured reconnaissance unit. In addition to this, the Company Commander at Port Francqui, Captain Ralph, was, according to Alexander, not very experienced and had allowed the troops to be dispersed in 'penny packets' all over the town. He had also offended the numerically superior ANC by occupying the civilian hotel which contained the only drinking bar available in Port Francqui. Alexander ended:

'Now that this has happened, I cannot militarily recommend the retention of the Ghana contingent in the Congo, because I feel that to do so might lead to the ruination of your fine young army, which should be back in this country being trained and expanded. I consider that you have done all you can, without harming your own army unnecessarily, to keep United Nations operations in the Congo alive and that it is up to other countries now to contribute contingents if they wish these operations to succeed. I therefore strongly recommend that you give me permission to arrange for the complete evacuation of the Ghana contingent from the Congo, starting 1 June.'

In spite of Alexander's attempts to shelve the blame for the Port Francqui massacre on to others, his own report is unsatisfactory. As Chief of Defence Staff of the Ghana Army it was his duty to see that Ghanaian troops were not placed in the kind of impossible position they found themselves in at Port Francqui. Having failed to get satisfaction from the UN Command when he complained of the dangerous situation, one might have expected a conscientious and efficient commander to have refused to have let the matter rest, especially when he considered the men for whom he was responsible were so dangerously placed. Yet he did not go himself to Port Francqui, and he was apparently content to leave the Ghanaian troops under the command of officers he considered, according to his own report, to be inexperienced.

His advice to withdraw Ghana's contingent at that very critical stage of the UN operation in the Congo was similarly ill-judged. Unfortunately he seemed to have had divided loyalties. In his own words: 'I often found it difficult to act on Nkrumah's orders without feeling that I might be hurting British interests.' If this kind of conflict existed in his mind, it would have been more honest to have resigned his post as Ghana's Chief of Defence Staff.

News of the incident at Port Francqui came as a terrible shock to the people of Ghana. The bereaved families of the men who lost their lives derived no comfort from the knowledge that their menfolk had died heroically while on active service with the United Nations. They were, like many others, at first stunned by the news and then bitterly angry at the senselessness of the killings and the exposure of the incompetence of the UN commanders in the Congo who were responsible for allowing their troops to be in such a fatally weak position.

Among the messages of condolence received at this time was one from the Secretary-General, Dag Hammarksjöld. I replied to him on 9 May as follows:

I am in receipt of your message NA/236 dated 4 May 1961, in which you send your condolences for the deplorable and unprovoked attack on Ghanaian troops by Mobutu's men. I thank you for these condolences.

To comment on the remainder of your message:

It is hard for those who are not soldiers to understand that the role assigned to and the orders given to United Nations contingents serving in the Congo have been of such a nature that they are in fact reduced to being policemen. A soldier is trained for war and is trained to take sound military precautions at all times. Young inexperienced officers and soldiers require clear, emphatic orders if occurrences of this nature are to be avoided in the future. I believe that UNOC Directive No. 6, Paragraph 7, states: 'As a peace force the UN Force may not take the initiative in the use of armed force. It is, however, entitled to use force in self-defence, but only as a last resort after other means, namely negotiation or persuasion, have failed.' It then goes on to state some of the circumstances under which force may be used and at the end says: 'The minimum force necessary will be used in all cases in order to prevent as far as possible a loss of human life or serious injury to persons.' This paragraph could hardly be more difficult for a young officer or NCO to interpret, and I believe it is one of the background reasons for the Port Francqui occurrence. Nor do I agree with you in your signal that 'Such attacks cannot be anticipated or planned against.' Every time a serious incident happens in the Congo, it is surely the duty of the senior military commander to make certain that the lessons from these occurrences are clearly brought out, in order that the troops under his command can take precautions to prevent such a situation arising again. I have never asked that United Nations Forces should be used in an unsanctioned offensive role but have on the other hand asserted that the safety and proper military handling of the troops entrusted to the United Nations Command are both essential, and in this connection good clear orders which enable United Nations troops to take effective military action if the Congolese appear to be becoming aggressive are part and parcel of proper military handling.

You say later on in your signal that United Nations Forces are now being reinforced, which should eliminate some of the dangers, but you also admit that recently United Nations Forces have been painfully weak. If they were inadequate to carry out the full task in the Congo, which covers an area bigger than Western Europe, surely it is taking unjustified risks to spread them in the 'penny packet' layout to which I referred. You also make the point that a great deal is left to the discretion of the local commanders. You are not unaware that many of the commanders in contingents given to the United Nations are militarily inexperienced, and their role in the Congo is about the most difficult that any soldier could be asked to execute. Therefore, if the higher Military Commander thinks that his junior is doing things which are militarily unsound, surely he must give some guidance. I, of course, do not agree with you that the equivalent of $2\frac{1}{2}$ battalions operating in an area partially occupied by three so-called armies and many warring tribes is a sound military estimate of a fair task.

I am glad to hear that the United Nations Force is being reinforced and, as you know, have always urged African countries to contribute generously.

It is for this reason that I felt we might seize the first opportunity of Sierra Leone's independence to interest her Government in the Congo operations. I was not unaware therefore that Sierra Leone was not yet a member of the United Nations when I made my suggestion. I should have thought that an approach to her could have been made through the United Kingdom Representative or that of another friendly Government at the United Nations.

As regards your last paragraph, as yet I have made no firm decision concerning the Ghana contingent serving in the Congo, although for training reasons I have decided that it must be reduced in numbers by early June. I will be communicating further with you on this matter.

Lastly, can you or your adviser in the Congo possibly now assert that any peace can be brought to the Congo unless the various so-called armies are brought to heel? Unless something really effective is done to bring their armies under proper control, the situation which now exists will continue to drag on and I can see no end to the chaos in the Congo. If this is the case, are you justified in asking countries to contribute contingents to an effort which cannot succeed?

I understand that plans are being put into effect to reorganise and retrain Mobutu's and Tshombe's forces. The gangs of these two gangsters are the cause of the continued struggle in the Congo. It might do a great deal to assuage fears and apprehensions of the political leaders of the countries contributing troops if a little more information of these plans were given to us.

My contingent in the Congo has now taken some military precautions to ensure that the ANC or whoever dares to attack them are adequately dealt with. Even if I do retain a contingent in the Congo it will be with the proviso that they are employed in a proper military role, and I will see that this is done.

A new appraisal of the military situation in the Congo was necessary. Ghanaian troops had been in the country since 15 July 1960. They were among the first to answer the call of the government of the Congo Republic for military aid in the early days of independence, and in proportion to the size of her army, Ghana sent the largest contingent of any state. We were justifiably proud of our contribution to the peace-keeping force but confidence in the handling of the UN operation was severely shaken by the tragedy at Port Francqui, where 40 Ghanaian soldiers lost their lives.

15 Adoula's Government and the Katanga Campaign

THE three months from 28 May 1961, when the conference ended at Coquilhatville after agreeing on the recall of Parliament, and 20 September 1961, when a cease-fire was arranged in Katanga, were perhaps the most eventful of the whole year. During those months, Tshombe was released in Leopoldville; the Congolese Parliament met at Lovanium and Adoula's Government was formed; the UN campaign against the mercenaries took place in Katanga; and Dag Hammarskjöld and Dr Wieschoff, his adviser, were killed in mysterious circumstances when the plane in which they were travelling crashed near Ndola.

The decision taken at Coquilhatville to summon Parliament followed weeks of talks and negotiations behind the scenes among the various Congolese leaders to decide the most suitable place for Parliament to meet. It was important that members from all parts of the Congo should feel able to attend in perfect safety and that the Parliamentary discussions should be free from outside pressures. The three possibilities seemed to be Lovanium University, some twelve miles outside Leopoldville; Stanleyville, the seat of Gizenga's government and the military base of Kamina.

On 12 May I sent the following telegram to Gizenga:

Reports circulating indicate that UN is assisting with plans to reconvene Parliament. In the interests of your administration and your personal safety please insist that Parliament reassemble only in Stanleyville, the seat of the legal successor to the Lumumba Government. This stand is necessary because of the possibility of your arrest and the fact that reports indicate that members of Parliament are under heavy pressure by outside powers who are determined to buy them off.

We are sending a special envoy to you in the next few days as Ghana's representative to your Government.

Soon afterwards, I learned that Gizenga was asking for the military base at Kamina to be neutralised so that the Congolese Parliament could meet there. I at once cabled (17 May):

Thank you for your message No. 215 of May 1 which I have just received. Since my last telegram to you about convening the Congolese Parliament in Stanleyville, I have learnt from a Reuter's report that you have asked that the military base at Kamina be neutralised as a venue for the meeting of the Congolese Parliament. I am in complete agreement with this proposal of yours as well as with your request that troops from Ghana, Sudan, Togo, Guinea, Mali and the United Arab Republic should provide protection for you and the other members of Parliament so that the meeting may be free from the coercion and intrigues of the military interventionists. I have today cabled Secretary-General of the United Nations expressing my support for your proposal.

Messages were sent to the heads of African states asking them to support Gizenga's suggestion. Characteristic of the telegrams I sent at this time was one dated 24 May to His Majesty King Moulay Hassan II, Rabat:

Honoured to inform Your Majesty that I support the suggestions of Premier Gizenga that the Congolese Parliament should meet in a neutralised Kamina. I am prepared to provide a contingent of Ghana troops to join troops from African countries to provide the necessary security to members of Parliament.

Reports suggest that it is imperative for Parliament to meet at the earliest possible moment and I appeal to Your Majesty to give vigorous support to any measure which may enable the Congolese Parliament to meet in a calm and free atmosphere.

On 12 June delegates from Stanleyville arrived in Leopoldville to discuss the recall of Parliament, and a week later, on 19 June, it was agreed that Parliament should meet at Lovanium under UN protection. The authorities in Leopoldville and Stanleyville had reached agreement and the UN had achieved its aim, but there remained the problem of Katangan representation. This problem appeared to be solved with the release of Tshombe on 22 June and his statement at a press conference in Leopoldville that he would be prepared to send a Conakat delegation to Lovanium. On 24 June he actually signed an agreement with the Leopoldville authorities in which he agreed that Parliament should be convened as soon as possible and that 'a new Government shall be constituted and shall come before the Chambers for a vote of confidence'. Among other articles in the agreement was a provision for the abolition of customs barriers between Katanga and the rest of the Congo and the establishment of a single diplomatic representation abroad.

Having signed this agreement, Tshombe returned to Elisabethville, where he received a hero's welcome. Within four days he was addressing the Katanga Assembly as though he had never made any pledge in Leopoldville. He made no mention of the agreement he had signed and in ending his speech with the words 'Long live an independent Katanga' he showed quite clearly that he did not intend to keep his word. Once again Tshombe had shown himself in his true colours as a dishonest, selfish politician whose only concern was his own private ambition and the business interests of his foreign supporters. Under his guidance the Katanga Assembly rejected the agreement with Leopoldville and the unification of the Congo seemed as remote as ever.

By then, Conor Cruise O'Brien had arrived in Elisabethville (14 June) as UN representative in Katanga, his task being to apply the Security Council Resolution of 21 February which called for the expulsion from the Congo of all 'foreign military and para-military personnel and advisers not under UN Command, and mercenaries'.

It is not my purpose to describe in detail the events which took place in Katanga during the months following O'Brien's arrival. In his book *To Katanga and Back* he has given a full account of the UN operation as he saw it. Others have written from different points of view and it may be many years before the full facts are known. But at this stage it is possible to make a few observations on the failure of this most direct attempt by the UN to expel mercenaries and 'advisers' from the Congo and to end the secession of Katanga.

During the first few weeks of his stay in Elisabethville, O'Brien was able to secure the expulsion of various foreigners from the Katangan capital. Colonel Weber left on 17 June. He was followed shortly afterwards by Professor Clemens. Others left of their own accord or were deported. But the UN was only scratching at the surface of the problem. The Katanga leaders could spare these so-called 'advisers'. The real test would come when the removal of foreign officers and mercenaries was attempted. These, Tshombe and his colleagues could not do without.

At the beginning of July, Mr Charles Muller, a principal private secretary of M. Henri Fayat, Under-Secretary of State for foreign affairs in the Belgian Government, arrived in Elisabethville with a list of Belgian political advisers suitable for expulsion from Katanga. The list contained the names of several people whose presence in Katanga was not of sufficient danger to justify their expulsion. Others on Spaak's list clearly should have left long before. Notable among these was George Thyssens, an implacable enemy of the UN and a well-known supporter of Katangan secession. O'Brien, after obtaining authority from the UN, managed to deport him but only after a struggle in Thyssen's apartment during which shots were fired. By way of retaliation, Munongo ordered the arrest of Muller and he too was expelled from Katanga.

In this atmosphere of rising tension it was not surprising that attempts to persuade the Katanga leaders to send deputies to Lovanium were unsuccessful. The Tunisian, Mahmoud Khiary, chief of civilian operations in the Congo, arrived in Elisabethville on 17 July as special emissary of the Secretary-General, to invite Tshombe to a summit meeting in Leopoldville and to allow Conakat deputies to attend the central Parliament. Khiary spent hours with Munongo, Kimba, Kibwe, Kiwele and Samalenghe trying to persuade them to co-operate. He pointed out the need for an African solution to the Congo problem, but his arguments fell on deaf ears. Encouraged by the knowledge that Britain, the U.S.A. and Southern Rhodesia sympathised with them in their resistance to UN pressure to end the secession, the Katanga leaders refused to participate either in any Summit or in the meetings of the central Parliament.

Nevertheless, by 19 July most deputies had arrived at Lovanium. Notable among the absentees was Antoine Gizenga, who claimed to be ill and remained in Stanleyville, and the delegation from Katanga. In general, members tended to support either the Bloc Nationaliste, representing the old Lumumbist parties, and the Bloc National Démocrate, representing parties mainly from Equateur and Leopoldville Provinces. The Bloc Nationaliste candidate, Kasongo, was elected President of the Chamber, while Koumoriko (Bloc National Démocrate) was successful in the Senate.

On 24 July, Kamitatu went to Stanleyville to try to persuade Gizenga to go to Lovanium, but without success. At about the same time, Tshombe decided to go to Brazzaville in the hope of seeing Kasavubu. Tshombe arrived in Brazzaville on 29 July, but Kasavubu refused to cross the river to see him and Tshombe for his part refused to meet him in Leopoldville.

However, after Ileo and his government had resigned on 1 August, Cyrille Adoula was asked to form a government of national union.

On 2 August, the Adoula Government was approved in the Chamber by 121 votes to none, with one abstention, and in the Senate by a unanimous vote. The composition of Adoula's government seemed reasonable enough. Ten of the members held the same positions as they had occupied in Lumumba's government. For example, Antoine Gizenga was made First Deputy Prime Minister, Justin Bomboko was in charge of Foreign Affairs and Christophe Gbenye was Minister of the Interior. The latter went to Stanleyville two days after his appointment to urge Gizenga to go to Leopoldville to take up his post as Deputy Minister. He returned with the news that Gizenga accepted the post, recognised Adoula's government and would shortly arrive in Leopoldville.

The first week of the new government was proceeding well. On 7 August deputies and senators from Katanga arrived at Lovanium to take part in the parliamentary proceedings and by 16 August Adoula felt sufficiently confident to visit Stanleyville, where he received a warm welcome from President and people.

But it was the lull before the storm. While the establishment of the Adoula government marked a step forward there had in fact been no solution to the main problems underlying Congolese disunity. Tshombe was still maintaining the secession of Katanga, while mercenaries and foreign 'advisers' remained in the country in spite of efforts by the UN to remove them.

There were in existence two main recruitment centres for mercenaries, in Bulawayo and Johannesburg. Recruits were lured by advertisements in daily newspapers which called for 'ex-servicemen looking for an interesting and adventurous career', but did not mention Katanga. The briefing given to them by Belgian officers serving in the Katangese gendarmerie gave them the impression that their task was the pacification and economic rehabilitation of areas made insecure by rebel activity and that consequently they would not be in conflict with the United Nations forces. Basic pay ranged from £100 to £180 a month plus a danger allowance, family allowance, insurance, and the offer of a free holiday after one year. With these conditions of service there was no lack of recruits and Adoula and his colleagues in the central government decided to take strong action to end the threat from Katanga once and for all.

On 24 August the government issued an ordinance ordering the evacuation of foreign officers and mercenaries serving in the Katanga gendarmerie and at the same time, in a covering letter to the UN, asked for UN help in expelling them. Early in the morning of 28 August, UN troops occupied key points in Elisabethville and began the arrest of mercenaries and foreign officers. Their activities were stopped, however, when two days later the Belgian Consul in Elisabethville assumed responsibility for rounding up the foreign servicemen. Although nearly 300 foreign officers were deported, many remained, and O'Brien decided to embark on a similar operation to that carried out on 28 August. This time, although UN troops met with fierce resistance from the Katanga gendarmerie, O'Brien proudly declared, 'Katanga's secession is at an end'.

The UN action and O'Brien's announcement, which to say the least was premature, caused immediate reactions in London and Salisbury. The British Foreign Office 'regretted' the intervention of the UN, while Sir Roy Welensky with typical directness denounced it. This was just the encouragement Tshombe needed. Fighting continued and Tshombe announced that he would wage total war on the UN.

In view of the critical situation, Hammarskjöld had already decided to go himself to the Congo. En route, he called to see me in Accra, where we had a most interesting discussion. He gave me the clear impression that he considered the solutions I had repeatedly advocated for the Congo were the correct ones, and that he intended to act in accordance with them.

Hammarskjöld arrived in Leopoldville on 13 September, and on 16 September he stated that he would go to Rhodesia to meet Tshombe to arrange a cease-fire. His plane left Leopoldville the following day for Ndola in Northern Rhodesia but it did not arrive. It was found wrecked, on the 18th, near to Ndola; the one survivor who later died being unable to give any explanation of the crash. There have been several theories about the affair, none of them entirely credible and the circumstances of Hammarskjöld's death remain obscure. But as in the case of the murder of Lumumba, there are doubtless people living who can throw light on the tragedy and one day perhaps they may be induced to tell what they know.

On hearing of Hammarskjöld's death I at once sent the following telegram to Ako Adjei in New York (20 September 1961):

I would like you to submit the following Note on the Katanga situation to the President of the General Assembly for circulation to the members of the General Assembly:

'There is a serious danger that owing to the sudden death of the Secretary-General of the United Nations and the temporary military set-back of the United Nations forces a cease-fire will be arranged in Katanga before the main objectives of the United Nations action in Katanga, namely, the maintenance of the unity and territorial integrity of the Congo, has been secured.

Ghana fully and completely supports the action taken by the United Nations in Katanga. The Government of Ghana considers it essential that all Member States of the United Nations, particularly those from Africa, should come to the immediate aid of the United Nations. The United Nations forces may have suffered a military set-back because they have been opposed by large numbers of mercenaries. The Government of Ghana has already drawn the attention of the United Nations General Assembly this year to the supply of Fouga Magister aircraft, made in France for Belgium under a NATO agreement, to the rebel forces in Katanga. According to the information of the Government of Ghana these very aircraft are attacking at this moment the forces of the United Nations.

By the decision of the United Nations the forces sent to restore order and secure the independence and territorial integrity of the Congo were lightly armed and were not furnished with military aircraft. Certain powers from outside the African continent who are intent on destroying the prestige of the United Nations and on maintaining colonial rule and exploitation in the African continent have taken advantage of this. They have flooded Katanga with heavy modern armament of all kinds. The object of these Powers is clearly to maintain a puppet regime in the province of Katanga in absolute defiance of the Central Government of the Congo and of the decisions of the Security Council.

In the opinion of the Ghana Government a cease-fire based upon a *de facto* recognition of a separatist State would have fatal consequences on international order and on the prestige and the very future of the United Nations.

There should therefore be no cease-fire in Katanga until that province has been absorbed completely into the Congo as a unitary, sovereign and independent State.'

However, the death of the Secretary-General caused little delay in the peace talks between Tshombe and the UN. Mahmoud Khiari took Hammarskjöld's place at Ndola and negotiated a provisional cease-fire to come into force on 21 September. According to the agreement, a joint commission consisting of four members having full powers was to be set up immediately 'to supervise the application of this agreement and to seek ways of placing the relations between the United Nations and the Katanga authorities on a basis of mutual understanding and harmony and also to fix the respective positions of each side's troops'. This provisional agreement was approved by UN headquarters on 24 September, and the same day negotiations began on a permanent cease-fire agreement. The new agreement was subsequently (23 October) approved in New York subject to certain reservations. Two days later, on 25 October, the Adoula Government was recognised by Ghana. Below is the text of a statement released by the Ministry of Foreign Affairs at that time:

The Government of Ghana has been informed that Mr Antoine Gizenga has agreed to co-operate with the Central Congolese Government recently elected by the Congolese Parliament and has assumed office as First Deputy Premier in Leopoldville.

The Government of Ghana has therefore decided to recognise the Central Congolese Government with Mr Adoula as Prime Minister and Mr Gizenga as his First Deputy.

16 Tshombe's Call for Total War

THE question of appointing a successor to Hammarskjöld was of immediate concern to all members of the UN involved in the Congo struggle. It seemed to me that a candidate from Burma would be a good choice and that he should be aided by three Assistant Secretaries-General, one from the East, another from the West and a third from the non-aligned nations. This was a proposal I had made at the Conference of Non-Aligned Countries held in Belgrade during the first week of September. It was the subject of a cable I sent to Ako Adjei in New York on 23 September:

I met Heads of Missions of the non-aligned countries in Accra today and informed them of my proposal for filling the vacant post of Secretary-General of the United Nations and also provided them with a copy of Mr Nehru's reply quoted below. I urged upon the representatives to ensure that their Governments bring my proposal to the notice of their representatives in New York. I expressed the need for very quick action to forestall a stalemate which might occur by the Great Powers taking irreconcilable positions. I realize that great lobbying for various proposals is at present in progress but it is imperative that the non-aligned powers should take immediate steps to put forward a positive proposal on the lines of my suggestion referred to above. If this is not done there is strong probability that a temporary plan may be put forward which would be fatal to our cause. You should therefore take active measures to ensure that the representatives of the non-aligned powers in the United Nations agree on a plan which is in accord with my proposals. You will see from Mr Nehru's telegram which I quote below that India agrees with this plan. I also consider that there should be set up an executive authority to deal with the

Congo situation effectively and in accordance with the Security Council's resolutions. I have already forwarded to Quaison-Sackey a copy of my proposal addressed to Mr Nehru and others.

Mr Nehru's reply is as follows:

Thank you for your message which reached me yesterday. The proposal you make about a candidate from Burma being put forward for the Secretary-Generalship, with three Assistant Secretaries-General, has much virtue in it and I would be happy if this is generally agreed to. I am anxious that immediate arrangements should be made for the appointment of some suitable Executive Authority to deal with the Congo situation. It would be unfortunate if nobody is to be in charge there while the United Nations is arguing about Mr Hammarskjöld's vacancy.

I am communicating your message to Krishna Menon, the leader of our Delegation in New York. These questions can only be dealt with after proper consultation there.

I strongly supported the subsequent appointment of U Thant of Burma as Secretary-General but regretted the failure to take up the suggestion I made at Belgrade of the appointment of three Assistant Secretaries-General and an executive body elected by the General Assembly, whose duty it would be to ensure that the decisions of both the General Assembly and the Security Council would be faithfully and promptly implemented by the Secretariat. I was convinced that an effective Secretariat working in the true interest of the United Nations Organisation would contribute greatly to the maintenance of peace and security in the world.

Although the provisional cease-fire agreement between the UN and Katanga was approved on 24 September, it soon became evident that further fighting was imminent. There were rumours that central government troops in Kasai were moving towards North Katanga. A further, more ominous sign of the general malaise was the return of Gizenga to Stanleyville. He went ostensibly to deal with family matters but he did not go back to Leopoldville.

By early November, both the UN and Katanga each accused the other of breaking the cease-fire agreements. In an attempt to discover the true state of affairs, I sent a special mission to the Congo consisting of A. Y. K. Djin and E. A. Hialekpor. They left for Leopoldville on 25 October 1961, and on arrival were met by representatives of the government including the Secretary to the Ministry of Foreign Affairs. On the following day the envoys called on Adoula and discussed with him the political situation in the Congo and Ghana's part in past events. Djin assured Adoula that Ghana's policy towards African affairs was unchanged. We stood for African unity and independence. In reply, Adoula told the envoys that the Congolese people very much appreciated Ghana's recognition of his Government. He went on to say that he stood by the same ideals held by Patrice Lumumba and that he would do all in his power to promote good relations between Ghana and the Congo.

In a later discussion, Adoula spoke of an offensive being prepared against Katanga and the reconciliation he claimed had taken place between Generals Lundula and Mobutu. Lundula, he said, had been reinstated and summoned to Leopoldville but the real difficulty facing the central government was the attitude of Gizenga. During the month he spent in Leopoldville he had been unco-operative and seemed obsessed with the fear that people were plotting to assassinate him. Although the Cabinet had given him a week to go to Stanleyville to settle some personal affairs, he had not returned.

During their stay in Leopoldville our envoys met Mobutu and had a discussion with him. He accused Gizenga of working against the government and of causing unnecessary and unreasonable arrests. Talks followed with Gbenye, the new Lumumbist Minister of the Interior. He too complained about Gizenga's intransigence and his failure to consult his followers before taking action. The envoys then saw Sendwe, Vice-Premier and President of the Balubakat, which controlled the north and west of Katanga. He told Djin and Hialekpor that his followers were in open revolt against Tshombe's puppet régime. They were fighting guerrilla warfare but needed modern weapons and skilled instructors. They would, he said, welcome help from Ghana.

In the report of their mission, Djin and Hialekpor recommended that Gizenga be invited to Ghana and told of the need to reach agreement with Adoula, Sendwe and Gbenye. Gizenga should also be asked to advise Lundula not to let his men face the brunt of the fighting in Katanga, since if they suffered heavy casualties this would only leave Mobutu and his soldiers in a stronger position on the collapse of Tshombe's régime. They ended their report: 'Ghana should advocate the use of force to bring an end to Katanga's secession and also to eliminate foreign mercenaries from the Congo.'

If only the problem of Tshombe's mercenaries could have been settled once and for all by the United Nations, the Congo would have been saved years of internal strife and bloodshed. As it was, these foreigners continued to cause trouble and remained as the major obstacle to the peaceful development of the country under a government freely chosen by the Congolese people. Until the Central government could keep order throughout the Congo with its own troops, the right solution would surely be a peace-keeping force from African countries, supplied under the OAU, or better still, under an African High Command controlled by a Union government.

In 1961, however, there was no OAU and no African High Command, though I had tried on several occasions to get one formed, and it seemed as though the solution could only come through a further effort of the United Nations. At the 973rd meeting of the Security Council on 13 November 1961 the Ethiopian delegate Mr Gebre-Egzy spoke of the build-up of the military strength of the mercenaries in Katanga. It was clear, he said, 'that Tshombe would not and could not evict of his own free accord the mercenaries serving with him. Without them Tshombe will crumble. Without them the interests of foreign companies cannot be defended.'

Shortly after the Ghanaian delegation left Leopoldville, I received a message from Adoula.

(*Translation*)

Dear Mr President,

I was greatly honoured by the visit of Ambassador Djin and Mr Hialekpor, the attaché, who handed me your kind letter dated the 25th October.

It is a pleasure for me to inform your Excellency that in reply to his message I shall very shortly be sending my Ambassador to inform him of my Government's decision regarding the resumption of diplomatic relations which were temporarily broken off with the Republic of Ghana.

I was deeply touched by your Excellency's expressions of sympathy and affection for the Government I have the honour of directing and I wish to assure Your Excellency of my gratitude.

Please accept the assurance of my highest esteem.

Nearly two weeks later, on 16 November, came a request from Jean Bolikango, President of PUNA (Adoula's Party), for an invitation for a three-man delegation to visit Accra:

I should be pleased if you would fix a precise date on which you would find it convenient to receive the delegation.

To my mind, this is the best procedure to adopt, partly in view of the present state of affairs and partly because of the importance I attach (depending of course on the merits of each case) to personal contacts established through correspondence.

While I await a prompt reply from you, please accept, Mr President, my thanks for the attention you will give to this letter as well as the assurance of my highest consideration.

The three-man delegation was asked to come to Accra in December. In the meantime, the situation in Katanga had further deteriorated. On 4 November about 2,000 troops from Stanleyville were reported to be moving from the Kindu area of Kivu into North Katanga. Tshombe was at that time in Europe, and during his absence from Elisabethville, Munongo stepped up the propaganda campaign against the United Nations. On 24 November, the Security Council approved a resolution sponsored by Ceylon, Liberia and the United Arab Republic demanding an immediate end to the secession of Katanga and authorising the Secretary-General to use force to remove the mercenaries. The Resolution further declared that 'all secessionist activities against the Republic of the Congo are contrary to the Loi Fondamentale and Security Council decisions'. It is of interest to note that the Resolution was adopted by 9 votes to none with 2 abstentions, France and the United Kingdom.

Tshombe's reaction to the Resolution was quickly shown in a speech made the following day in which he bitterly attacked the UN and called on the people of Katanga to take up arms so that 'not one United Nations mercenary should feel himself safe anywhere'. Three days later, Brian Urquhart and George Ivan Smith, the UN representatives in Katanga, were attacked and beaten up during a cocktail party by members of the Katanga gendarmerie. On 1 December, O'Brien resigned from UN service and he and General McKeown made it clear that they considered Britain and France responsible for sabotaging the UN's effort to end the secession of Katanga.

By then, the Katanga gendarmerie had begun to erect barricades at various points on roads leading to Elisabethville airport and there were many reports of attacks on UN personnel. On 5 December, UN forces went into action to clear the road to the airport, with the result that 38 Katangans and two mercenaries were killed. The next day, UN planes bombed Katangan-held airports and military installations. The gloves were finally off. Tshombe called the entire population to arms and declared that the fighting would continue until the last UN soldier had left Katanga or been killed. It was a call for total war.

While the American government gave full support to the UN action, Britain wavered. O'Brien's accusations against Britain, accusing her of wrecking the earlier UN effort, had led me to send a note to the British Prime Minister, Mr Harold Macmillan, on 6 December 1961, in these terms:

Recent statements made by Dr O'Brien and General McKeown concerning United Nations operations in Katanga have caused me some concern. I know that I can speak to you in all sincerity because you appreciate the necessity for frankness in the issues that arise between your country and mine. The statements made by these high officials of the United Nations in the Congo indicate that Great Britain and France deliberately hampered the operations in the Congo in clear contravention of the Security Council Resolutions.

If these allegations are true they would constitute, in my view, a serious indictment, since we are all dedicated to the paramount necessity for upholding and maintaining the ideal of the United Nations as the surest guarantee of world peace and security. I know that you hold the view that as members of the United Nations we must do everything we can to help this world organisation to carry out its responsibilities as effectively as possible and to complete its difficult assignment in the Congo. Your Government has already made quite a significant contribution to the United Nations operations in the Congo.

It may well be, therefore, that your Government is not in any way connected with the specific acts which formed the subject of complaint by Dr O'Brien and General McKeown. There is no doubt, however, that certain mercenaries of British origin and from Rhodesia have unfortunately played a very prominent part in the resistance of Moise Tshombe to United Nations operations in the Congo.

I am sure you will agree that unless firm action is taken by your Government to restrain such irresponsible elements from involving themselves in the armed insurrection of the Katanga Provincial Administration against the Central Congolese Government, it will be difficult to exonerate Britain from some of the charges now being made against her.

The Congo situation is becoming a running sore which must be healed quickly before it is allowed to fester and poison international relations to the extent that I am afraid it is beginning to do. I wish to appeal most earnestly to you, therefore, Mr Prime Minister, to continue to lend your full support and influence to United Nations action in the Congo and to the steps now being taken to bring the Katanga secession to an end. Until the secession of the Provincial Administration has been ended and the unity and territorial integrity of the Congo (including Katanga) preserved, we cannot remove the cold war or the continuing threat to peace in Africa.

I felt that I would be failing in my duty to you as a friend if I did not make my feelings in the matter known personally to you. I hope that I do not appeal to you in vain.

Fighting continued in the streets of Elisabethville. But the UN forces were discouraged by the lack of support for their action outside the Congo. On 12 December, M. Spaak stated before the Belgian Chamber that the UN action was inadmissible and the Chamber called for a cease-fire. The next day, Britain also called for an end to the fighting.

When Abbé Fulbert Youlou, President of Congo (Brazzaville), asked me to use my influence to end the fighting in Katanga, I again stressed the need for an end to the secession. I wrote to him (14 December 1961):

Am grateful for your telegram requesting me to intervene in the Katanga situation in order to end the fighting taking place there. I would like to point out that only Tshombe is responsible for the fighting now forced upon the United Nations Command in the Congo. By breaking with his foreign mercenaries and working in harmony with his brother Africans Tshombe can bring an end immediately to hostility in the Congo. I call upon you in view of your close association with Tshombe to encourage him to accept his proper status as Chairman of the provincial administration of Katanga which is constitutionally an integral part of independent Congo. You can use your good offices to persuade Tshombe to this course, since by his selfish collaboration with foreign business and financial interests mainly concerned with the exploitation of the resources of the Congo he is making himself Traitor Number One to the cause of Africa's freedom, independence and unity. I hope that you will heed my appeal knowing how highly you regard the dignity and welfare of our people and how much you value peace and goodwill at this time.

Six days later (20 December) I sent the following telegram to Tshombe:

I should like to support the appeal of President Kennedy calling upon you to negotiate immediately with Prime Minister Adoula. I consider that unless you do this at once and come to understanding with the Central Congolese in terms of the *Loi Fondamentale* on the basis of which the independence of the Congo was framed, you cannot escape responsibility for the loss of lives which the military operations in Katanga will inevitably cause. You can help to bring about peace and harmony in the Congo and assist the progress and welfare of our brothers in the Congo by heeding President Kennedy's appeal to you to negotiate with Prime Minister Adoula. You know that Ghana has always stood and will continue to stand for the unity, sovereignty and territorial integrity of the Congo, including the Province of Katanga as an integral part of the Congo Republic. We have done so because of our desire to see peace and prosperity established in the Congo. I call upon you therefore to heed the voice of those who have the progress and welfare of the Congo at heart and accept your constitutional status as Chairman of the Provincial Administration of Katanga. If you fail to do this you will expose all Africa to the grave risk of the cold war and of interference from big business interests whose sole interest is in the exploitation of Africans.

By then, the Katanga gendarmerie had been getting the worst of the fighting. United Nations troops had captured their headquarters at Camp Massart, and Sir Roy Welensky had stated that he would give asylum to Tshombe and his government if necessary.

On 19 December, Adoula and Tshombe met under UN protection for talks at Kitona in the Lower Congo, and on 21 December, Tshombe made the following declaration:

The President of the Government of the Province of Katanga:
> Accepts the application of the Fundamental Law of 19 May 1960.
> Recognises the indissoluble unity of the Republic of the Congo.
> Recognises President Kasavubu as Head of State.
> Recognises the authority of the Central Government over all parts of the Republic.
> Agrees to the participation of representatives of the Province of Katanga in the Governmental Commission to be convened at Leopoldville on 3 January 1962, with a view to study and consideration of the draft Constitution.
> Pledges himself to take all necessary steps to enable deputies and senators of the Province of Katanga to discharge, from 27 December 1961, their national mandate within the Government of the Republic.

7

Agrees to the placing of Katanga gendarmerie under the authority of the President of the Republic.

Pledges himself to ensure respect for the resolutions of the General Assembly and the Security Council and to facilitate their implementation.

With typical cunning, however, Tshombe sent a copy of the declaration and a note to Ralphe Bunche, Under-Secretary of State for Special Political Affairs of the United Nations, drawing his attention to the fact 'that the haste with which my journey was made did not allow me to consult the competent authorities of Katanga so as to be authorised to speak on their behalf. I accordingly propose to do this on my return and to inform the Central Government of the steps to be taken with a view to the application of the enclosed declaration.'

Doubtless Tshombe was thinking of the agreement made with the Leopoldville government earlier in the year, when he was a prisoner there, and the ease and speed with which the Assembly in Elisabethville promptly rejected it on his return.

Clearly Adoula was not taken in by Tshombe's promises, as is shown in the note sent to me after the Kitona meeting:

(Translation)

I have the honour to acknowledge receipt of your telegram and to thank you sincerely for your support of the Central Government in its action to end the secession of the Province of Katanga.

The Congo crisis should by now have found a favourable solution if those responsible for the administration of the province of Katanga had shown good faith in honouring their promises to the Central Government and to the Congolese people as a whole. But the actual fact clearly shows that far from finding a peaceful solution to the problems caused by the secession of Katanga, Mr Tshombe is rather playing for time in order to reinforce the Gendarmerie with mercenaries so as to firmly establish his régime in the pay of the imperialists. The Kitona talks took place exclusively between Congolese and ended with an undertaking on the part of Mr Tshombe to respect the enforcement of the Loi Fondamentale in the whole of the Congolese territory. This solution would have been a happy one if Tshombe had not once again failed to honour his word on his return to Elisabethville. However, the Government has decided to find a rapid solution to this dispute. This is why it hopes it can always count on your support and that of the people of Ghana for which it is most grateful.

In my reply I said that Ghana would firmly support the Congo government 'until victory is won . . . Katanga is an integral part of the Congo and its unity must be preserved by all means.' This was in line with the policy consistently pursued by the Ghana government since Tshombe first declared the secession of Katanga; a policy we have never deviated from, of supporting the cause of Congo unity and independence.

In order to help Adoula's government to achieve unity, the Ghanaian envoys Djin and Hialekpor arrived in Stanleyville on 21 December to try and persuade Gizenga to return to Leopoldville to co-operate with the central government. They told Gizenga that I would arrange for Ghanaian soldiers to be stationed in Leopoldville, since he feared Mobutu's troops. But Gizenga would not commit himself to return to Leopoldville. He said he would wait and see what happened as a result of the Kitona talks. He declared that he was not against Adoula's government, but he had only agreed to serve in that government subject to the fulfilment of certain conditions and nothing had since been done. The central government, he said, had accused him of being unco-operative, but it was the central government which was not co-operating with him.

In a report of their mission, our envoys strongly suggested first, that the Casablanca Powers should meet at Foreign Ministers' level in order to discuss Gizenga's return to Leopoldville, and that if he persisted in his present attitude, the Lumumbists should be asked to select another leader who should have the full backing of the Casablanca Powers. Secondly, the Casablanca Powers should urge U Thant to send a strong Afro-Asian contingent to Leopoldville to check the threats of Mobutu's army and thereby enable the Lumumbist ministers to act freely according to their consciences. Thirdly, a committee of three, which I had suggested should be appointed, should start to meet at least twice a week and submit its decisions to the government. Finally, the Ghana Embassy in Leopoldville should be reopened and the Ghanaian ambassador should make himself available to advise the Lumumbists.

In January 1962, I sent the following message to Adoula:

In pursuit of our declared intention to assist the Congolese Government in every possible way, we have decided to reopen our Embassy in Leopoldville and to appoint an Ambassador of considerable experience in the affairs of the Congo who will be at hand to give every necessary assistance in your struggle for the unity and independence of the Congo. I should be most grateful if you would ensure that the necessary approval is granted for the Agreement which is being sought through the normal diplomatic channels for the appointment of our Ambassador.

In his reply, Adoula stated that negotiations for the reopening of the Embassy and the accreditation of an Ambassador to the Republic of the Congo should proceed through the Ministry of Foreign Affairs in Leopoldville. It seemed, early in the new year of 1962, that there might at last be some chance of Adoula's government succeeding. Tshombe had been checked, though the Congo was still far from united and the problem of the foreign mercenaries remained.

17 The Imprisonment of Gizenga and the Adoula/Tshombe Talks

GIZENGA, on his return to Stanleyville soon after Adoula's government had been formed, created a new political Party called PANALU (Parti National Lumumbiste). This, and his continued refusal to go back to Leopoldville to take up his duties as Vice-Premier in the central government, led to increasing tension in Stanleyville and throughout Orientale Province.

On 29 November 1961, Gizenga violently attacked Adoula's government, particularly in connection with the secession of Katanga. Yet the final rift did not come until early in the new year. On 8 January 1962, The Chamber of Representatives in Leopoldville passed a resolution by 66 votes to 2 with 7 abstentions, requesting the government to order Gizenga to return to Leopoldville within 48 hours to answer charges of secessionism and of maintaining a private militia. On 10 May, Gizenga sent a message to the central Parliament saying that if he was accused of some crime, the courts and not Parliament should deal with it. He would return to Leopoldville as soon as the decision taken by Parliament in September 1961, regarding the return of Katanga into a united Congo, had been fully implemented. Two days later, the Congolese Parliament passed a motion of censure on Gizenga by 67 votes to 1 with 4 abstentions. Seventy-two out of a total of 137 deputies were present. Certain speakers argued that since the Vice-Premier had engaged in 'open rebellion' he was subject to arrest without further formalities. Gizenga was accordingly stripped of his position as Vice-Premier and it was rumoured that General Lundula had received orders from Leopoldville to arrest him.

A clash had already taken place in Camp Kitele in Stanleyville, between troops of General Lundula's Congolese National Army and gendarmes loyal to Gizenga. Six of Lundula's men and eight gendarmes had been killed. On 13 January, Lundula asked the UN for help to restore order. This was granted and the gendarmerie was disarmed. It was then the turn of Gizenga to appeal to the UN. On 16 January, he asked for a guard to protect his home. But after consultation with Adoula, UN representatives decided that protection was not necessary as Gizenga's life was not considered to be in danger. Four days afterwards, on 20 January, Gizenga was taken to Leopold-ville aboard a UN aircraft.

There was great concern among his followers and friends for his safety. Although I had tried, through the Ghana mission to Stanley-ville in December 1961, to persuade Gizenga to return to Leopold-ville to co-operate with Adoula, I understood Gizenga's stand, and I did not want to see yet another crime committed against a Lumumbist. I therefore sent a message to our permanent representative in New York, informing him of the despatch of Ghanaian troops to the Congo:

> In response to United Nations appeal, I am sending Ghana troops to Congo. I would further like to express my great concern about the trend of affairs in the Congo, with particular reference to Gizenga. You should therefore convey my concern to the Secretary-General of the United Nations about this state of affairs and to obtain from him an assurance that the Ghana troops in the Congo will not be involved in any action that could lead to the murder of another Lumumbist. You should also emphasise, for record purposes, that I reserve the right to withdraw the Ghana troops from the Congo with Ghana government planes at any time that the interests of the government of Ghana will require such action.

On 22 January, Gizenga was given a villa by the central government and he declared he no longer needed UN protection. This was followed by a motion, presented by 15 deputies in the Congolese Parliament, for the immediate liberation of Gizenga. The latter had by then been removed to a small island in the mouth of the Congo River. Adoula was in New York at the time and it was decided to postpone a vote until his return.

When he got back, Adoula asked for a vote of confidence in the way in which he had handled the Gizenga affair. By 66 votes to 10 with one abstention, the Chamber expressed support for the Prime Minister. As time went on, however, growing concern was felt for Gizenga's health. His mother and two wives protested to the UN about the treatment he was receiving. They said he was eating only once a day and was under constant guard in a tiny cell; and further-more, the climate of the island was unhealthy. On 3 April, I sent the following note to U Thant:

I have been constrained to bring to your Excellency's notice many and repeated reports that have reached me concerning Mr Gizenga's present state of health. Although these reports are sent from widely divergent sources, they all seem to agree on the basic point that Mr Gizenga's health is deteriorating and that unless urgent and vigorous measures are taken to arrest this, the result may be fatal.

Whatever may be the cause of Mr Gizenga's detention there should be no room, on humanitarian grounds, for harbouring any doubt about his personal well-being and welfare. Indeed, we must accept the view that pending a decision on his political future the United Nations has immediate and ultimate responsibility for his safety and protection.

In these circumstances, if anything should happen to him, not only would this create serious consternation among the Congolese people and the peoples of Africa but I feel sure that it would do incalculable harm to the prestige and honour of the United Nations.

I write to you now, your Excellency, as the first stalwart cham-pion of the United Nations Charter and also because of your pas-sionate devotion to the cause of humanity, your unflinching ad-herence to the ideals of liberty and for the great concern you have shown for the affairs of the Congo since your assumption of office as Acting Secretary-General of the United Nations. For these reasons, I feel sure that you will pay heed to my appeal to you concerning the safety of Mr Gizenga and the necessity to assuage mounting fears about his physical and mental health. You will also agree that even if it could be said that his health was in very good condition now, he must suffer severe mental strain and agony from his present relegation to a state of solitude and isolation without any definite indications regarding his fate or future.

It appears that, for reasons of which I am not aware, the Congo-lese authorities would like to keep him away from all political activity while efforts are being made to resolve the grave constitu-tional impasse in the country. If so, as a contribution to these efforts, the Government of Ghana would be glad to offer tempo-rary political asylum to Mr Gizenga under the usual conditions, until such time that he could resume normal life in the Congo.

I shall be glad to learn your views about this, and whether the proposal is acceptable to the Congolese authorities.

The question of Gizenga's health could not have seemed of very high priority to Adoula at that time, since the next stage of the struggle with Tshombe had already begun. Arms were being smuggled into Katanga and although the Katanga Assembly ratified (15 February) the Kitona agreement between Adoula and Tshombe, certain reservations were made. For example, 'military operations and other hostile acts against Katanga authorities must immediately cease', and 'Katanga must have in the central government at least as many portfolios as the Leopoldville group, including Defence. The Central Government must affirm the Congo's attachment to the free world and its opposition to international communism.' Finally, 'the United Nations must cease all interference in Katanga affairs and withdraw its troops.'

Even more unpromising for the future was the communiqué published by Jenakat (Katanga National Youth Movement) on the eve of the Assembly's ratification of the Kitona agreement, stating that it still considered Katanga independent no matter what political structure was adopted for the Congo. Jenakat claimed, in its communiqué, to have 20,000 members.

Once again, Tshombe was to wreck any hopes of a peaceful solution in the Congo. I sent a telegram to U Thant (13 January 1962) assuring him of Ghana's support for strong UN action:

As I have said many times before, it is imperative to keep the cold war out of the Congo and to prevent the colonialists from developing further intrigues in that young Republic in an effort to curb its freedom and sovereignty.

Steadfast and strong measures are necessary to counteract these tendencies designed to balkanise Africa and prevent its unity. You can rest assured, Mr Secretary-General, that the Government of Ghana will continue to give vigorous support to any policies you may adopt in implementation of the decisions of the Security Council.

Early in March a 12-man Ghanaian UN patrol was attacked by Katanga gendarmes near Kamina. It extricated itself without casualties after a 75-minute skirmish during which the Ghanaian patrol had been forced to send back to its base for 81 mm mortars to repulse the attack. Tshombe falsely claimed that 1,200 UN troops had launched a surprise mortar and machine gun attack on the Kamina base.

Adoula and UN officials had been trying for some time to persuade Tshombe to go to Leopoldville for talks, and there was some cause for optimism when the Katanga government issued a statement saying that Tshombe had agreed to a meeting with Adoula in Leopoldville if adequate guarantees were given for his safety. The two leaders did in fact meet in Leopoldville on Sunday 18 March, after a period of delay during which both Adoula and Tshombe stood on their dignity, each insisting on maximum respect. When the talks did actually begin, they took place in strict secrecy in Adoula's residence. But progress was painfully slow. It seemed that Tshombe, as usual, was playing for time. He refused to discuss the core of the problem, Katanga's secession, confining himself to claiming that his terms of reference did not entitle him to take final decisions and that anything agreed upon had to be ratified by the Katanga Provincial Assembly. It was the same old cat and mouse game he had employed on several previous occasions.

At the end of March it was feared that the talks would break down completely. Adoula insisted on treating Tshombe as a provincial president, while Tshombe asserted he was head of an independent state. However, both saw the need for compromise. Tshombe realised he could not in fact maintain an independent Katanga and Adoula recognised the necessity for gaining the economic strength which Katanga could give to the central government.

On 6 April, I sent a telegram to Tshombe's foreign minister, Kimba:

I thank you for your telegram of 3rd April and wish to inform you that I have always stood for the discontinuance of foreign interference in the affairs of the Congo and will continue to work for the independence, integrity and unity of the Congo Republic.

It is my view that peace and unity can only be restored in the Congo through respect of the *Loi Fondamentale* which is the constitutional basis of the independence of the Congo. In this regard it is my earnest hope that you and other members of the Katanga Administration will resist all separatist tendencies and work sincerely for the unity and integrity of the Congo. Unless your leaders in the Congo turn away from the dangerous machinations of the foreign powers in the Congo, the constant intrigues of these powers will only serve to prolong a settlement in the Congo by exaggerating even the smallest differences among the people. If you do not free yourselves from these entanglements you cannot keep the Congo free and united. It is for this reason that I appealed to the United Nations for the temporary withdrawal of the Diplomatic

Corps from the Congo until a peaceful settlement of outstanding problems had been effected. At a time when millions of Africans call for unity as the only guarantee of the independence, welfare and progress of our continent, it is extremely unprogressive and dangerous to encourage in any way the elements of separatism now unfortunately at work in the Congo. If the Katanga administration does not unite unconditionally with the Central Congolese Government, and thereby restore the unity and territorial integrity of the Congo, the Cold War will tear the Congo apart and leave a bitter strife in its wake.

Doubtless the domestic difficulties facing Adoula encouraged Tshombe in his independent attitude. In Leopoldville, while the talks were going on, the 60,000 strong Congolese Workers' Union threatened to call a two-day strike in protest against the excessive salaries paid to members of Parliament. Congolese MPs were being paid £3,600 a year, while the average worker's wage was only £144 a year. The two presidents of the Chamber and the Senate received about £760 a month; ministers drew £550, and ordinary MPs £300 a month. The Union claimed that MPs had been selling maps of gold mines and other mines to Europeans and had been buying expensive cars, banking their money abroad and dipping into public funds.

These grievances were symptomatic of the general unrest and economic distress caused by two years of political instability. Until the political problems were solved there was little hope of economic improvement. I have always maintained that political independence must precede economic emancipation. It is the same with Congo unity as with African unity; political unity is an essential first step towards effective economic advance.

Adoula evidently also saw the urgent need for political solutions. On 16 April, the central government asked the UN to send two battalions of troops to South Kasai, to end Kasai's secession. The Kasai leader, Albert Kalondji, was at that time awaiting trial in Leopoldville, and Adoula was determined to settle the problem of Kasai once and for all. He sent me a note on 10 April expressing his deep concern about the worsening situation and telling me of the measures he proposed to take. I replied (17 April):

I have read with great sympathy your letter of 10 April 1962, together with its enclosures, and feel equally concerned about the worsening of the position in the Congo. You are no doubt aware, Your Excellency, that this situation has arisen as a result of the obstructionist and imperialist chicanery and manoeuvres which have rendered the United Nations action, or any action on our part, ineffective in the Congo.

I completely support the line of action proposed in your letter, since it is in full accord with the stand taken by the Government of Ghana on the Congo issue from the very outset. You will remember the line I took at the United Nations which I still think is the only line; this is also the Lumumbist line, on which alone the complete and total liberation of the Congo can be established. This stand is furthermore endorsed by the Security Council Resolution of July 1960.

In response to your appeal, I wish to assure Your Excellency that I and the Government of Ghana are ever prepared to offer whatever assistance can help achieve peace in the Congo and preserve the territorial integrity of the Country. In order to demonstrate our readiness to help, I have charged Mr M. F. Dei-Anang, Ambassador Extraordinary and Plenipotentiary, the bearer of this Note, who is visiting Leopoldville for Easter and who has full powers, to discuss with you and the United Nations Chargé de Mission, the various issues raised in your letter.

By his experience and prudence, I am sure that Mr Dei-Anang will discharge this duty to your satisfaction and approbation.

Please accept, Your Excellency, the assurances of my highest esteem and brotherly sentiments.

Then came news of the return of Tshombe to Elisabethville. As predicted, the talks had broken down. Adoula accused Tshombe of 'shuffling and speechifying', while Tshombe, in a statement made in Elisabethville, said that Katanga should join some larger complex of African States on the continental level. When pressed to return to Leopoldville to resume talks with Adoula, Tshombe was reported to be ill with fever.

In the meantime, Adoula's two other main opponents were being effectively dealt with, if only temporarily. Already under detention, Gizenga was, on 8 May, stripped of his parliamentary immunity. The voting was 64 in favour; 22 against, with 8 abstentions. At about the same time, Kalondji was sentenced to five years' imprisonment 'for the arbitrary arrest and ill-treatment of political opponents'.

By the end of May, as a result of UN pressure, Adoula and Tshombe at last agreed to set up four commissions to study the main problems existing between them. These commissions, to which UN technicians were to be seconded as experts, were to be concerned with military, monetary, economic and financial, and transport and communications problems. The two leaders also agreed to integrate the Katanga gendarmerie into the National Congolese Army. Observers said that it was the first concrete measure to be adopted by the Congolese leaders since the resumption of talks.

But how sincere was Tshombe? If he intended unity within the Congo Republic, why did he still encourage the recruitment of mercenaries? Reports coming from the Congo revealed the arrival of more mercenaries. U Thant, contemplating the likelihood of another breakdown in the talks between Adoula and Tshombe, said that he might have to secure a fresh mandate from the Security Council. 'The position is,' he said, 'that many member states who are paying for the operation do not favour any fresh United Nations involvement in the Congo, while many who do not pay their share have been advocating a more vigorous policy.' It was rumoured that the UN was planning to place the Congo under UN trusteeship. But UN representative Gardiner strongly denied the suggestion.

Some ten days later, on 21 June, Tshombe alleged that ANC troops had attacked certain towns in Katanga. This caused a temporary interruption in the talks, which Gardiner had great difficulty in ending. He did manage to save the talks and Adoula announced a Cabinet reshuffle to include Katanga members. But his success was very short-lived. At the end of June, Tshombe was proudly telling a crowd in Elisabethville that he had signed nothing after his month's stay in the Congolese capital; Adoula at the same time announced that all peaceful means of ending Katanga's secession appeared to be exhausted.

I have vivid memories of those tragic days, when it seemed as though no solutions had been reached after two complete years of apparently wasted effort. Tshombe, backed by Union Minière and foreign mercenaries, seemed as strong as ever in Katanga. In other parts of the Congo, however, there were signs of a revival of Lumumbism. Plans were going ahead for the erection of a statue in Stanleyville to 'Lumumba the Liberator'.

In Leopoldville, a meeting was held to mark the revival of the Bureau of the National Movement of the Congo (MNC), the biggest political party of the Congo, founded by Lumumba. The chairman of the Party, Christophe Gbenye, recalled the disastrous events of 1960 which caused the Bureau to close and called for two minutes' silence for Lumumba.

Reflecting on the whole tragic drama of the Congo I decided to put my thoughts on paper and to send a note to leaders of all African independent states:

I am writing this letter to you in view of present developments in Africa. This continent of ours is passing through a decisive phase in its history. The forces of liberation which have already won remarkable successes are bending all their energies towards the complete liquidation of colonialism in all its forms and manifestations.

The imperialists, for their part, are making gigantic efforts individually and collectively, by a series of disguises and subterfuges, to keep and even to reinforce their position in Africa. It is therefore incumbent upon us to unite our forces politically and economically against this new threat in Africa; otherwise, in our separate existence we shall be compelled to sell out, disintegrate or perish.

Africa is considered by the imperialists as 'the richest prey on earth', because of its immense agricultural and mineral wealth and its power resources. The dramatic events that have taken place in the Congo are a particularly clear and positive illustration of the determination of the imperialists and colonialists not to let slip this prey.

As far as the imperialists are concerned, Africa is not only 'the richest prey on earth', but also their last chance: the imperialists' sphere of domination is daily shrinking. In Europe, a number of countries have severed their ties with the capitalist system and have embarked upon the socialist system. Indeed, events of far-reaching importance have taken place in Europe, Asia and more recently in Latin America, which have irretrievably undermined the foundations of colonialist domination in Africa. The colonialists are well aware that their only chance of survival lies in the maintenance and strengthening of their economic and neo-colonialist position in Africa. The survival of colonialism would relegate the African people to a life of misery and oppression. Similarly, if we permit neo-colonialism to have a foothold, in whatever form, in Africa, we would cause it to undermine the strength, progress and prosperity which we should derive from African unity and non-alignment.

We must not be unhappy instruments manipulated by foreign powers to promote disunity among us, or to make us victims of their intrigues and machinations, which would retard our progress and development.

We the leaders of Africa have therefore heavy responsibilities towards our people in Africa. We must assume these responsibilities fully, and carry them out firmly, courageously and consistently. Our Governments must therefore keep steadfast faith with Africa, strengthen the hands of all Freedom Fighters and encourage all those who are fighting by any means for the total liberation and unity of our continent.

Having measured the explosive power of the African liberation movement, the imperialists and colonialists are combining artifice with strength, in an attempt to pervert our aspirations and use them for their own ends. They have granted us independence taking great care to station on our soil such links as can still contribute to the maintenance of their interests.

Before transferring power, they either leave no constitution behind at all, or they draw up for the people protracted and unworkable constitutional devices which take little or no account of our conditions and way of life and which have a great effect in engendering discord and creating disunity on the very threshold of independence.

The imperialists and colonialists also impose upon us monster agreements which guarantee the continued use of military bases, agreements which for all practical purposes seek to perpetuate the essentials of colonialism.

Even countries that have discarded the political shackles of the old colonial days are not automatically insulated from a possible return of colonialism. Unless we firmly and steadfastly resist these dangerous tactics of the imperialists and their agents who blow hot and cold, exerting pressure, distributing smiles, fomenting plots, professing friendship and practising blackmail, we are liable to swerve from the right path of true service to Africa and its people. This is particularly so when we wrestle, as we are all doing now, with economic or financial problems in our respective territories. Such a situation is obviously a good opportunity for foreign capital to come in and, if not carefully guarded, to spread its monopolistic tentacles over the principal resources and sectors of our economy, forestalling or sabotaging any attempt to overhaul and transform the colonial structures that we have inherited.

Conscious of our responsibilities towards Africa and its people, we must guard against any attempts by the imperialists, colonialists and neo-colonialists to use financial aid as a means of economic infiltration, and, ultimately of political subjection. They are well aware of the difficulties facing us. These include problems of balkanisation, the weakness of our national economics resulting from centuries of colonial exploitation, glaring inequalities in our state of development and disabilities in regard to disease, illiteracy and technological experience. Of course, the imperialists and colonialists miss no opportunity for employing these disabilities to foment trouble and to create suspicion, distrust and confusion among us. They also know that if Africa becomes united with a continental government, the power and strength derived from this unity would deal a death-blow to colonialism. They are further aware of the fact that the slogan 'African Unity' has gripped the masses, holding them so firmly in its embrace, that it would be a great risk and folly to oppose it openly.

We must not, and should not, subscribe to any idea of imperialist-inspired regrouping. Regional groupings may have a tendency to deflect us from our ultimate goal of African Unity. In this sense, such groupings could be regarded as a wider and subtle form of balkanisation. We must therefore be firm and ready to oppose any attempt to bring about such a regrouping which would only aggravate or exaggerate the position of our present artificial divisions and boundaries. If we fail to do this, I fear that the following other consequences could follow:

(a) Neutralising the efforts of the African States pursuing a national policy that is independent and democratic, by setting these States fairly and squarely within a unity, which the imperialists control through the interposition of third parties;

(b) Reinstating and even consolidating politically governments that may easily fall prey to neo-colonialism;

(c) Attenuating or completely paralysing the Liberation Movements in territories that are still under colonial rule by depriving the Freedom Fighters of effective support from the independent African States;

(d) Liquidating the Afro-Asian group at the United Nations Organisation and, generally speaking, breaking up the anti-imperialist front;

(e) Finally, turning Africa into an economically affiliated and dependent bloc, subordinated to foreign powers.

It would be playing into the hands of the colonialists and neo-colonialists and unwittingly encompassing our own destruction and that of Africa as a whole, if we were to allow ourselves to be controlled, influenced or 'tele-guided' by foreign powers. That is why some of us view with dismay and concern the recent decision, taken at the Bangui Conference, to set up a Franco-African Community having 'close links' with France and expressing its identity as a group at the United Nations. It is obvious that such a unit or community could retard our progress towards African Unity. Some time ago, I had occasion to welcome one of our leaders on an official visit to Ghana and I made a statement at a public dinner party in his honour. I said:

'It is only in an African Community that the African territories can achieve an effective personality in the political, economic, military as well as social and cultural fields. This African Community should not be subordinated in any way to any "rapprochement" between any foreign governments or institutions whether it be in the British Commonwealth or the French Community. The African Community should remain completely independent, exclusively African and subject to no interference from outside, and detached from any other community.'

And I went on:

'As I have said before on several occasions, it is time for Africans to discard completely the labels which have been handed down to us by the imperialists and colonialists. There is not time to be lost. The independent African States owe it as a duty to themselves and to the world to join together in an effective union to find solutions to the urgent and painful problems now facing Africa.

The basis of the Union of African States is clear. It is based on a fundamental need to maintain between African States a common identity and a common approach to African problems. The alternative to this is chaos and confusion.'

Now we are deep in confusion. Our attempts to help the Congo maintain its independence are still meeting with grave obstacles. Many parts of Africa are still under colonial domination, while others agree to play second fiddle to the neo-colonialists. In the Independent African States that are fighting hard to safeguard their independence and tread the path of genuine development, the colonialists, imperialists and their agents strive by all possible methods —corruption, subversion, assassination, murder and protracted constitutional devices—to destroy these efforts and thus maintain their domination over Africa. It is clear that only a unified and progressive point of view on our part can strengthen and encourage our Freedom Fighters now engaged in a life and death struggle with the colonialists, and also bring about true independence and unity for Africa. I sincerely believe that a Continental Government of Africa is both possible and a necessity, a definite prerequisite to Africa's survival.

When I speak of African Unity, I mean the political and economic unification of the African Continent. It is the only way if we are to survive as a people; and this, in my view, should seek three objectives:

Firstly, we should have an over-all economic planning on a continental basis which would increase the industrial and economic power of Africa. So long as we remain disunited, so long as we remain balkanised, regionally or territorially, we will be at the mercy of colonialism and imperialism.

There is a great contrast in this respect between Africa and Europe today. Whereas Europe is making frantic efforts in the direction of economic and political integration, Africa is sadly being torn apart by the manoeuvres and intrigues of neo-colonialism.

Secondly, we should aim at the creation of a joint military Command. I do not see any wisdom in our present separate efforts to build up or maintain vast military forces for self-defence which, in any case, would be ineffective in any major conflict. If we examine this problem realistically, we would be able to ask ourselves this pertinent question: which single State in Africa today can protect itself against an imperialist aggressor?

Recently, anti-apartheid leaders have alleged that South Africa in conjunction with other settler governments in Africa is building great military might with all the latest weapons of destruction, in order to crush African nationalism. If this is true, only the unity of Africa can prevent South Africa and other settlers from achieving such an aim. If we do not unite and combine our military forces for common defence, the individual States, out of a sense of insecurity, may be drawn into making defence pacts which will endanger the security of us all. There is also the expenditure aspect of this problem. The maintenance of military forces imposes a heavy burden on even the most wealthy States. For young African States, who need every penny they can get for development, it is ridiculous for each State individually to assume such a heavy burden when the weight of this burden could easily be lightened by sharing it among ourselves.

The third objective which we should have in Africa comes from the first two which I have just described. If we in Africa set up a common economic planning organisation and a joint military command, it follows that we shall have to adopt a common foreign policy to give political direction to our national continental defence and our national continental economic and industrial development planning. We must begin to build our own continental Common Market and continental monetary zone.

It should be possible to devise some constitutional structure which secures these objectives and yet preserves the sovereignty of each country joining the Union. For example, countries in such a union will naturally maintain their own constitutions, continue to use their national flags, their national anthems and other symbols of sovereignty which they don't have to surrender. The forces that unite us are greater than the superficial differences which divide us at present.

I have referred to the need for economic planning on a continental basis. It is most important that African leaders must now begin to find the best and quickest means by which we can pool our economic resources together for our mutual benefit. If we achieve this, we shall raise in Africa a great industrial, economic and financial power comparable to anything the world has seen in our time. Let us keep our hands off anything which may now divide us.

Allow me here to express my absolute faith in the triumph of Africa's cause, namely, the total liberation and the political and economic unification of our African Continent.

18 Attempts at Economic Sanctions and a Federal Solution

THE UN Secretary-General, U Thant, put his finger on the root cause of the continuing Congo crisis when he warned, in July 1962, that he might have to ask for new powers, 'The problem of the Congo is the problem of Katanga. The problem of Katanga is the problem of finances. The problem of finances is the problem of the Union Minière.'

After the failure of the Adoula/Tshombe talks the UN were convinced that the only way, short of force, of ending Katanga's secession was to bring economic pressure to bear on Tshombe. They hoped to persuade Union Minière to switch their payments of royalties, export and special taxes from Katanga to the Central Government. These payments, amounting to about £15 million a year, represented about 70 per cent of Katanga's entire budget and enabled Tshombe to maintain a militia of 12,000 men. It was thought that if Tshombe was deprived of this support the Congo could be reunified and the Central Government would be able to make use of the additional revenue to increase the efficiency of its administration.

But the immense financial power of Union Minière was only one aspect of its strength, as the UN learned to its cost. Behind the company lay a powerful administrative machine capable of influencing the policy of governments. In July 1962, the Belgian Foreign Minister, Paul-Henri Spaak, was unable to achieve any change in his country's policy towards the Congo because of pressure from interests inside Union Minière, which provided an effective pro-Tshombe lobby throughout the world.

A brief glimpse of the structure of Union Minière reveals the extent of the interests involved. The largest holding company is Belgian, the legendary Société Générale, and about one-third of its profits come from Union Miniére. But the control of Société Générale over Union Minière is not complete. They and their associated Compagnie du Katanga owned, in 1962, only 20 per cent of the voting shares. The public controlled 36 per cent and 24 per cent had been appropriated by the Katanga government. The other big shareholder was Tanganyika Concessions with 20 per cent of the votes. The Chairman of 'Tanks', Captain Charles Waterhouse, was on the Board of Union Minière together with Lord Selborne and Sir Ulick Alexander, each of them exercising important right-wing influence.

In Union Minière itself, the majority of those who directed company policy in 1962 were convinced that they depended for their survival on Tshombe and that Tshombe depended on them for money. They argued that whatever the rights or wrongs of Katanga's secession, the existence of an independent Katanga was a vital fact and had to be recognised as such. 'We are not in politics,' one Union Minière spokesman explained, 'we have to pay taxes to whoever's in power.' The point was taken up by Mr Paul Gillet, Chairman of Union Minière, in his address to shareholders at the annual general meeting held in Brussels on 24 May 1962, when the net profit was given as 1,526,580,449 francs:

> Union Minière deplores the existence of political deadlock in the relations between the Central Government and that of Katanga. At every possible occasion we have expressed the wish for an agreement upon which the future of a considerable number of African and European nationals depends.
>
> But in the meantime, we must comply with the decisions of the authority which has, moreover, the means of imposing them.

The Chairman concluded, 'It has been truthfully said that in the Congolese disaster, one single thing resists and that is private enterprise. Union Minière can testify to this.'

During the military operations in Katanga in September and December 1961, according to the report of the Board of Directors, mining extraction was generally maintained 'at a level comparable to that of the preceding year'. While the 1961 production of copper was down by some 7,000 tons on the 1960 figure, production of cobalt increased (8,326 tons in 1961, against 8,222 tons in 1960) and the electricity energy produced by the power stations in Haut-Katanga amounted to 2,034 million kw (against 2,008 million kw in 1960).

The resilience of Union Minière to political unrest and even military operations, reflected in its 'business as usual' attitude, explains in great measure the continuing strength of Tshombe. As long as Union Minière flourished and financed his government through the payment of royalties and other taxes, he could afford to employ mercenaries to defend him and could be sure of a sympathetic hearing among business circles abroad.

On 12 July, celebrations were held in Elisabethville to commemorate the second anniversary of Katanga's secession. Some 2,000 troops took part, instead of the 300 as promised by Tshombe. A few days later, a crowd of about 10,000 women were involved in an ugly incident near a UN roadblock guarded by Indian soldiers outside Elisabethville. Some of the women danced provocatively in front of the soldiers and rolled in the dust at their feet. Others set fire to the dry grass surrounding the Indian positions. Many of the yelling women clawed at the soldiers' uniforms, until the men could stand it no longer and the order was given to fire into the air. Five women were injured in scuffles with soldiers using rifle butts before the demonstration finally ended.

Much publicity was given to the incident in the world press. Those behind Tshombe made the most of the fact that UN troops had used a show of force to disperse a crowd of women. On a three-day visit to Finland, U Thant despairingly doubted if he could do business with 'such a bunch of clowns' as Tshombe and his ministers.

In Britain and America, policy-makers were going into the question of applying economic sanctions against Katanga. The British government was apparently not in favour of taking such a step and the view was widely held in America that this was due 'to the interests which Britain has in Katanga, particularly in the Union Minière and in some of the railways'.[1] But then came news of a private scheme devised by certain British businessmen to bring economic pressure to bear on Tshombe. The plan was for a 10 per cent garnishee on the copper companies' revenue. Its originators, who wished to remain anonymous, were prominent businessmen who had a close knowledge of mining and industry in Africa. Most of them were Conservatives who disagreed with Lord Home's policy towards the Congo. They sent the plan by unofficial channels to the UN and the State Department in Washington. Although the plan was not adopted, it was encouraging to know that at least some business opinion in London was in favour of active steps to end Katanga's secession.

On 25 July, Tshombe announced that Katanga would adopt a scorched earth policy and fight guerrilla warfare if the UN again attempted to use force to integrate Katanga with the rest of the Congo.

[1] Report from Washington in *The Times*, 20 July 1962.

He rejected the UN plan to tax Katanga's mineral resources in order to help finance the central government. Undaunted, U Thant continued to try to get British, American and Belgian support for economic pressure against Tshombe. The first stage of his plan was to freeze assets of Union Minière and then to divert to the Central Government the taxes paid by the Company to Katanga. The American government was reported to be in favour of the plan but Britain and Belgium held back.

This division among the ranks of his enemies played right into Tshombe's hands. He openly boasted that he had enough money and arms to carry on a guerrilla war for years. One diplomat described his attitude as 'cock-a-hoop'.

A death-blow to the sanctions plan occurred when Union Minière, at the end of July, rejected the suggestion that it should pay its taxes and royalties to the Leopoldville government, saying that it had to obey the local government or suffer the consequences. Then Home formally announced in the House of Lords that Britain opposed sanctions. The decision was taken in spite of President Kennedy's personal intervention on the side of action against Union Minière.

In a report to the Security Council written by the Officer in Charge of ONUC, 20 August 1962, blame for the stalemate in the Congo was laid squarely on Tshombe's shoulders, 'I have felt it my duty to say that the delays and evasive tactics which have been so artfully employed by Mr Tshombe are dangerous and cannot be indefinitely tolerated either by the United Nations or by the Central Congolese Government.' Yet without the financial support of Union Minière, and the refusal of Britain and Belgium to apply economic sanctions, Tshombe could not have indulged in 'delays and evasive tactics'.

The Katangese President appeared to score another political victory when, on 29 July, Adoula formally proposed a new constitution for the Congo on federal lines. Each province was to control its own local administration but the federal government was to be responsible for foreign affairs, defence, currency, customs, foreign trade, immigration and communications. He called on UN jurists to draw up a final document for presentation to Parliament in September.

The proposal for a federation was a significant concession to Tshombe. In Elisabethville, he declared it was 'what we always wanted and I am happy to say we now have an opportunity to find a solution to the constitutional problems'. But U Thant was less optimistic. On 2 August he again said that the crux of the Congo problem was the big mining companies. Nevertheless, he asked Nigeria, Switzerland and Canada to provide one expert each to draw up a federal constitution for the Congo. At Adoula's request, a fourth expert was included from India.

The idea that the Congo should have a federal form of government filled me with alarm. It would seriously weaken the central government in Leopoldville and would delay urgent measures for the political and economic reconstruction of the country. If ever a country needed the strength and dynamism of a unitary form of government, that country was the Congo. Separatism would simply enable Tshombe to pursue his selfish policies regardless of the general good of the Congolese people as a whole.

There was a time before our own independence, when a small section of our people, backed by alien interests, urged the adoption in Ghana of a federal form of government. They demanded the virtual secession of Ashanti, the Northern Region and what was formerly British Togoland, from the sphere of the central Ghanaian government: and this in a country of some 6½ million inhabitants. The Ghanaian people clearly showed what they thought of such a ridiculous idea in the general election of 1956 which returned the CPP to power for the third time with an overwhelming majority. The CPP was, of course, pledged to a unitary form of government in Ghana.

Unfortunately, no general election could be held in the Congo in 1962 to test the opinion of the Congolese people. It seemed that Tshombe was getting it all his own way. At the beginning of August his position was strengthened as a result of a new agreement made between Union Minière and the Katanga Central Bank. According to this agreement, the Company would supply convertible currency and be repaid in Katanga francs. The effect would be that the Company, which sold its produce for dollars and other hard currencies, would no longer wait until sales were made before making the currency available to the Katanga exchange control. The increased reserves would obviously strengthen Tshombe in his struggle with Adoula and the central government.

Once again, tension began to rise sharply as Adoula's government instructed all firms in the Congo to shut down their branches in Katanga if they wanted to continue operating in the rest of the country; and Tshombe, for his part, continued to play for time. He knew that he had nothing to fear as long as Britain and the U.S.A. failed to agree on tactics to bring Katanga to heel. Throughout the whole Congo crisis, Tshombe always seemed to have just enough political support from among the western powers to prevent the United Nations efforts from ending the secession.

In Leopoldville, Adoula was in no mood for further talks with

Tshombe. He said he would rather not go through gruelling sessions with the wily Katanga leader once more, 'only to see the results of our talks float down the Congo River on the last day'. The kind of despair experienced among Congolese officials in those days was well summed up by one of them when he remarked, 'We have less to say about Katanga with every day that passes. Our fate is decided in Washington, London, Paris and Brussels. Debates in the House of Commons or the American Senate are more significant than decisions of our own Parliament.' What a sad commentary on affairs in an 'independent' state.

On 17 August 1962 I sent a telegram to Adoula advising against the adoption of a federal constitution:

Since it was announced that the United Nations would appoint four experts to assist your government to draw up a federal constitution, progressive African opinion has become restive and I personally have become considerably anxious that such a step would constitute a backward move for the Republic of the Congo.

In order to repair effectively, and quickly, the serious damage done to Africa as a result of imperialism and colonialism, emergent African states need strong unitary governments capable of exercising a central authority for the mobilisation of the national effort and the co-ordination of reconstruction and progress.

Even your present constitution, which is only semi-federal, enabled Katanga to attempt to secede and has actually created difficulties for the Republic of the Congo, which otherwise by now would have found its feet truly placed on the road to progress and stability. What then if you allow a fully federal constitution to be imposed upon the Congo, causing the dissipation of your national energies and resources?

In the name of Africa, I entreat you and your colleagues in the Government of the Congo to set your face resolutely against imposing on your country a federal constitution which would act as a permanent bar to the unity of the Congo and militate severely against all stability, progress and prosperity.

I send you sincere greetings and assure you that all of us are in this struggle together for the total liquidation of imperialism and colonialism and for African Unity. I have no doubt that true sons of Africa everywhere solidly support you and the present Central Government of the Congo, and wish that the Congo will soon be free itself from neo-colonialism and the collective imperialism now hampering her.

I am publishing this telegram in the hope that it will strengthen your hand.

In the meantime, fighting had broken out in the Mukato-Kyayo area and the UN warned the Katanga Government that unless it stopped its troops in the northern part of the Province from attacking, the UN would have to intervene 'with all means at its disposal'. Tshombe was at that time on one of his frequent visits to Salisbury to consult Welensky. In his absence, Katanga's foreign minister asserted that the Katangese had been attacked by Congolese troops but that orders had been given to end all movement.

This did not indicate any weakness on the part of the Katanga Government. On the contrary, Tshombe was more confident than ever before. He was convinced that time was on his side and that Britain was more concerned with safeguarding commercial interests than with supporting Adoula's government. He therefore considered that very little would be done to coerce Katanga into federating with the rest of the Congo or into making substantial financial concessions to the Central Government.

19 U Thant's Plan for Reconciliation

IT was clear that the next few months would be critical for the Congo. Tshombe's government would be faced with the new federal constitution drawn up by UN experts and the UN would be responsible for its implementation; a difficult, if not impossible task in view of the lack of support from some of the western powers, notably Britain, for any kind of effective pressure on Katanga.

The 17th Session of the UN General Assembly was due to open on 18 September and Ghana requested the inclusion of the Congo problem on the agenda. This was granted. It was well known by then that U Thant was determined that a supreme effort should be made to solve the question and that he was in favour of strong measures, if necessary, to compel Tshombe to accept re-unification. On 22 August it was reported that U Thant had given the Katanga President a week to ten days in which to agree to enter a federal system in the Congo and to share the revenues from the Province's copper and cobalt mines, or else face severe economic sanctions. But Tshombe was evidently about to begin a ten-day tour of Katanga instead of preparing for constitutional talks.

U Thant put details of his plan before the Security Council. He proposed a 'quite brief' period for Katanga to consider re-unification proposals, to be followed by trade and financial sanctions if reconciliation efforts were spurned. There was to be a 50/50 split of all taxes, duties and mining royalties between the Congolese Central Government and the Katanga provincial authorities. A Congo Monetary Council was to be set up to control all foreign exchange and to make available for the essential needs of Katanga at least half of the revenues coming out of the Province. There was to be a national plan for currency unification 'in the shortest possible time'. The Katanga gendarmerie was to be merged into the Central Congolese army within two months and all Katanga's diplomatic offices abroad were to be closed so that only the Central Government maintained foreign representation.

It was reported at first that Tshombe had cautiously welcomed U Thant's plan but as the days went by, Adoula's position seemed to be weakening. Having halved his unwieldy cabinet two months previously he now faced the possibility of a strange alliance against him from Conakat deputies and Gizengists. Furthermore, although Britain, the U.S.A. and the Central Congolese Government had approved the UN plan to unite the Congo, Britain had made it clear that she only approved the constitutional and financial proposals made by U Thant and not the threat of economic and financial sanctions against Katanga. Once again, it looked as though the UN effort was to lack teeth.

In this situation, Adoula sent me the following note (28 August 1962), knowing that the Congo problem would be discussed at the Commonwealth Prime Ministers' Conference due to start on 10 September:

(Translation)

I have the honour to address you personally, and through you, the noble nation whose fortunes you direct. It is with confidence that I do so, convinced that the appeal launched by my country will be heard.

The Republic of the Congo, whose population is almost 15 million and whose size is three times that of France and eighty times that of Belgium, has been, as you are aware, independent since 30 June 1960. Unfortunately, her independence was not achieved without difficulties being created everywhere in the way of the Congolese authorities which took over the reins of power from the Belgians.

Your Excellency will no doubt recall the numerous debates and resolutions passed in New York, the seat of the United Nations Organisation, both by the Security Council and by the General Assembly. The external forces engaged in the systematic sabotage of the independence of the Republic of the Congo extend far beyond the limits of small Belgium and are the result of a series of manoeuvres carried out and supported by financial interests who wish to exploit for themselves the mineral and agricultural resources of our territory.

These interests have succeeded in keeping the Republic of the

Congo in a state of chaos through the secession of one of the Provinces of our Republic, Katanga, whose inexhaustible mineral wealth naturally provoked their greed. The relative success of these manoeuvres is due to the active solidarity and the complicity of the capitalists to which must be added South Africa, the paradise of the most intransigent racialists.

Furthermore, the role played by certain British interests in this plot was most conspicuous. In fact, British financial interests and other allied interests are very large in South Katanga. In the Rhodesias, Nyasaland and South Africa they are larger still. In order to continue to benefit and even add to the excessive privileges acquired by certain mining and agricultural firms during the Belgian colonial days, these interests have been providing the secessionist regime through the intermediary of the permanent settlers in South Katanga and in Rhodesia, facilities and assistance of all kinds within the framework of internationally accepted rights.

In spite of the presence of the UN emergency forces in the Republic of Congo who are operating under the resolutions passed in New York by a great majority of member States of the United Nations, we are compelled to point out the hypocrisy which characterises the attitude of certain Western Powers who pretend to abide by the UN Charter while openly or secretly obstructing the full implementation of the resolutions passed, especially, whenever they are not in their interests. The Central Government of the Republic of Congo is convinced that peace and prosperity in Africa are the only factors which could solve the Congo crisis, not only against the people of Congo and their legally and democratically established Government, but equally against the whole of Africa.

This problem which has now been included in the agenda of the next General Assembly of the United Nations cannot be omitted in the discussions of the Commonwealth Prime Ministers' Conference which will be held in London starting from 10 September 1962.

United behind its Central Government, the Congolese people are convinced that Your Excellency will use all your influence, in the light of the information at your disposal, to get the financial interests to adopt a more realistic attitude vis-à-vis the Katanga secession which runs the risk of becoming an incurable sore in the heart of Africa, with all the consequences which this involves, if not brought to an end very rapidly.

The Republic of the Congo, since 30 June 1960, has been governed by a provisional constitution, 'La Loi Fondamentale', which was passed by the Belgian Parliament and signed by the King of the Belgians on 19 May 1960. This 'Loi Fondamentale' was drawn up at the end of the political Conference held in January and February 1960, at which delegates of the Belgian Government and Congolese political leaders from all the Provinces and of various political shades were represented. During this Conference all the Congolese political parties had the opportunity to put their views across. There were supporters for a unitary form of Government as well as those for a federal form of Government.

The principles which were finally retained and which helped in formulating the 'Loi Fondamentale', therefore, constitute a compromise of all the views expressed at the 'Round Table Conference'.

Considering the provisional nature of this 'Loi Fondamentale', it is left to the National institutions resulting from elections to the Legislative Assembly to review some of the Articles, amend or remove them or adapt them to conform closely to Congolese standards. This is the task which my Government has now set itself.

Wishing to obtain a change or an adaptation of this law by some other means, such is the spirit which animates the financial interests who have provoked, organised and maintained the secession of Katanga with the object of setting up in the heart of Africa an oasis where their profitable factories, already abundant, would increase tenfold and where the emancipation of the popular masses would be according to the rhythm controlled and imposed by them.

The Central Government of the Republic of the Congo has the responsibility to protect the Congolese people against the action of people who aim, in fact, at the destruction of the Republic and who are consequently enemies of our people in particular and of Africans in general. The Congolese people and the Government over which I preside place all their hopes in those who, like Your Excellency, will be able to understand our intentions and support our efforts with a view to preserving the unity of the Republic and hence the happiness, prosperity and peace in this important part in the heart of Africa. I am fully convinced that our appeal will not be in vain and that Your Excellency will take to heart to make the most of the merit of our attitude and the pressing necessity of ending immediately a situation which cannot fail to gravely compromise the legitimate interests not only of my compatriots, but of all the countries enamoured with a real love of freedom.

It is in this firm hope that I request Your Excellency to accept the assurances of my highest consideration and the expression of the warmest recognition of my country for the support which the Nation at the head of which you have the honour to be, will have given it.

On the last day of the ten-day ultimatum, Tshombe agreed to U Thant's plan. But few people rejoiced. They knew Tshombe's record and waited to see if he really intended to act on it. In the meantime, developments caused a further weakening of Adoula's position.

The first was the escape from prison, reported on 10 September, of Albert Kalondji, the 'Emperor' of South Kasai, and the subsequent revolt in the Province by Baluba supporters of Kalondji. A state of emergency was declared in South Kasai by the Central Government.

The second was the announcement by Tshombe of an offensive by ANC troops in north Katanga. Tshombe declared that the troops were acting on orders from Mobutu. But UN aircraft reported no signs of military action, and Mobutu denied an attack had been made. It looked as though Tshombe might be trying to foment hostilities; hardly the action of a leader sincerely intending to work for the unity of the Congo.

The third development was the decision taken early in October by four major political parties in the Congo to oppose the federation plan. The parties concerned were the National Movement of the Congo, the African Solidarity Party, Balubakat and the National Union Party. Their joint declaration, in which they rejected federation, ended as follows:

... in the name of the security and tranquillity of Africa as a whole, the Congolese nationalists denounce federation as a policy of betrayal of national interests to please foreign powers.

We denounce the unbearable foreign intervention, the cause of our current crisis, and the intervention by United Nations which usurps the right to settle the future of our country without our participation, and thus to circumvent the legitimate national institutions.

Clearly, some positive steps would have to be taken by the UN if Adoula was to be saved. On 11 October, it was reported that U Thant intended to ask the Security Council for a mandate to impose economic sanctions against Katanga. This was in spite of Tshombe's claim that he had placed $2m. (about £714,000) at the disposal of the Central Congolese Government. Adoula and his colleagues simply regarded the gesture as an attempt to throw dust in their eyes, particularly as Katanga was no nearer to integration with the Congo and reports were circulating in Leopoldville of a renewed build-up of mercenaries in Katanga.

Robert Gardiner confirmed in New York that the strength of foreign mercenaries in Katanga 'remains as significant as ever', and that 'most of them were in civilian dress and employment, which made it difficult to distinguish them from the local Europeans'. He also reported evidence of increased air strength.

On 16 October, the proposed new federal constitution was handed over by Adoula to the Presidents or representatives of the 21 new provinces into which the Congo was to be divided. A conspicuous absentee was Moise Tshombe. On the same day, a cease-fire was signed in Katanga by Joseph Ngalula of the Central Congolese Government, Joseph Yav of Katanga, and Eliud Mathu (UN). But Adoula rejected the cease-fire and insisted on carrying out U Thant's plan. He said that the cease-fire agreement was made without instructions and he urged the UN to apply sanctions against Tshombe.

It was by then obvious that U Thant's plan was not going to work. Fighting broke out again in north Katanga, and Tshombe's planes bombed villages in the area. Even in Leopoldville all was not well. Both Houses of the Congolese Parliament failed to muster a quorum for the session of 5 November. This was the session before which Adoula wanted to put the new constitution. Some of the deputies were in detention. Others were afraid to attend.

Gardiner, in an attempt to deliver a decisive blow for unity, issued an ultimatum to Tshombe calling on him to end Katanga's secession or else face economic sanctions. The only result seems to have been the summoning of Gardiner to New York for consultations with U Thant and the visit of Tshombe to Rhodesia. It was rumoured that Tshombe had gone to the Rhodesian capital to negotiate for arms, and this seemed likely in view of his admitted military action in north Katanga.

There followed a wave of lawlessness in Leopoldville Province and Kasavubu declared a state of emergency. This declaration was nullified by the Lower House of the Congolese Parliament. Furthermore, signatures were gathered for a motion of censure.

In New York, the despairing U Thant threatened not to offer himself for re-election if the Congo crisis was not settled. M. Spaak, the Belgian Foreign Minister, was engaged in talks with the Secretary-General in an attempt to find a solution. The use of sanctions was unlikely but as a last resort, pressure might be put on Katanga by checking rail and road communications. M. Spaak told U Thant that Belgium would support plans to end Katanga's secession. Both President Kennedy and the Belgian Foreign Minister advocated 'severe economic measures' unless substantial progress towards the reunification of the Congo was made 'within a very short period of time'.

Meanwhile, in Leopoldville, the Chamber of Representatives of the Congolese Parliament adopted two resolutions calling for the release of unlawfully arrested members and the immediate lifting of the state of emergency. On 29 November, a motion of censure on the Congolese government received 50 votes to 47 against, but failed to obtain the two-thirds majority necessary for it to be carried.

U Thant was determined to embark on a tougher policy. At the beginning of December, Brigadier Indar Rkhye (India), Chief Military Adviser at the United Nations, left for the Congo to review and possibly reorganise the 18,000 strong UN force. But Britain was uneasy about U Thant's plans and again the UN was virtually paralysed by indecision among the western powers. Adoula was insisting that Union Minière pay the whole of its taxes to the central government; while it was rumoured that Katanga might join an association of African-governed East and Central African States.

On 11 December, the world press gave prominence to the delivery of a note from the UN to Tshombe, accusing him of sabotaging U Thant's plan for reunification. It said all phases of the plan would be put into action 'in the period immediately ahead'. At the same time, Gardiner sent a note to Tshombe telling him that UN forces would not attack but would defend themselves if attacked. He added that the UN would call on member states to take action 'designed to impress upon you and your colleagues the advisability of abandoning your policy of secession and civil war'. M. Spaak joined the assault on Katanga by referring to Tshombe as 'merely a powerful rebel'. Even Union Minière was moved to issue a communiqué deploring the possibility of a renewal of fighting in Katanga.

As before, economic issues were to the forefront. U Thant sent letters to certain States asking them to co-operate in an economic boycott of Katanga, while Adoula specifically asked Britain, Belgium, France, U.S.A. and 13 other countries to stop importing Katanga's copper and cobalt. Faced with the possibility of economic sanctions at last, Kibwe, Deputy President and Finance Minister of Katanga, went to Salisbury for talks with Welensky.

U Thant's measures to bring pressure to bear on Katanga included a ban on exports and imports for Katanga without Congolese Government authorisation. The Central Government was to ask neighbouring nations for their co-operation in the control of arms and smuggling. Belgium was to withdraw 'technicians' and there was to be a cessation of air traffic in and out of Elisabethville. Finally, all governments were to be asked to refuse to grant entry visas to Katangese, or to permit entry if they carried other documents besides a Congolese passport.

It seemed that at last the UN meant business. But again, Britain reaffirmed her opposition to measures against Katanga. Here it must be stated that the view was widely held that the British Foreign Secretary, the Earl of Home, was personally in favour of a stiffer attitude but that some of his Cabinet colleagues were less determined. It is noteworthy that over eighty Conservative back-benchers signed a motion, on 14 December 1962, urging the government to take an immediate initiative in the Security Council against the use of force or economic coercion to impose a political solution on the Congo.

This occurred shortly after the Chamber of Deputies in Leopold-ville had decided to suspend U Thant's plan for the reunification of the Congo on federal lines. The wheel had come full circle. Both in Elisabethville and Leopoldville the proposed UN solution was unacceptable.

In view of this, and the near-bankruptcy of UNO, it was scarcely surprising that U Thant faced a highly critical UN General Assembly. There were, in December 1962, angry debates on the question of financing the UN operation in the Congo (ONUC), and also the UN Emergency Force (UNEF) operating as a peace-keeping force in the Middle East. The USSR and others were refusing to contribute to either of 'those two illegal operations' on the ground that the Security Council's resolution of 14 July 1960 had been implemented in violation of the UN Charter, under which the Security Council alone determined which States were to participate in any action undertaken for the maintenance of peace and security (Article 48 of the Charter). In a speech to the 961st Meeting of the General Assembly on 3 December 1962, the Soviet delegate, Mr Chernyshev, pointed out that it was obvious that the agreements which should have been negotiated under Article 43 of the Charter had never been concluded and that Dag Hammarskjöld had himself chosen the Member States which were to participate in that operation. Similarly,

8

the financing of the Congo operation had been provided for in violation of the Charter, since Hammarskjöld had submitted the matter directly to the General Assembly, which had no jurisdiction over it, whereas he should have addressed himself to the Security Council. That was why, Chernyshev said, the Soviet Union had always refused to recognise the decision by the General Assembly that those expenses should be borne by all Member States on the basis of the regular scale of assessments. The western powers had tried to press the argument that all expenses of the Organisation came under Article 17 of the Charter, even if they had been incurred for activities undertaken in violation of the Charter. However, the question of financing could not in his view be separated from the question of the legality of the actions themselves. The USSR would not help to finance either UNEF or ONUC, and did not recognise the validity of the advisory opinion of the International Court of Justice.[1]

Assessments for financing UNEF and ONUC had been made only up to the end of June 1962, while between them they continued to cost over $11·5m. a month. Excluding the assessment made at the 16th session, 49 states owed a total of $25·25m. to the UNEF Special Account and 60 states owed $47·5m. to the Congo *ad hoc* account. Everything possible had to be done if the collapse of the Organisation was to be prevented.

At the 967th Meeting of the General Assembly, held on 10 December 1962, Mr Romanov (Ukrainian Soviet Socialist Republic) argued that events in the Congo and the Middle East had been precipitated by a small number of states for the sole purpose of bringing about the economic enslavement of young and defenceless countries. He said that the country (Congo) was a prey to the monopolists of a few countries who, indifferent to the fate of the Congolese people, were concerned only to pursue their dismemberment of the country and thus to consolidate their positions, especially in Katanga. While they supported the Central Government in public, they were in practice weakening it, for they paid their taxes to the puppet Tshombe. The United States representative had twice stated at the present session that his country had no connexion with the

---

[1] In Resolution 1731 (XVI) of 20 December 1961, the General Assembly had asked for an advisory opinion from the International Court of Justice on the question of whether certain expenditures authorised by the Assembly in connection with UN operations in the Congo and the Middle East were 'expenses of the Organisation' within the meaning of Article 17, para. 2 of the Charter. The Court answered the question in the affirmative in its opinion of 20 July 1962.

unhappy events in the Congo, giving as evidence the fact that there were no U.S. soldiers there. But there was no need of soldiers to exploit the wealth of the Congo; what was needed was capital, and the U.S. monoplies were second only to those of Belgium in the extent of their investments in the Congo.[1]

While not necessarily agreeing with all that Mr Romanov had to say, it could not be denied that economic interests guided the policy and actions of the western powers in the Congo. It explains the continuing reluctance to apply economic sanctions against Katanga and goes a long way to explaining the whole of European and American involvement in the Congo. If the Congo had not been so rich in mineral resources and the happy hunting ground of foreign monopolists, it would not have attracted such anxious attention and might have been left to solve its own problems.

[1] Official Records, UN General Assembly, 17th Session, 967th Meeting, 10 December 1962.

20 End of Katanga's Secession

DURING the last two weeks of December 1962 relations between the Katanga government and the UN steadily deteriorated. Tshombe declared that he would adopt a scorched earth policy if force was used to compel Katanga to re-unite with the Congo. It was reckoned that he had at his command some 40,000 troops and gendarmerie, approximately 400 mercenaries and at least 20 aircraft. U Thant made it clear that he intended to press on with reunification in spite of continuing disagreement between Britain and America over the amount of pressure to be used.

In Elisabethville, students attacked the American consulate and gave a favourable demonstration outside the British consulate. They thanked Derek Dodson, the British consul, for Britain's stand against the U.S.A. on the Katanga issue. This division among the ranks of the enemy must have been immensely cheering for Tshombe's supporters. However, in the third week of December, the UN General Assembly authorised the extension of the UN Congo operation until 30 June 1963.

It was at this time that three developments occurred, which were to have great significance for the future. First, the Indian government announced its decision to withdraw Indian forces from the Congo by February 1963. Second, the chief of the U.S. military mission to the Congo, General Louis Truman, arrived in Elisabethville for talks with UN officers and officials. Third, Jomo Kenyatta and Tom Mboya, together with other East African leaders, arrived in Leopoldville to discuss Katanga's secession, their arrival coinciding with the opening in Leopoldville of the Pan-African Freedom Movement for East, Central and South Africa. India's declared intention to withdraw her forces in February indicated the growing feeling of disillusionment among many States which had previously supported the UN effort. The appearance of a U.S. military mission in the Congo demonstrated the increasing American participation in the Congo's affairs; a straw in the wind whose importance was not fully recognised until later. Finally, and most encouraging, was the East African mission, indicating the mounting awareness among African leaders that only an African solution could provide the answer to the Congo problem.

Fighting broke out in Elisabethville on 28 December, when UN troops were ordered to attack 'in self-defence' against Katanga soldiers using small arms and mortar bombs. The British consul, Dodson, tried unsuccessfully to arrange a cease-fire, and Tshombe was escorted round the city to be shown how his men were taking the initiative in firing on UN positions. He apparently ordered a cease-fire, but his orders were not obeyed and Elisabethville began to take on the air of a besieged town. The radio was silent and electricity and water supplies were cut off. Robert Gardiner expressed what was in many people's minds when he said, 'I have been wondering about this Katanga myth and Tshombe. I have been asking myself, if Tshombe's orders to his gendarmes are not obeyed, then who is running the gendarmerie? Does the ineffectiveness extend to the political affairs of Katanga?'

For a short time, the whereabouts of Tshombe was a mystery, but when UN forces succeeded in gaining control of Elisabethville by the end of the second day of fighting it was revealed that he was in Salisbury. Through the intervention of Britain he was told by U Thant that he could return to negotiate with the Central Government. It seemed that UN objectives had been achieved in Katanga; Tshombe had been brought to heel with the minimum of bloodshed and, what was more important in western eyes, Union Minière was still working normally.

UN forces then proceeded to take Kamina and to extend their military control in Katanga. In the meantime, U Thant was engaged in obtaining Tshombe's agreement to the following proposals:

1 Senior army officers in Katanga should go to Leopoldville to take an oath of allegiance to Kasavubu, thus integrating the Katanga gendarmerie with the ANC.
2 Representatives of the Katanga National Bank should be authorised to go to Leopoldville 'forthwith'.
3 Full liberty of movement should be given to all UN forces and civilians throughout Katanga.

4 There should be co-operation with the UN in devising a plan for the immediate expulsion of all mercenaries from Katanga.

5 The authority of the Central Government's customs and immigration officers should be accepted.

Tshombe, however, was not behaving like a defeated man. Flying to Kolwezi, about 220 miles east of Elisabethville, he held a cabinet meeting and accused the UN of 'blatant hypocrisy and flagrant lies'. On 2 January, it was rumoured that he was in Jadotville, the second largest town in Katanga and was making conditions about his return to Elisabethville, stipulating that he must be met by the U.S., Belgian and British consuls. The following day UN forces took Jadotville.

Adoula, who had announced on 1 January 1963 the closing of Parliament until 1 March, was justifiably angry with the UN for allowing Tshombe to return. He was further dismayed when Britain blocked a U.S. move to have its policy statement of 4 January 1963, calling on Tshombe to abandon resistance and integrate Katanga, issued as a tripartite Anglo-American-Belgian declaration. Britain argued that Adoula had not implemented the federal constitution and that the British government was against the use of force in Katanga. The British newspaper, the *Sunday Telegraph* of 6 January 1963, reported that 'the British decision leaves this country, in appearance at least, as Mr Tshombe's only major protector among the Western powers'. Adoula's government seemed near to collapse, yet he proudly rejected an offer of financial aid from Britain, amounting to £750,000, because of Britain's 'subversive activities in the African Republic'.

On 9 January, Tshombe returned to Elisabethville, where he received a great welcome. At first the UN placed him under house arrest, but he was soon allowed freedom of movement in Elisabethville. On hearing of this, I sent the following message to U Thant (11 January 1963):

I am greatly perturbed to note that no action has as yet been taken to implement the Security Council resolution of 21 February 1961, which provided that the persons responsible for the murder of Patrice Lumumba and his colleagues should be prosecuted.

Your Excellency will recall that the United Nations Commission of leading international jurists appointed to examine the evidence available and to establish responsibility for the murder named Tshombe, Munongo and Kibwe as being directly concerned with the assassination of the Congolese leaders.

Until such time as Tshombe and his accomplices are brought to trial for their part in the murder of Lumumba and the others mentioned, I consider it highly improper for the United Nations to have any further dealings with Tshombe either in his capacity as so-called President of the illegal state of Katanga or in his position as an official of the Provincial Administration of the Katanga Province of the Central Congolese Government which my Government has already recognised as the sole sovereign authority in Leopoldville, Congo.

The latest decision of the United Nations Secretariat to permit freedom of movement to Tshombe in Elisabethville following closely upon the announcement of his being placed under house arrest, is an example of the vacillation and lack of resolution in the Secretariat's handling of the Congo situation that has made it impossible for so long to reach a settlement of the Congo problem. I am sure you will appreciate that much needless suffering could have been avoided in the Congo if the United Nations had taken firm steps to restrain the secessionist activities of the illegal Tshombe régime in Katanga, and the Republic of Congo would have been set on its rightful course to progress and development. Previous attempts at negotiation with Tshombe have provided a sorry history of prevarication and dishonesty on the part of Tshombe. This should give us all clear proof that Tshombe is a man whose word cannot be trusted. Time is running out for the United Nations in the Congo. If the United Nations fails in this, it will have discredited itself in the eyes of the world. I am sure that by your own resolution and firmness you will be able to resolve the Congo situation once and for all. I hope therefore, that I do not appeal to you in vain.

The Secretary-General replied the following day, 12 January 1963:

I acknowledge receipt of Your Excellency's recent message which was delivered to me by your Permanent Representative to the United Nations in a covering note of 11 January 1963.

I read the very serious allegations in your letter with deep concern, but I am sure that you would not have made them were it not for either misinformation or misunderstanding on your part about what the United Nations is doing in Katanga, or a combination of the two. I assure you that the misapprehensions implicit in these allegations are entirely unfounded.

First of all, as regards Mr Tshombe, the policy I have followed in the conduct of the United Nations Operation in the Congo is to adhere strictly to the mandates defined for the operation by the resolutions of United Nations organs, and to avoid all actions of an arbitrary nature which could not be soundly based in terms of our authority. I have never heard it questioned by anyone, including the Central Government, that Mr Tshombe is the legitimate president of the province of Katanga. It is on this basis and on this basis alone that the United Nations has dealt with him from the beginning. The United Nations has never at any time dealt with Mr Tshombe 'in his capacity as so-called president of the illegal state of Katanga', as you state it, because the United Nations has never at any time or in any way recognized the secession of Katanga. To the contrary, as your Excellency surely knows, the United Nations has consistently and persistently done all that it can to bring an end to the secessionist ambitions of Mr Tshombe and others in Katanga, and in this the troops of the Ghana contingent in ONUC and one of your own countrymen, Mr Robert Gardiner, have given invaluable assistance.

As regards the decision to permit Mr Tshombe's return to Elisabethville and his freedom of movement, there was in my view no other course that could be legally taken by the United Nations. I note your reference to the Security Council Resolution of 21 February 1961. Mr Tshombe, as head of the provincial government, has been in and out of Elisabethville constantly since the United Nations first came there in early August 1960. He was, to the best of my knowledge, legally chosen for the position and has a firm legal claim to it. There has been and there is no basis on which the United Nations could restrict his movements or intervene with his right to perform his official duties except for the reasons that have been stated by me publicly, namely if he or any other Katangese official should overtly incite to violence against ONUC or should advocate a scorched-earth policy. Should he do this we will certainly take him in hand. We are not, however, in Katanga or elsewhere in the Congo, intervening in internal political affairs; we are not putting officials in office or taking them out of office; we are not supporting or opposing any official and we have no intention of doing so, for that would be entirely beyond our mandate and would have the United Nations Operation pursuing a political course, which, in my view, would prove ruinous to it.

Moreover, the Central Government, at the time Mr Tshombe was permitted to return to Elisabethville and to his responsibilities, had not and has not yet taken any action against Mr Tshombe. There is no warrant for his arrest, there are no formal charges against him, there is no legal process concerning him and there has been no attempt to have him removed from office. In this connexion I must point out that ONUC does not try ever to substitute itself for the legitimate Government of the Congo, which is the Central Government, at Leopoldville.

I must take exception to your Excellency's statement about the 'vacillation and lack of resolution in the Secretariat handling of the Congo situation'. Here again an allegation is made which is without foundation. The Secretariat, which I head and for whose acts I assume full responsibility, has been exerting every effort in the most diligent way to carry out the mandates given to the United Nations operation by the various resolutions. The policy has rightfully been to exert first every possible effort to achieve a peaceful resolution of the problem of Katanga, and I need not detail for you the long and varied efforts we have exerted towards this end, including the Kitona talks, the Leopoldville talks and most recently the Plan of National Reconciliation. The employment of force has been always an action of last resort, but as the record of ONUC will amply attest, we have not hesitated to employ it when it becomes necessary. Indeed, the most striking examples of this have been in the recent successful actions at Elisabethville, Kipushi, Jadotville and Kaminaville. In the latter action, in fact, the troops of the Ghana contingent participated most valiantly. In the conduct of the operation in the Congo we have adhered also to another and highly practical principle, namely that of thorough preparation of both political and military levels before any move is undertaken. It may well be that you have mistaken this for 'vacillation' but I assure you that we would not be as far advanced in the Congo as we are today had not this principle been adhered to. To move on any other basis would be to court a setback and this we always seek to avoid. Incidentally, only this morning, the Ethiopian troops were given a friendly welcome by the people as they entered the important Katangese railroad city of Sakania.

It will be of interest to Your Excellency, I am sure, to know that on 11 January, just prior to the receipt of your letter, I was visited by the representatives of all African members of the United Nations here who gave me unqualified endorsement of the policies we are following in the Congo.

Since we had learnt of the substance of your letter from Press releases out of Accra prior to its receipt by me, I am sure that you will not mind my intention to release my reply to you.

I may assure Your Excellency of my confidence that through perseverance and steadfastness in the policy we have been pursuing, the Congo difficulties with which the United Nations is concerned will before long be resolved. In this unrelenting effort I very much hope for Your Excellency's continuing understanding and support.

U Thant's high-sounding phrases seemed rather hollow when one remembered the very different treatment accorded to Lumumba, the legitimate prime minister of the Congo, who was at a crucial moment denied the right to broadcast to his people, while his political opponents received every consideration from the UN, including a very timely grant of money to pay Mobutu's soldiers.

I replied to the Secretary-General's note on 16 January:

I thank you for your reply to my recent message to you. I note that you say you have read the very serious allegations in my letter with deep concern but you are sure that I would not have made them were it not for either misinformation or misunderstanding on my part. I am afraid that if there is any misinformation or misunderstanding it is in the United Nations Secretariat.

For example, you say in your letter to me, 'Moreover, the Central Government, at the time Mr Tshombe was permitted to return to Elisabethville and to his responsibilities, had not and has not yet taken any action against Mr Tshombe'. In fact, as long ago as 8 and 9 September 1961, the two Chambers of the Congolese Parliament authorised his arrest. You say 'There is no warrant for his arrest'. In fact, a warrant was issued by the then appropriate officer, Adrien de Loof, of the Parquest General at Leopoldville on 9 September 1961. You say 'there are no formal charges against him, there is no legal process concerning him'. In fact, Tshombe was charged with sedition, murder, arbitrary arrests and bodily torture under Articles 43, 44, 67, 180, 189, 192 and 193 of the Congolese Penal Code. United Nations Authorities in the Congo agreed to execute this warrant but failed to carry out their promise. This failure is responsible for the subsequent delay in settling the Katanga problem, for the unfortunate loss of life which has since occurred and the great expense occasioned in the protracted operations which have since been necessary. The history of this sorry affair is another example of the vacillation and lack of resolution in the Secretariat's handling of the Congo situation about which I complained to you in my message of 11 January.

Paragraph 4 of the Security Council's Resolution of 21 February 1961 is as follows: 'The Security Council . . . decides that an immediate and impartial investigation be held in order to ascertain the circumstances of the death of Mr Lumumba and his colleagues and that the perpetrators of these crimes be punished.'

In accordance with the Security Council decision an impartial investigation was held by an International Commission of Jurists acting under the authority of the United Nations. This Commission named Tshombe, Munongo and Kibwe as being directly concerned in the assassination of Lumumba and his colleagues. The Resolution of the Security Council thus imposes an obligation on all member States, including the Republic of the Congo, to take active steps to see that the perpetrators of these murders are brought to trial, and, if convicted, punished. I trust that you will bring this point forcefully to the attention of the Government of the Congo. Any amnesty or pardon which prevented the bringing to trial and the punishment of those responsible for Mr Lumumba's murder would be a clear violation of a Resolution of the Security Council. I feel I must add that it is not for the Secretariat to pick and choose and decide which Resolution of the Security Council it will enforce and which it will ignore. If it is your view that the Security Council Resolution of 21 February is now no longer appropriate, then it seems to be your clear duty to invite the Security Council to rescind it. Short of a reversal by the Security Council of their previous decision, I do not consider that the Secretariat has any excuse for refraining from taking all possible active steps to see that the Resolution is implemented.

You further say in your letter to me, 'We are not, however, in Katanga or elsewhere in the Congo intervening in internal political affairs . . . and we have no intention of so doing, for that would be entirely beyond our mandate'. I am in complete agreement with your views on this point and therefore I regret that your name should have been associated with the so-called 'U Thant Plan' which proposes fundamental constitutional changes for the Republic of Congo.

I consider that there is extreme danger in the United Nations attempting to put forward what the Secretariat, and those who advise it accepts, considers to be a suitable Constitution for the Congo. This, in my opinion, is entirely a matter for the Congolese people and Government. They should be given the utmost liberty to choose whatever form of Constitution seems best to them. To use the United Nations for the purpose of forcing a Federal

Constitution upon the Congo is, I should have thought, far beyond any mandate given to the Secretariat by any Resolution of any United Nations organ.

While you say in your letter to me that the United Nations Secretariat have never at any time dealt with Mr Tshombe in his capacity as the so-called President of the illegal State of Katanga but have always dealt with him as the legitimate President of the Province of Katanga, in fact the way in which he is even today being treated is entirely different from the way in which the United Nations authorities deal with the other provincial administrations in the Congo. Despite the fact that Tshombe was elected Chairman of the provincial administration of Katanga there are three valid reasons why the United Nations should have no further dealings with him in that or in any other capacity. The first reason is that Tshombe and his provincial government stand, in the judgment of a United Nations organ, under the gravest suspicion of having murdered the Prime Minister of the Congo, Patrice Lumumba, at whose invitation the United Nations came to the Congo. The second reason is that this Provincial Chairman and his council have three times levied war against United Nations forces, as well as engaging in continual hostilities against the forces of the Central Government and loyal Congolese citizens throughout Katanga. The third reason is that Tshombe and his provincial council have a record of consistently repudiating, whenever convenient, all agreements entered into by them, so that if they are protected in office as provincial authorities they will certainly in their own time, whatever they say now, renew their secessionist activities. For all these reasons the only correct policy with regard to Tshombe and his accomplices is to detain them, pending their being brought to trial before the appropriate judicial authorities, in accordance with the Resolution of 21 February.

In his note of 21 January, U Thant agreed that 'mandats d'amener' had been issued in the names of Tshombe and other Katangese ministers in September 1961, but he considered they had 'long since lost whatever practical meaning they may have had. Since their issuance in September 1961, Mr Tshombe has met with Prime Minister Adoula at Kitona in December of that year, and at Leopoldville for many weeks between March 1962 and June 1962, without any suggestion from Congolese authorities that any legal action against him was pending.' He went on to assert that the proposed new federal constitution for the Congo was drawn up by international experts recruited by the UN as a form of technical assistance, at the request of the Central Government. As for his own plan for national reconciliation, 'it was merely a proposal submitted by me to Mr Adoula and Mr Tshombe, which they were entirely free to accept or reject'. He denied that Tshombe was being treated differently from other provincial presidents.

There seemed little point in prolonging the dialogue with U Thant and I decided to inform Adoula of our exchange of views in the hope that his government might take some positive steps to bring Tshombe to justice. In my note of 16 January to the Congolese prime minister I said:

I have instructed my Chargé d'Affaires in Leopoldville to put before Your Excellency some exchange of views which have taken place between the United Nations Secretary-General and myself.

In my letter to the Secretary-General, a copy of which is attached for your information, I invited attention to the Security Council Resolution of 21 February 1961, which decided that 'an immediate and impartial investigation be held in order to ascertain the circumstances of the death of Lumumba and his colleagues and that the perpetrators of these crimes be punished'.

You will recall that the International Commission of Jurists who conducted the investigation into the circumstances of the death of Lumumba and his colleagues stated that there was sufficient evidence of complicity in the death of these Congolese leaders on the part of Tshombe, Munongo and Kibwe to justify their being brought to trial.

In spite of this, I have been greatly concerned to note that no action has as yet been taken to bring the offenders to trial. The object of my letter to the Secretary-General was thus to invite the Secretary-General's attention to this grave anomaly and to ensure that action is taken in accordance with the Security Council's resolution mentioned above. My Chargé has authority to show Your Excellency the full text of U Thant's reply in which he makes the following main points:

(a) The UN is not in the Congo to intervene in internal affairs;
(b) The UN has no authority to arrest Tshombe until the Central Congolese Government has issued a warrant for his arrest.

You will note that I insisted in my letter to the Secretary-General on the United Nations responsibility to ensure that the murderers of Lumumba—including Tshombe and Munongo—are brought to trial. I believe that in doing so I was acting in accordance with your own views, as I know the abhorrence with which you regard this crime.

I am also sure that punishment of the murderers of Lumumba and his colleagues will have a most dramatic effect in appeasing the national conscience of the Congolese people and rally them fully to the support of the Central Government.

I am, of course, aware of the pressures which, in present circumstances, are being brought to bear on your Government and I hope that you will welcome some external initiative from me, particularly as Ghana is a member of the Security Council. For these reasons, if the arrest of Tshombe can be assisted by the United Nations on the initiative being taken by your Government, as the Secretary-General's reply leads me to believe, I am firmly of the opinion that you will have the whole world on your side, if you decide that the time has come to issue a fresh warrant for Tshombe's arrest.

As regards the Secretary-General's reference to his respect for the principle of non-intervention in Congolese affairs, it should be observed that this has not prevented him from attempting to put forward what he considers to be a suitable Constitution for the Congo. In my opinion, the drawing up of a Constitution for any Government is supremely a matter for its own people and Government. You should therefore be given the utmost liberty to choose whatever form of Constitution seems best suited to your country's requirements and temperament.

It is also my view that the so-called U Thant Plan was only a compromise for securing a settlement, so as to avoid the use of force and to prevent unnecessary bloodshed. Now that Tshombe's intransigence has compelled the UN to resort to the use of force to secure a settlement, I do not consider that you should feel yourself in any way bound to accept this plan. A logical consequence of Tshombe's military defeat is that the Congolese Government should be given a free hand to decide what form of Constitution they will have—a purely internal matter.

If you take this view, my Government will support it in the Security Council and at the United Nations. I realise full well the compromises which are necessary in order to obtain and maintain independence but I would impress upon you the grave dangers of disintegration to which a too flexible federal system exposes a newly developing state. The whole record of the Katanga episode shows that even a limited grant of provincial powers to the present rulers of Katanga carries in itself the seed not merely of a renewed secession of Katanga itself but of the ceaseless provocation of disorders, corruption and covert intervention in the other provinces of the Congo.

Finally, may I express to you my personal good wishes for the future success of your Government and for the speedy solution of the many difficulties with which you have to contend.

At the time of writing to Adoula, Tshombe was reported to be in Ndola, Northern Rhodesia, looking 'tired and dishevelled'. He said he intended returning to Elisabethville, but had gone to Ndola to meet members of his Cabinet. Significantly, about £2,800,000 to £3,500,000 was reported missing from the Katanga National Bank in Elisabethville. Some records and files were also missing. Later, on 9 February, a former RAF officer said that Tshombe had ordered a Belgian pilot to fly out 300 million Katangan francs, then valued at about £2 million, to Angola during the last days of the disintegrating régime. He believed also that an amount between £1,800,000 and £5,400,000 in American dollars was driven to Northern Rhodesia and later flown to banks in Geneva and Brussels. The money flown to Angola was packed in 60 boxes, each holding 5 million francs, and flown in the President's Dakota by Jan van Rissingen, a Belgian who had been operating a parachute school. It was handed over to Portuguese security forces in Angola. There it was apparently converted into gold coin and ingots before being transported by various routes to Switzerland, where it was protected by traditional Swiss banking secrecy.

On 14 January, the day on which an agreement was reported between the Central Government and Union Minière on a division of revenue and tax payments, Tshombe was said to be in Kolwezi, having flown there from Ndola. It was stated that he had declared his willingness to end Katanga's secession and on 16 January he officially informed the Central Government, in a written statement that the secession was at an end. Two days later, UN forces entered Kolwezi without fighting.

Shortly afterwards, Tshombe announced that he was leaving Katanga 'for health reasons'. Gizenga was freed and Joseph Ileo, representing the Central Government, arrived in Elisabethville on 23 January 1963 to take up his post as Minister Resident.

21 Proposals for an All-African Force

In February 1963, Adoula visited Elisabethville and received quite a friendly welcome. He then went on to Brussels to negotiate with Belgian government officials. At the end of his visit he remarked, 'You need us, and we need you.' At about the same time it was announced that the Congo Government was to receive 'aid' from the U.S.A. amounting to £8 million, mainly in the form of agricultural products.

While fully understanding Adoula's difficult position, it seemed to me that he was becoming controlled by the American and Belgian ambassadors, working closely with the UN Secretariat. As far as Belgium was concerned, its purposes would be served in the Congo if it could maintain stooges in charge of the administration throughout the country. America's main interest, on the other hand, was to secure economic domination. Only the Congolese people could bring about any radical change in the situation and this was dependent on their Parliament being allowed to function without undue outside interference.

As a means of helping the Congolese people in their difficult task, the Ghana government decided to keep up the pressure against Tshombe by asking for an early meeting of the Security Council to consider his position under existing UN resolutions. It was Ghana's last year as a member of the Security Council and vital, therefore, that our position there should be used to the full in trying to solve African problems. At the time of making the request, Tshombe was known to be contemplating a return to Elisabethville. He did, in fact, return in the middle of March, having paid the customary visit to Salisbury. At the Rhodesian airport he declared, 'You thought that I had run away—nothing of it. If we shall have to die we shall die together. . . . I have been given a new set of eyes (his spectacles) to see and watch you better.' On his arrival in the Katanga capital he was wildly cheered, while in Katanga villages there were reports of villagers arming themselves for rebellion in support of Tshombe.

In this situation it might have been expected that Ghana's attempt to get the Tshombe question discussed in the Security Council would have been welcomed by the Congo Government. But the contrary was the case. The Congo's Minister of Foreign Affairs, Bomboko, called it 'flagrant interference in the internal affairs of the Republic'. As a result, and in order not to embarrass the Central Congolese Government, we agreed that our approach to the Security Council on the Tshombe issue should be suspended for the time being. In view of later events, when Tshombe's real supporters came out into the open, one may imagine the nature of foreign pressure being exercised on the Central Government in Leopoldville at that time. It was unlikely that Adoula himself, or his colleagues, had suddenly become supporters of Tshombe.

While this confused state of affairs persisted it was not surprising that certain member nations of the UN became increasingly critical of the Organisation's activities. The Soviet Union demanded UN withdrawal from the Congo. As soon as news of the Soviet demand reached me I impressed upon the USSR representative in Ghana the dangers of such a withdrawal at a time when the Central Government was trying to establish its authority throughout the Congo. The Commander-in-Chief of the UN forces in the Congo, Lieutenant General Kebbede Gebre, had warned that civil war might break out if UN forces were withdrawn. As it was, there was already fighting in various parts of the country. Sizeable rebel forces were at large in South Kasai, where there had been almost continuous turmoil for $2\frac{1}{2}$ years; and in Katanga there were reports of many skirmishes between supporters of Tshombe and troops of the Central Government.

On 11 March, I sent this message to Adoula inviting him to Ghana:

Mr A. Y. K. Djin, Member of Parliament, who is well known to you, has brought me a full report of the discussions which you had with him during his recent visit to Leopoldville. Owing to the extreme importance of the matters discussed concerning affairs in the Congo I have decided to send him to you again as leader of a special delegation. Mr Djin and his delegation have been charged by me to bring you a personal invitation to pay a brief private visit to Ghana during which you and I can hold a tête-à-tête on the urgent issues with which you are now confronted in the Congo.

Mr Djin will be assisted in his mission by the Reverend S. A. Dzirasa, Member of Parliament and Deputy Foreign Minister, together with Messrs Bonsu and Ofori Atta. As I have repeatedly pointed out on previous occasions, the Congo is the very heart of Africa. It is because of this that I personally, and indeed all sincere African nationalists, have from the very beginning hailed the Congo Republic and taken the keenest interest in her affairs.

The relationship between the Republic of Ghana and the Republic of the Congo as you know has been a very close one from the very beginning, and it is my ardent wish that we should make this relationship even closer since we in Ghana regard the Congolese as our brothers and sisters.

In view of this I thought it would be a very good thing if Your Excellency and I could have a private meeting. If you are able to accept this invitation I shall be most happy to send a special plane to convey you and your entourage to Ghana. I hope you will be able to indicate soon whether you are able to accept this invitation.

The visit did not take place. However, on receiving news of the formation by Adoula of a new government to include more members of the Lumumbist Party (MNC), steps were taken to appoint an ambassador to the Congo.

It seemed that Adoula had no strong following anywhere. His government did not enjoy either the confidence or the backing of Parliament. Divisions among the Nationalist Front showed members of Parliament divided on essential objectives. The Nationalist Front, forged by Lumumba, consisting of the MNC, the Parti Solidaire Africain (once led by Gizenga, but then under Kamitatu, the Minister of the Interior), the Balubakat under Jason Sendwe of North Katanga and CEREA based in Kivu, lacked a single acclaimed leader. There was even talk that members of the Nationalist Front had been bribed by Tshombe, who had been distributing largesse when he was in Leopoldville. In an appraisal of the Congo situation, Quaison-Sackey, head of our permanent mission to the United Nations, wrote (21 March):

In my opinion, Ghana can play an effective role in the Congo. Our ideas are supported by the young men most of whom I have met both in Leopoldville and at the United Nations. . . . The future of the Congo cannot be predicted, but I cannot see real stability for a number of years to come, so long as every Power seems to be fishing in the troubled waters of that territory. The United States has been trying to sign a secret mutual defence pact with Adoula's Government; the Belgians have returned and are managing to control affairs again; Britain, France and Portugal are doing their bit in Katanga; Greece, Italy, Nationalist China and Japan are all gaining a foothold and very soon too the Soviet Union will endeavour to have a 'share'.

Throughout May, June and July there was increasing unrest in the Congo. At the beginning of June, Tshombe was reported to have fled from Elisabethville to avoid arrest by the Central Government. It was rumoured that a warrant for his arrest had been issued after the capture of papers showing that he planned to announce secession again. This news was followed by accounts of a Congolese army 'shooting spree' in Kolwezi. On 16 June, Tshombe, having arrived in France 'to consult an eye specialist', was detained at Orly airport for a time, and told that he could not remain in France. Ten days later, on 26 June, he was removed as head of the Katanga Provincial Government by a law passed in the Congolese Parliament. In July Adoula visited Britain to ask for aid. During his four-day official visit he was given VIP[1] treatment and succeeded in obtaining a substantial grant for the purchase of equipment, but economic discontent had by then led to a serious situation in Leopoldville. This was symptomatic of widespread disappointment in the country over the unprogressive economic and social programme of Adoula's Government.

At the beginning of August, the Congolese Government ordered the army to carry out manoeuvres in the centre of Leopoldville, in an attempt to prevent rioting. The Government feared an explosion of popular discontent leading to violence. A similar situation had ended Abbe Youlou's régime in Brazzaville ten days before. But the mood of the working population was expressed in the words of Alphonse Kithima, Secretary-General of the Confederation of Free Trade Unions when he threatened to break off all negotiations with the Government unless the orders for manoeuvres were cancelled, 'We cannot and will not negotiate with bayonets in our backs. . . . We are not seeking the overthrow of the Government, but the moment it turns against us we will turn against the Government.'

Following these developments closely, I considered the time had come for further efforts to press for an African solution in the Congo. It had been clearly demonstrated just how hopeless it was for the

[1] Very important person.

Central Government to depend on disinterested help from western powers. The Congolese people themselves would have to find their own solutions but while they needed aid, this aid should come from African countries. I sent a message to Adoula on 19 August:

I have been giving serious consideration to the indications that the Secretary-General of the United Nations may have to withdraw the United Nations troops from the Congo at the end of this year and I am writing to you in all earnestness as a brother to put to you my own views on this question.

I know that you have for some time now been considering various plans for providing suitable arrangements to fill in the vacuum which will be created by the withdrawal, because you are naturally anxious to avoid insecurity and instability in the Congo.

I share your anxiety in this and wish to put a positive proposal to you for your urgent consideration. In order to eliminate the interplay of power politics over the Congo situation, allow its Government more time to achieve complete stability and to retrain the ANC, my proposal is that there should be a small all-African force of a brigade strength or so commanded by a Brigadier, to take over from the United Nations well in advance of its withdrawal from the Congo. You should naturally have the final say in the selection of the troops and their commander. The force would be at the disposal of the Congolese Government for a period to be determined by the contributing African States in consultation with you.

I consider that the Independent African States should be capable of providing this force and financing it amongst themselves, using only such technical assistance as the United Nations may be called upon to contribute. I am sure that if we in Africa undertook this responsibility jointly in aid of a sister African State, we would be setting a healthy example of African self-help, and make unnecessary the use of foreign troops with the attendant dangers with which we are all familiar.

I am informing the United Nations' Secretary-General about my suggestion and will consult the other Heads of State and Government if you agree to this.

The Congolese Prime Minister, however, asked for the support of the Ghana Government for the continuance of UN forces in the Congo until mid-1964. He wanted to see a highly mobile force of 3,000 men maintained. In a note to the Secretary-General, he said that he considered that the time had not yet come to terminate the

UN Military Mission in the Congo. U Thant replied to Adoula on 16 September, regretting that he could not comply with his request to prolong the stationing of UN troops there:

To my great regret, I have no choice but to inform you that as of now I lack the means of granting your request. The explanation of this is that the General Assembly, in its fourth special session last May, adopted a resolution which appropriated funds and authorised me to expend money for the United Nations Force in the Congo only until 31 December 1963. Therefore, any extension of the Force beyond the end of this year will require new action by the General Assembly providing financial support for the Force.

U Thant added that the UN would give serious consideration to Adoula's request, but that an effective UN Force would need to consist of not less than 5,000 to 6,000 officers and men.

On 19 September, I sent a cable to Mr Botsio, our representative in New York:

I would like you and Quaison-Sackey to take immediate steps to discuss with the African Group the plan which I have already put to the Secretary-General and Premier Adoula for an All-African Brigade in the Congo in the event of the UN Military Mission now in the Congo being withdrawn at the end of this year. Quaison-Sackey already has a copy of my letter making this proposal. You should impress upon the African Group that unconfirmed reports indicate that the United States, Belgium and Britain are considering an alternative plan to keep a small mobile UN force of between 2,000 and 3,000 men in the Congo during the first six months of 1964. If this happened, there is no doubt that the western powers would retain undue political influence in the Congo, to the detriment of the sovereignty and independence not only of the Congo but of Africa as a whole. I am sure that if you discuss these proposals with the African representatives they and also the Asian Group would co-operate with you in sponsoring a joint approach to the UN on this most crucial problem. Please report progress on this as soon as possible.

A few days later, on 25 September, I sent a message to Adoula:

I am very grateful for your kind message dated 10th September 1963 in reply to my letter of 19 August 1963.

I have noted your own desire that we should support the plan to keep a United Nations force of 3,000 men in the Congo until about June 1964. I fear, however, that with the present financial position of the United Nations in such a low state, the Secretary-General will be unable to maintain such a force without having to place undue reliance on contributions in men and material mainly from the colonial and other Powers who are member States of the United Nations, and who have a vested interest in our affairs in Africa. If this happens, it will give these foreign Powers an undue say and influence in the affairs of the Congo, in particular, and of Africa in general. I am sure that neither our Congolese brothers nor our compatriots in other parts of Africa would wish to put up with this state of affairs.

It is owing to my anxiety about this and a strong desire to keep away the danger of neo-colonialism from the Congo and Africa, that I have ventured to put forward this proposal to the Independent African States as a way out of the present difficulty.

I do earnestly implore you, therefore, to view this problem in this light, so that a joint effort on the part of the African States may be made to assist the Congo. I consider that it is now time for the African States to offer such assistance jointly rather than leave it to foreign powers and agents. We must admit that the United Nations has done more than enough in present circumstances.

I enclose for Your Excellency's information a copy of the letter I have addressed to the other Heads of Independent African States on this matter.

The following note addressed to Heads of Independent African States was despatched the same day as my letter to Adoula:

A few weeks ago, I wrote to the Prime Minister of Congo, Leopoldville, Mr Cyrille Adoula, and U Thant, Secretary-General of the United Nations, in regard to the intention of the Secretary-General to withdraw the United Nations Forces from the Congo by the end of this year.

I am of the opinion that we in Africa must show great concern about the consequences of the proposal to withdraw the United Nations forces from the Congo before effective arrangements have been made by the Congolese Government to keep the peace.

If the United Nations forces are withdrawn before the Congolese National Forces are in a position to take over completely, there is no doubt that too much strain will be placed on the Government of the Congo in its efforts to maintain law and order in present circumstances.

I feel certain that it is the desire of all of us to ensure that we can be of assistance to one another within the framework of the Addis Adaba spirit. My proposal to the Congolese Government and the Secretary-General of the United Nations was therefore to the effect that the Governments of Africa, with the consent of the Congolese authorities, should be invited to consider the possibility of maintaining at least one brigade in the Congo at the expense of the African States and with such technical assistance from the United Nations as may be deemed necessary.

In view of the fact that the United Nations Secretary-General's intention to withdraw the United Nations forces from the Congo has now been put before the United Nations General Assembly, I am sending you a copy of my message to Premier Adoula and U Thant in the expectation that it will be possible for Your Excellency to authorise your representative in the United Nations to discuss with his colleagues there the question of the African States providing military assistance for the Congo while the Congolese Government is taking steps to retrain and regroup the Congolese National Army.

I hope that Your Excellency will wish to give this proposal your most urgent and sympathetic consideration.

On 2 October, I followed up with a message to Mr Botsio, who was leading the Ghana delegation at the UN:

With reference to our telephone conversation of this morning, you should make it quite clear to U Thant that he would help the cause of the Congolese people and of Africa better if he could give his full moral support to the proposal that an All-African Brigade should take over from the UN after its withdrawal from the Congo. U Thant should also impress upon Adoula and Kasavubu that this is the safest way out of the present difficulty in the Congo. I know that Russia will not contribute to the support of a limited UN force in the Congo. In any case, such a force maintained only by a few UN member states would leave the Congo under the mercy of these states. I must emphasise that the African States are capable of keeping a Brigade in the Congo, with UN technical assistance, until the Congolese National army is ready to take over from an all-African army. Indeed, Ghana and Algeria alone should be able to undertake this responsibility and thus eliminate the risk of interference in Congolese affairs by interested foreign Powers. You should also insist that this question is particularly an African problem and not one for the Congolese people alone because none of us can escape the consequences of a strongly-entrenched neo-colonialist force in the Congo. I am sending a copy of this message to Premier Ben Bella of Algeria for his information and a copy to Premier Adoula.

When I sent this message, anarchy was spreading in the Congo and the Congolese Parliament had been sent into recess by Kasavubu while a new constitution was being worked out. Adoula decided to go to New York himself to support the Congo's application for membership of the World Bank, and to ask the UN to maintain its force in the Congo after 31 December 1963.

After prolonged discussions in the UN it was finally agreed that a limited UN Force should stay in the Congo for an extra six months. The news was received in Leopoldville on 15 October without any enthusiasm or interest. The tasks of the UN were stipulated to be to retrain the Congolese Army; to remove the threat of Katangese gendarmes who had been roaming the South Katangan bush with modern weapons for over a year; to guarantee the Congo's borders and to help Adoula's Government to keep law and order internally. The diminished UN Force of some 5,000 men was to be maintained by fixed contributions from member States which had so far made financial allocations for the upkeep of the UN forces in the Congo.

On hearing of this arrangement I sent an immediate message to Botsio informing him of a telegram sent to the Secretary-General in which I said that the Ghana Government had decided to bear the full cost of its contingent which might be required to serve under the UN in the Congo after the withdrawal. In these circumstances the Government did not propose to make any direct contribution towards the upkeep of the diminished UN forces. Botsio was asked to point out to the Secretary-General that although the arrangement to retain a diminished UN force in the Congo until the end of June 1964 had been adopted, it would in my view be necessary still for the African States to organise themselves so that they could provide an All-African contingent for assisting the Congolese Government to keep law and order, if this became necessary after the final withdrawal of UN forces in June 1964, 'It is imperative to look forward so far in advance in view of our experience of the Congo situation. You should therefore do everything possible to secure the agreement of the African Group and U Thant to this proposal.'

On his return to Leopoldville, Adoula faced growing trouble. A number of grievances had accumulated. For example, Primary school teachers had been on strike for six weeks because some £6 million due to them since independence had gone astray either at central or provincial government level. There were frequent charges being made of corruption and incompetence against various government officials. The situation became so serious that Kasavubu declared a state of emergency in the Leopoldville area on 20 October and announced the establishment of an emergency committee to deal with 'trouble makers and threats against established institutions'. The latter was the answer to the Trade Union ultimatum giving the Prime Minister a short time in which to set up a 'Government of National Safety'. The three main Trade Union leaders, Alphonse Kithima, Remy Siwa and Andre Boliko, were arrested for leading a strike of teachers and civil servants in the capital, thereby 'endangering the security of the state'.

On the advice of experts of the International Monetary Fund, the Congo devalued the franc. It was the first step in a two stage devaluation designed to halt inflation and to get the Congolese economy on its feet. At the same time, the Congolese Government announced a 25% increase in minimum wage rates, tighter fiscal control and public works projects costing between 5,000 million and 6,000 million francs to provide work for the unemployed.

But while measures were being devised to improve social and economic conditions, rumours began to circulate of troop movements in an area of Angola some 20 miles west of Dilolo, near the Congolese border. The troops were reported to be led by white mercenaries. Adoula had written to me during his visit to New York, expressing concern about developments in Angola and I had replied on 23 October:

> I thank you for your letter of 14 October 1963, which you sent me during your visit to the United Nations General Assembly concerning the reported plans of the Portuguese colonialists in the Congo.
>
> I agree with you that, in the spirit of our Addis Ababa declarations, we should present a united front to any threat that may be directed against the sovereignty and integrity of any part of our continent. I am therefore happy to assure you that, with this understanding, the Government and people of Ghana shall stand firmly behind the Congo, as we have always done, in the interests of the safety and security of Africa as a whole.

It was several months before the UN took serious note of the build up of mercenary forces, though there were persistent reports of the training in Angola of former Katangese gendarmes. In his Report of 16 March 1964 to the Security Council, the Secretary-General stated that he had received reliable reports that some 400 former members of the Katanga gendarmerie, who were employed by mining companies in the Kolwezi and Jadotville areas of the Congo had left their jobs and gone to Angola. The men were asserted to be acting in response to a mobilisation order, and were said to be directed in their movements by two persons known to have been active as mercenaries during the period of Katanga's attempted secession. U Thant's Report continued:

A later report put the estimated number of the former Katangese gendarmes who had left the Kolwezi and Jadotville areas at some 600. The same report also stated that according to information received from trustworthy sources, there were at the beginning of March of this year, about 1,800 former Katangese gendarmes receiving training in Angola around Teixeira da Souza; that with the gendarmes in Angola were about 20 mercenaries and that more mercenaries had been recently recruited in Europe on behalf of Mr. Moise Tshombe and instructed to proceed to Vila Luso, where a mercenary camp had already been set up.

The foregoing information seems to bear out reports received earlier concerning the activities in Angola of ex-Katangese gendarmes commanded by mercenaries. Certain documents on this subject, submitted to the Fourth Committee at its 1493rd meeting on 27 November 1963, by Mr Holden Roberto, were circulated by decision of the Committee to the Members of the General Assembly (A/C.4/625 and Add 1). Those documents in sections II and III indicated that, in January of last year, 130 mercenaries and 200 Katangese gendarmes had left Kolwezi for Dilolo whence they subsequently crossed into Angola. One hundred of the mercenaries were then repatriated, leaving 30 in Angola, together with the 200 ex-gendarmes. It was also indicated that these men in Angola had been organised into military units and were engaged in military training and related activities. They were said to remain under the command of Mr Tshombe and his emissaries.

In view of this report and the new threat to the peace of the Congo which was implied in it, a note was sent by the Secretary-General to the Permanent Representative of Portugal at the UN, asking for information. The Portuguese Chargé d'Affaires replied on 13 March 1964 that 'the Portuguese Government has studied with attention the letter under reference and, having carried out the necessary investigations, can categorically affirm that the rumours which Your Excellency mentions are devoid of foundation'.

Just how insincere was Portugal's reply became all too apparent later. But to return to the closing weeks of 1963: on 1 December, Auguste Mabika-Kalanda, Congolese Foreign Minister, was arrested in Leopoldville for plotting against the security of the state, his arrest being rumoured to have some connection with the issue of a diplomatic passport to Tshombe, then in Madrid. A week later, came news of the release of the Trade Union leaders, Boliko, Kithima, Siwa and Booka. Adoula's Government was clearly trying to rally support for the grim struggle which lay ahead.

In a supreme effort to win the support of the Secretary-General for the replacement of the military forces of the UN by an All-African Force, I sent the following letter on 16 December 1963, which I quote in full:

Is there any need to stress to you what independence of the Congo must mean to every African leader who regards the freedom and prosperity of the whole African continent as indivisible? But even for those who think in national, sectional or regional terms, any form of foreign control over the Congo Republic constitutes an immediate and substantial threat to their own independence.

Geographically, strategically and politically, the Congo is the most vital region of Africa. Military control of the Congo by any foreign power would give it easy access to most of the continent South of the Sahara.

Geographically, it owes its importance not only to its central position, but to its vast area and tremendous resources. Although these resources have hardly been tapped, they have already enriched foreign interests to a degree which has made them adamant to continue with the exploitation of the Congo's wealth, and has aroused the cupidity of others to share in this exploitation.

The strategic importance of the Congo derives from its geographical features. Foreign Powers which have concerned themselves with what they like to call 'the defence of Africa'—by which they mean the defence, on the African continent, of interests which are mainly contrary to those of the African people—clearly regard the Congo as the key to the military control of Africa. This is the significance of the aid which Belgium received from her allies to build great military bases at Kitona in the West and Kamina in the East of the Congo. This is the reason why there are eight international airports, thirty principal and over a hundred secondary and local airports in the Congo.

The Congo represents 'strategic space' to Western military and civilian experts when considering the likelihood of a war with their enemies from bases in Africa. The size and pivotal position of the Congo furnish the greatest military advantages, either for the purpose of attack or defence when fighting in Africa. In the geographical theories of men like Mackinder and Haushofer, the Congo is the area from which the domination of Africa can be ensured, and this assumption is shared by leading political scientists who do not necessarily agree with all the geo-political theories. There is a consensus of opinion among western strategists that the Congo must be in hands friendly to the West. This can mean nothing else in the final analysis, but that the West must have control over the Government of the Congo. If the Soviet Union had made such a claim over the Congo, we would be justified in accusing it of seeking to drag the Congo into the defence system of the Eastern Bloc. We do not want to bring the Cold War into Africa. The Congo should be independent and neutral—it should be absolutely free and sovereign, and should not be controlled by either the East or the West.

In fact this is precisely what the West has prevented in the Congo. The Central Government is constrained to believe that its interests coincide with western interests. The future is not even left in such uncertain hands. The future is ensured by seeing to it that the Congolese Army, although theoretically under the Central Government, is in fact managed principally by two Western Powers through the so-called 'Binza Group'.

For military planners and economic exploiters alike, the fact that a Government subservient to foreign Powers can only perpetuate the present misery, stagnation and disorder of the people of the Congo, while reserving greater horror for them in the event of war, is unfortunately a matter of indifference.

The political importance of the Congo is, of course, closely related to its strategic and economic importance. This combined importance must attract military intervention, as well as all the subtler forms practised in all Independent African States where foreign interests seek to retain their former colonial privileges.

The Congo is not only politically important because of its vast resources and strategic space in the event of a global or continental war, but because it is the buffer state between independent Africa in the North, and the territories of colonialism and white supremacy in the South. Northwards stands free Africa determined on a free continent: Southwards, Angola begins and stretches to the stronghold of colonial and racial oppression, the Republic of South Africa.

It will require not only the most pervasive system of foreign intrigue, but direct intervention to prevent the Congolese people from coming to the aid of their brothers in Angola fighting for freedom. They have made and continue to make heavy sacrifices towards this end.

It will require not only a Congo vitiated and corrupted by neo-colonialism, but a hostile Congolese Government openly siding with colonialism and white supremacy, to prevent independent Africa from using the Congo as a corridor and a base for all possible aid to the peoples of Angola and Southern Africa fighting for their liberation.

Thus, the degree of the Congo's independence will substantially determine the ultimate fate of the whole Continent of Africa. Free Africa will never abandon its struggle to end colonialism and to expel white supremacy from the whole continent. An independent Congo will be unreservedly on Africa's side in that struggle, whilst Congo with a Government controlled by imperialism and neo-colonialism, because of its geographical position, will be assisting Portuguese colonialism and South African apartheid even by playing a neutral or semi-passive role.

The South African Republic, Portugal and the settler régime of Southern Rhodesia are well aware of the Congo's strategic and political importance. This accounted for their open and constant support for the Tshombe secessionist régime in Katanga, even at the risk of colliding with the forces of the United Nations. The colonialist alliance, for the same reasons, cannot cease from intervening in the Congo's affairs now, from undermining the Congo's stability and from urging their friends in the West to maintain control over the Congo's Government. Secession, disruption and neo-colonialist control in the Congo are considered essential political aims by the colonial territories in Southern Africa.

These reasons amply suffice to show why, and in what sense, certain powers have involved themselves in the political life of the Congo. Sections of the Press in some of these countries have even had the effrontery to rebuke us, leaders of Independent African States, for our efforts to sustain the independence of the Congo.

Thus, when I wrote letters of advice to Patrice Lumumba, the Press raised the cry that this constituted interference in the internal affairs of the Congo; but when the tools and thugs of the Union Minière murdered the same Patrice Lumumba, no one in these quarters referred to that as interference in the internal affairs of the Congo. One newspaper, with a very large circulation in the city of New York, could find no other comment than the words, 'Another Red gone to hell'. For, of course, all this conspiracy against the Congo is carried on under the banner of anti-Communism. Lumumba was not killed because he was thought to be a Communist, but because he was a nationalist leader threatening the monopolies of the Union Minière. It was for that reason that all who wished to keep the Congo weak, subservient and divided became his enemies; and for that reason that, even today, those in the Congo who sincerely hold to his principles and convictions are persecuted and imprisoned.

We are now approaching another turning point in the history of the Congo. The United Nations forces, sooner or later, will have to withdraw. The question is, what will follow that withdrawal? Will there be, at the behest of outside influence, a military coup, with General Mobutu, or someone in a similar position, taking over power, and perhaps with the return of Moise Tshombe, the puppet of the Union Minière, to a position of influence? There are indications that preparations are being made for such an outcome, which would turn the Congo back into a colony in all but name. What is the significance, for example, of the retraining programme which has been announced for the Congolese Army? This programme is placed in the hands of a group of NATO countries and their allies. At present, Congolese paratroopers are being trained by Israeli Air Force personnel and the ground Forces by some hundred Belgian Army officers. This is a very strange programme indeed for a non-aligned country, and the Congo, from the formation of the Adoula Government in July 1961, has declared itself to be a non-aligned country. M. Adoula and M. Gizenga, indeed, attended together the Conference of the non-aligned countries at Belgrade. M. Gizenga is now in captivity and M. Adoula has allowed NATO to take over the training of his Army. I cannot believe M. Adoula would have committed himself to such course, in clear contradiction with his declared policy of non-alignment, were he a free agent. The sad fact is that in Leopoldville now, as at all times since the betrayal and murder of Patrice Lumumba, the dominant interests are those of a group of Western Powers. We have sympathy for M. Adoula in this very difficult situation, but can we consider him to be speaking for the Congolese people while he remains politically and militarily dependent on outside powers?

Even when M. Adoula makes a token assertion of independence by allowing the AGIP Oil Company to operate in the Congo in competition with the existing American and Belgian Companies, his position as Prime Minister is openly threatened.

The fact is that nothing and nobody can help the Congolese people to free themselves unless the African nations come to their help in unity and in accordance with the spirit of Addis Ababa. The African nations must insist that the United Nations force in the Congo shall be an All-African one, under African Command; that it should be this force, and not NATO, which should be in charge of the retraining programme for the Congolese Army, and that this programme should include the stamping out of bribery and corruption and the removal of officers who are working as agents for foreign powers.

In order that the Congolese people and their representatives shall be able to express their wishes freely, the first step necessary is the reorganisation of the Army, placing it on such a footing that it can no longer be used as a tool of foreign interests or employed for the terrorising, imprisoning and murder of patriots. The NATO retraining programme will not secure these ends: indeed, it will secure precisely the opposite of these ends because officers who are 'pro-NATO'—that is to say, who are prepared to serve foreign countries rather than their own—will be placed in key positions. This will perpetuate all the evils which have afflicted the Congo. The only thing, therefore, which can save the Congo is the kind of programme I have described. Technically, such a programme is perfectly possible. The obstacles in the way are not technical but political, arising from the conception which certain western powers have of their interests in the Congo; a conception which, I believe, must in the long run end in disaster.

I must urge you, Mr Secretary-General, to use your great office, for the sake of the African people and in the interests of world peace, to set in motion consultative machinery for replacing the military forces of the United Nations by an All-African Force under the provisions of the Addis Ababa Charter, as soon as the period of the present mandate of the United Nations expires.

22 The Return of Tshombe

DURING the first few months of 1964, Adoula's government made unsuccessful efforts to consolidate its position in the face of growing dangers both from within the Congo and from outside. To those of us who were most closely concerned with the situation, it appeared as if it was only a question of time before his government fell.

Within the Congo, guerrilla bands consisting mainly of youths between the ages of 13 and 18 (the *Jeunesse*), led by Pierre Mulele, increased their hold on the richest and most thickly populated parts of the Congo in Kwilu Province, some 350 miles east of Leopoldville. Mulele was then an almost legendary figure. It was said that he possessed magical powers and could inspire the Jeunesse to carry out the most daring military feats. On 7 February, the Congolese Chief of Staff, Lieutenant Colonel Eugene Ebaya, was reported killed in action in Kwilu Province. This news so shocked Mobutu that he went himself to the fighting area to assess the situation and estimated there were some 15,000 young warriors operating against the Central Government in small, mobile battalions.

Across the Congo River, in Brazzaville, another equally dangerous situation faced Adoula. For it was there that his political opponents had their base. These opponents were members of the Lumumba Nationalist Parties, namely the MNC/Lumumba, the PSA/Gizenga, the African Democratic Union (UDA) and the Convention People's Party (PNCP) who, in November 1963, had formed a co-ordinating Committee called the Comité National de Libération (CNL), under the leadership of Christophe Gbenye. Adoula regarded the move as constituting a government in exile and made it known that he regarded any intercourse with the opposition leaders in Brazzaville as a most unfriendly act.

Gbenye did, in fact, write to me shortly after the formation of the

CNL asking if I would receive a delegation to explain in detail the aims of the organisation and this led to various accusations being made by Central Government supporters of Ghanaian help for the Gbenye group.

A strong international surveillance backed by western intelligence was placed on Gbenye and his colleagues, to find out their supporters and their plans. As a result, two Russian diplomats were arrested on 19 November 1963 and documents connected with the CNL were found on them. It was expected that the Leopoldville Government would issue a strong statement against the Brazzaville Government for harbouring the so-called government in exile, though Brazzaville had only provided political asylum to Gbenye and his group and had not given any form of recognition or aid to them.

Ghana was not the only country thought by some to be assisting the Gbenye liberation movement at that time. Mali and the UAR were also suspected, and Adoula's government considered closing our embassies in Leopoldville. On 23 November, our representative in the Congo was instructed to deny Ghanaian support for the CNL and to protest against a hostile reference to Ghana, Mali and the UAR which appeared in the 269th edition of the daily paper *Le Progrès* of 22 November 1963. In this article, entitled '*Boris Vovonine Left Yesterday*', the writer described the departure of the two Soviet Embassy officials banished from Leopoldville for their connections with opposition members in Brazzaville, and ended, 'We know that certain African countries are courting the Committee of Liberation of Mr Gbenye. The Government is attentively studying the files so that it might send their representatives away to their respective countries. We have in mind Mali, Ghana and the United Arab Republic, only to mention a few.'

Our representative, in a *Note Verbale* delivered to the Leopoldville government on 23 November, considered the article tendentious and liable to damage the good relations which had always existed between the Republic of Ghana and the Republic of Congo (Leopoldville), since the formation of the Central Government presided over by Adoula. The *Note* continued:

Those who inspired the said article being avowed enemies of African unity want to sow seeds of confusion in the minds of those readers of *Le Progrès* who are not in a position to appraise the article. Thus they want to set the Congolese people against certain African countries. Their aim in doing so is to isolate the Congo by setting it against the rest of Africa.

9

The Embassy is convinced that the Congolese Government, aware of the gravity of this manoeuvre having for its objective the destruction of the unity created among African countries in Addis Ababa, are taking steps to thwart this move. The Embassy of Ghana hereby solemnly affirms that its Government is firmly determined to abide at all costs by the principles of Addis Ababa to which it freely and willingly subscribed. The foreign policy of the Republic of Ghana based as it is on non-interference in the internal affairs of other states, its diplomatic representatives in the Congo cannot take any action which is likely to be prejudicial to this principle. The Embassy is sure that the Congolese Government will not allow ignorant people who do not weigh the possible consequences of their actions, to play into the hands of our common enemy whose sole aim is to destroy African unity. Consequently, the Embassy of Ghana is suggesting to the Congolese Government measures which will put an end to the fresh campaign launched in *Le Progrès* against certain African countries. Better still, the Congolese authorities should make an official and public declaration denouncing the disloyal inspirators of this manoeuvre aimed at dislocating the Organisation of African Unity.

In addition to the worsening military situation within the Congo and the threat to Adoula's government from opposition leaders in Brazzaville, there was the constant danger of a return of Tshombe. Headlines such as 'Tshombe forms army in Angola', and 'Tshombe to stage a come-back?' appeared in the world press. It was common knowledge, particularly since U Thant's report of 4 March on the subject of the training of Tshombe's soldiers in Angola, that Tshombe was building up his forces probably with a view to returning when the UN troops were withdrawn at the end of June.

On 21 March, I sent the following note to Adoula:

News reaching me from very reliable sources indicates that a reconcentration of the Katanga Army is being undertaken and that Moise Tshombe will try to return to the scene after United Nations' troops are withdrawn at the end of June this year. This report has only recently been confirmed by Dr Ralph Bunche, Under-Secretary for Political Affairs in the United Nations Secretariat.

I have again and again urged you, Mr Prime Minister, and President Kasavubu to take early steps for the UN troops to be replaced by an All-African Force under the provisions of the Addis Ababa Charter. As recently as the end of last year, I addressed the Secretary-General of the United Nations in the same vein, asking him to use his great office for the sake of the African people and in the interest of world peace to set in motion consultative machinery for replacing the UN force by an All-African Force. Unfortunately, through the machinations of foreign powers and vested interests, my advice has gone unheeded.

I appreciate the difficulties with which you are confronted in your efforts to safeguard the integrity and sovereignty of the Congo with an Army—the Congolese National Army—which is known to be managed principally by two Western Powers through the so-called 'Binza Group'. I am confident, however, that with careful handling of the situation and especially with the sympathetic understanding of the African States, a move by your Government calling upon the OAU to assist, would immediately receive not only the combined support and strength of all progressive forces in Africa, but would promptly scare off those powers who are determined to bring chaos into the Congo. In this way the enemies of the Congo will fail to make it their centre of operations with Moise Tshombe as their agent. Nor can they wreck the African revolution or dismember the Congo and render it impotent.

I do not need to stress that geographically, strategically and politically, the Congo is the most vital region of Africa. Military control of the Congo by any foreign power would give it easy access to most of the continent south of the Sahara. The Congo is not only politically important because of its vast resources and strategic position in the event of a global or continental war, but because it is the buffer State between Independent Africa in the north, and the territories of colonialism and white supremacy and domination in the south. The South African Republic, Portugal and the settler regime of Southern Rhodesia are all aware of the Congo's strategic and political importance. This is the reason for their open and constant support for Moise Tshombe's secessionist manoeuvres in Katanga, even at the risk of colliding with the forces of the United Nations.

In my letter of 23 December 1963 to the Secretary-General of the United Nations, I asked the question: What would follow the withdrawal of the UN Forces? Would there be at the behest of outside influences a military coup with Mobutu or someone in a similar position taking over power and perhaps with the return of Moise Tshombe, puppet of the Union Miniere, to a position of influence? I then stated that there were indications that preparations were being made for such an outcome which would turn the Congo back into a colony.

We have delayed too long. Whilst we wait and give reasons for inaction, Moise Tshombe is acting. There are unconfirmed reports that he has recently been running between Angola and South Africa, plotting against you and your Government. We have less than three months before the UN Forces depart. In the name, therefore, of the Congolese people, in the interest of world peace and of the African revolution, I urge you as a loyal compatriot, to take immediate steps through the machinery of the OAU for an All-African Force to be formed NOW to replace the UN Force.

Because of the pressing nature of this problem, and because the future of the Congo affects the very independence of all independent African States, I am copying this letter to all Heads of State and Governments of the OAU for their urgent consideration.

At the beginning of April, Tshombe visited London to address a meeting of the Royal Institute of International Affairs (Chatham House). He was given VIP treatment by the British Government and although he claimed that his visit was 'entirely private' it was obvious that he intended to make contact with the Katanga lobby in Parliament to sound out the possibility of support for his return to the Congo when UN forces pulled out at the end of June. In his address to Chatham House, he called for a new provisional government in the Congo in which he and other exiled politicians would become reconciled with Adoula. He denounced the existing rule in the Congo as 'the law of the jungle' and called for a revival of the U Thant plan for federation.

Shortly after Tshombe's visit to London ended, Mobutu arrived in Britain to ask for military aid. The agreement by UN members that all military aid to the Congo should be channelled through the UN was then virtually a dead letter. It was being ignored by the Americans, by the Belgians who were training staff officers, the Italians, who were providing air training and by the Israelis who were instructing pilots. Mobutu spoke in London of the danger facing his government from pro-Tshombe guerrilla forces in Portuguese Angola. He estimated their numbers at between 3,000 and 5,000 men.

Yet in spite of this growing threat to his administration, Adoula insisted that his government was capable of managing its own affairs on the withdrawal of UN troops. In reply to my note of 21 March he sent the following letter (17 April 1964):

(*Translation*)

Your anxiety about Moise Tshombe's fresh efforts to start further trouble in Katanga is justified. The Portuguese authorities in

Angola are not hesitating to capitalise on his indignation in order to divert us from our rightful duty to our brothers in Angola.

We know that the Portuguese authorities are at present providing accommodation at Villa Luso and Teixeira da Souza for some of the men of the former Katangese gendarmerie as well as European mercenaries still in the pay of the ex-President of Katanga.

It is quite unnecessary of course to say that these measures can have no effect upon us, because our determination to preserve our territorial integrity is matched by our will to discharge our responsibilities towards our brothers who are engaged in an out-and-out struggle for independence.

We are fully conscious of the role we are called upon to play in Africa's liberation struggle in view of our geographical position. We are equally conscious of the strategic as well as the potential role of our country and the part it must bear in the maintenance of peace in Africa and the world. It is this pre-occupation, coupled with our determination to free ourselves from any circumstance that may vitiate our sovereignty, that inspired us in the recovery of the bases at Kamina and Kitona. We are happy and proud that the only remaining bases at present on our soil are those serving the cause of African liberation.

Although we intend to carry out a policy of non-alignment and friendship with all the nations of the world which respect us, we also mean to remain the sole masters of our destiny and take decisions affecting our country in all freedom of conscience and independence of action.

That is why we consider the departure of the United Nations troops as a normal step in the course of things. It is indeed quite inconceivable (and there has never been any question in this respect), that troops should be indefinitely stationed on our soil. We are in fact pleased to be able to pay high tribute to the Secretary-General of the United Nations who has never lost sight of this reality.

We have made a very close and detailed study of all the consequences attendant upon the completion of the task of the United Nations troops in the Congo. Our conclusion is that it is undesirable, in the present circumstances, to have them replaced by other forces, even though these forces are African. This could only have the effect of postponing the day when the Congolese themselves should take their own affairs into their own hands, and would run counter to our determination to assume our own responsibilities ourselves.

The Congolese people who have been steeled through three years of painful experience, but none the less full of useful lessons, will know how to frustrate attempts to parcel up or fragment her territory, or set up any kind of hegemony on its soil. They also know that they can count on our army which takes orders from us and us alone, in defending the territorial integrity of the Congo and facing any possible aggression, from any source whatever. The Government which I have headed for the past three years, and which has never shrunk from claiming its responsibilities, still intends to place confidence in our people and army, and will always do so.

It is from that confidence that we drew strength and upon it that we rely to consolidate our national unity. Such is our policy and such our intentions and we have full faith in the future of our country and our continent. We are equally convinced that if any danger were to threaten our country from outside, all our African brothers who are associated with us by so many friendly ties and the Charter of Addis Ababa, will not hesitate to come to our assistance, as they would to any other African State.

We know that Ghana will be among the first of such States to help, and this is no mere polite form of words, it is our firmly held conviction. We have in fact had an opportunity of appreciating through your correspondence with M. Tshombe, the steadfast firmness with which you opposed secession. This was not in the least surprising to us, because it is an attitude that squares with the struggle and unremitting fight you have waged for the African cause.

We should like you to know that we are extremely appreciative of this, and recall with deep feeling and gratitude the sacrifices made by the sons of Ghana on Congolese soil. I have no doubt that this attitude and those sacrifices are the best bond of friendship between our two peoples.

I am sending a copy of this letter to all the Heads of State and Government in Africa, so that they may know the position of the Congolese Government as regards your suggestions.

Finally, I should like to ask you, Mr. President and Dear Brother, to accept the expression of my very high esteem.

Adoula's confidence in his government's ability to maintain order in the Congo seemed misplaced in view of the almost daily reports of fighting and sabotage. On 18 May, two companies of the ANC were reported to be surrounded by about 400 'terrorists' at Kikwit in the Province of Kwilu. Three days later, saboteurs, believed to come from

Brazzaville, blacked out half of Leopoldville by blowing up key electric power cables. Their plastic bomb attack was the fourth in ten days. It was said that the Congolese Government was considering asking the UN for military aid in fighting the Jeunesse revolt in Kivu Province, but that such aid was unlikely to be granted.

At the end of May, the revolts in the Congo spread. The nationalists took Albertville. Apparently ANC troops in North Katanga were reluctant to engage the enemy. According to officials in Leopoldville, the nationalists were led by Justin Soumialot, operating from Burundi, and he was thought to have at his command about 3,000 to 7,000 men. In fact, it was more likely that all the nationalists were in sympathy with the National Liberation Committee based in Brazzaville, who were determined to liberate the Congo from neo-colonialists and their Congolese helpers, notably the pro-western Prime Minister, Cyrille Adoula.

The 'rebel' government at Albertville was short-lived. But on the first of June, pygmies, using modern weapons, were reported to have routed two companies of ANC commandos. So it went on, and the ding-dong battle for power in the Congo seemed no nearer solution. Yet the UN went ahead with its plans to withdraw its forces, and Adoula stubbornly refused to ask for an All-African Force to replace them.

Then came the expected news that Tshombe was on the move again. The kind of chaos existing in the Congo was just the kind of situation he needed in order to slip back into power. On 8 June he was reported in Paris. Four days later he was in Mali, on the first leg of an African tour prior to his return to the Congo. I received a note from President Modibo Keita of Mali dated 17 June, in which he told me of Tshombe's visit:

(*Translation*)

I have the honour to inform you that I have had a visit from Moise Tshombe from the 10th to the 12th of this month. He asked to come and I thought I should agree to meet him in the interest of Africa and having regard to the particular importance of the Congo in the struggle for African liberty and dignity and the special role which this country now plays in the fight to free Angola and Central Africa from colonialism and to eliminate apartheid in South Africa.

I think that to fulfil these obligations Congo must find national unity by the goodwill and effort of all her sons. The Republic of Mali attaches overwhelming importance to achieving the liberation of Africa and asserting African dignity. Mali has therefore decided to look favourably on all proposals which could help towards these objectives. Within this framework and to this sole end Mali has accepted Tshombe's visit and will ultimately receive other leading personalities from Congo.

I replied at once:

I have the honour to acknowledge receipt of your letter dated 17 June in which you informed me about your meeting with Tshombe.

I must confess that I was somewhat disturbed and surprised at the news which reached me from Press sources about Tshombe's visit to Mali before your official confirmation of this event arrived. You will perhaps have heard that Tshombe made similar overtures to meet me in regard to the situation in the Congo, but that I refused as a matter of principle to receive him. How could I in the name of Africa hold discussions with a man who not only betrayed his country but a great number of his own compatriots including our late beloved Lumumba, whose spirit of defiance and love for Africa sustained him in the fight against colonialism and imperialism in the Congo.

Your letter under reference gave no indication as to the nature or results of the discussions that took place between you and Tshombe. Tshombe no doubt may wish to go back to the Congo, but whether he will do so or not, the Congolese people themselves will ultimately decide. We who are concerned with the fate of the Congo must do our best to ensure that the territorial integrity of the Congo including Katanga is not undermined, and any reconciliation achieved must reflect the progressive will of the people of the Congo.

But the people of the Congo were getting little chance to decide their own future. Foreign influence was increasing all the time, and in an effort to prevent the Congolese government from applying to the OAU for help, approaches were made to certain 'reliable' African States to sent troops if necessary, the U.S. secretly agreeing to pay all costs. At least twelve U.S. rocket-firing planes, piloted by Americans and a mercenary group of Cuban exiles, were known to be operating in the Congo. Villages in Kivu were bombed. Yet the U.S. State Department strenuously denied taking any part in action against the freedom fighters.

With no UN troops left in any part of Katanga, and with only a Nigerian battalion of 900 men in Leopoldville, there were reports of tension all over the Republic. Of 23 provinces, only eleven were reported quiet. In Albertville, a new Mulelist government exercised control.

During the last days of June 1964, Tshombe, who had returned to Madrid, left the Spanish capital to begin a triumphant journey back to the Congo. On 24 June, men and women cheered and sang in the streets of Elisabethville when they heard that Tshombe was on his way back, and that he was returning at the invitation of the Central Government.

Tshombe arrived in Leopoldville on 26 June, where he was expected to join the government and perhaps become prime minister. His return demonstrated the desperation of the Leopoldville government, for it was well known that President Kasavubu distrusted him and that Adoula disliked him. Symbolically, within 24 hours of Tshombe's return, his bitterest enemy, Jason Sendwe, Provincial President of North Katanga was assassinated, together with two other leaders in Albertville. As a correspondent in the London *Financial Times* observed (29 June), ' In many ways it's just like the old days; even the foreign mercenaries are ready and willing to fly in at a moment's notice (and a price). . . .'

Adoula's government, having finished its term of office at midnight on 30 June, resigned, and within four days Tshombe was presenting a list of ministers to Kasavubu, to form a transitional government. On 10 July, Tshombe was sworn in as Prime Minister of the Congo and he received a rousing welcome when he toured Leopoldville. In an attempt to reconcile all the dissident elements in the Congo he included in his Cabinet Albert Kalondji, former head of the South Kasai secessionist movement, who returned from Europe to become Minister of Agriculture. André Lubaya, a member of the CNL, also obtained a Cabinet post; and Antoine Gizenga was released from prison where he had been for two and a half years. Godefroid Munongo became Minister of the Interior, while Tshombe himself, as Prime Minister, took over the three important ministries of External Affairs, Information and External Commerce.

To say that Tshombe's premiership came as a surprise and a shock to many people is an understatement. Most of Africa's leaders were horrified. They were at the time in Cairo attending a summit meeting of the OAU and refused to allow him to join the conference. Some of them forecast that Tshombe's government could not possibly last more than a few months. Fighting had broken out in the Stanleyville area, and there was a general increase in military activity against the central government.

But, as often in the past, observers of the Congo scene underestimated the extent of western support for Tshombe. As always, the underlying motives for this support were economic in nature. Since the war, the U.S.A. had bought practically all the uranium in the Congo. By 1964, U.S. capital had launched into the petroleum business. Four oil companies—Société Congolaise des Pétroles Shell (Anglo-Dutch), Petrocongo (Belgian), Mobil Oil Congo and Texaco Africa Limited (both U.S.)—had associated with the giant international oil cartels to form a new company, the Société Congolaise de Raffinge, its purpose being to negotiate with the Congolese Government for the construction of the country's first refinery.

These interests, and others like them, were the powerful indirect guarantees of Tshombe's continuance in office, so long as he 'delivered the goods' in the form of establishing conditions favourable to them. But, as subsequent events proved, a puppet regime bolstered by foreign interests was no match for the unconquerable fighters for freedom who continued to operate throughout the Congo during the whole of Tshombe's premiership.

23 Foreign Military Intervention

THE Tshombe-Munongo government was regarded by large numbers of Congolese as an illegal government, since it was formed in violation of resolutions passed during the Round Table Conference held in Brussels in February 1960 and did not follow the Loi Fondamentale. The latter provided, in Article 69, that the Houses of Parliament would meet by right on the first Mondays of the months of March and September, and that they should remain in session at least 40 days each year. Article 70 stipulated that 'The adjournment of the Houses during session pronounced by the Head of State, cannot exceed the period of one month, neither can it be renewed during the same session, without the prior approval of both Houses.' Yet in September 1963, when Adoula's government was in difficulties, President Kasavubu sent members of Parliament and senators away 'on holiday', and ordered a military guard to be put on the Parliament buildings to prevent the representatives of the Congolese people from meeting there. Kasavubu then transferred the work of Parliament to a group of men chosen by him. This assembly drafted the Presidential 'constitution' on which he based his rule.

In order to seek endorsement of this 'constitution' a referendum was held, but it was of doubtful value since no campaign against the government was allowed and the principal Lumumbists were either in exile or in jail. Apparently there were no electoral lists and certain people voted as many as ten times. A reporter in Katanga wrote:

This is how the notorious referendum was conducted in Eastern Katanga. Contrary to the principles of a true referendum, the population of Elisabethville had no freedom to vote. The population was forced to say 'Yes' . . . It had been forbidden in the first place to conduct any form of campaign against the constitutional project under pain of running serious risks going as far as imprisonment. This has been announced officially on the inter-provincial radio by Mr Kapwasa Antoine, President of the Regional Referendum Committee.

The writer went on to report that he was given, at the polling station, a paper marked 'Yes', which he was forced to put into a box; and another ballot paper marked 'No', which he was told to tear up. All this took place in the presence of soldiers and armed policemen. Not surprisingly, it was eventually declared that the 'constitution' had been approved by some two million 'Yes' votes.

It was by using the Presidential powers conferred on him by this 'constitution' that Kasavubu nominated Tshombe as Prime Minister in July 1964 and approved the ministerial team selected by him. The new government was not approved by the Congolese Parliament, nor, it seems, was it formed as a result of the freely expressed wishes of the Congolese people. With such an unpromising background, it was small wonder that Tshombe found it impossible to achieve national reconciliation. He failed from the start to realise that in the task of nation-building, political solutions must precede military or economic solutions. I know of no case where a fully roused people, fighting for what they sincerely believe to be their legitimate rights, has been permanently subdued by armed strength alone.

Almost as soon as Tshombe's government was announced, fighting flared up again in the Eastern Congo, and on 4 August, Stanleyville fell to the freedom fighters. As the guerrilla leader, Soumialot, remarked, 'This revolution is nothing more than the anger of the Congolese people in the face of injustice.' In a broadcast from Stanleyville shortly after its capture he declared that he was the new Lumumba, 'Lumumba said that someone stronger than himself would come to complete his work. That man is me . . . I have come to Stanleyville. I will come soon to Leopoldville.'

Soumialot was then 42 years old. Born in Samba, in the extreme south of Kivu Province, Soumialot's real name is Sumayili. His present name is the French form of the Arabic name he has in his native Bakussu tribe, one of the 'Arabised' tribes of the Eastern Congo. He began his career as a company clerk, but soon became a keen follower of Lumumba. The latter appointed him district commissioner of Kindu and, later, provincial Minister of Justice. He went on 'fellowship' visits to Prague and Peking and this led to the charge being made against him that he was a communist.

The freedom fighters of Africa are, of course, well used to being called communists. It is a form of abuse used frequently in the western press to describe anyone who challenges the *status quo*, who is against neo-colonialism and imperialism or who believes in socialism. Similarly, in many parts of the world, nationalists are described as 'rebels', 'agitators' or 'terrorists', the intention being to suggest the lowest possible motives for their actions and to rouse public opinion against them.

Soumialot, and those who fought with him, claimed to be true nationalists, the heirs of Lumumba, who were determined to establish a genuinely independent Congo. Yet they seldom achieved the name 'nationalists' or 'freedom fighters' except in the press of countries sympathetic to their cause. Tshombe and his foreign supporters insisted that they were 'rebels' who were terrorising the population for their own selfish gain, and that they must be crushed without mercy.

The American government was particularly concerned to 'restore stability'. On 13 August it was reported that four U.S. transport planes were on their way to the Congo, carrying 50 paratroopers to protect American aircraft and other U.S. property in the Congo. According to the *U.S. News and World Report*, 'The U.S. Mission in the Congo is a minor version of the American military mission now playing a major role in South Vietnam's shooting war.' In the editorial of the *New York Times* (12 June 1964) the following comment appeared:

> While President Johnson was telling the American Bar Association how troubled and turbulent the world is and how the United States lives with crisis and danger, American planes and soldiers were on their way to the Congo. There they will find as much trouble, turbulence and danger as exists at any spot on the globe. Thus, the United States is getting itself militarily involved in still another conflict; and it is doing so unilaterally. This time the United Nations is not taking part. A vacuum has to be filled and, as is becoming the custom, the United States is to fill it.

In view of the Congo's mineral wealth, the American action was not a surprise. Neither was Tshombe's action in stepping up the campaign for mercenaries. He had, after all, long experience of their worth.

Large numbers of mercenaries were recruited again. There were OAS supporters, and adventurers of all kinds. To many Congolese they were known simply as the 'Terrible Ones', the return of whom was linked inseparably with Moise Tshombe. *The Times* reported on 15 September that there were then between 400 and 500 mercenaries in the Congo. In addition to the mercenaries, Tshombe reorganised and armed his ex-Katanga gendarmes estimated by him to number some 15,000 men.

How different were the enemies of Tshombe's government. They claimed to have no foreign military aid and no foreign technicians. As Soumialot, National Director of Propaganda and Press Relations of the Mouvement Nationale Congolais, told the reactionary Ian Colvin of the *Daily Telegraph* on 6 August, 'My men have fought with clubs and spears and the only other weapons that they have were captured from the Congolese National Army.' Ian Colvin went on to report that in a week's roaming around Stanleyville he had seen no evidence at all of foreign participation. His view was supported later by the western-orientated Colin Legum, who wrote in the *Observer* (27 September 1964) thst it was incorrect to identify the Congolese 'rebellion' with Chinese Communism. 'It is not the Chinese who triggered off the rebellion. It grew out of the rotten conditions in the Congo.'

The success of the nationalists, using very inadequate arms, can be explained in no other way than in the support they obtained from the population of the areas in which they operated. Time and again, Tshombe's mercenaries would retake villages and towns, only to lose them again as soon as they moved on; the nationalists having temporarily retreated into the forest.

On 26 August, I decided to send a note to Kasavubu suggesting a conference in the Congo to end the civil war:

I have had the pleasure of receiving the Special Mission of the Congolese Government led by Mr Lubaya,[1] Minister of Health, and have had full discussions with them concerning the present situation in the Congo.

Africans everywhere are extremely concerned that with the departure of United Nations troops from the Congo, it has not been possible to maintain peace and security in the Congo. Instead, we are witnessing what is virtually a civil war, with brother killing brother. It seems to me, therefore, that Mr Moise Tshombe's proposals for national reconciliation, pacification and economic development cannot be achieved if the military situation in the Congo is not brought to a speedy and just end.

Military action in the Congo cannot solve the present problem

[1] M. André Lubaya was sent to Accra by Tshombe to explain his position to me, since I was considered to be against his policies.

of the Congo. It will merely aggravate and prolong this awful spectacle of fratricidal strife. As you are well aware, the occasion for fighting in the Congo is being actually exploited in their own interests by foreign Powers with the consequent danger of the serious interplay of the 'cold war' in Africa; a situation which every true African patriot must deplore.

To bring about a permanent solution which all of us seek, there should be a conference of the leaders of political parties and the leaders of warring factions in the Congo. The major object of such a conference is to find ways and means of bringing an end to the fratricidal strife now going on in the Congo. I propose that such a conference should be conducted under the auspices of the Organisation of African Unity acting through a Special Commission of Mediation chosen from five African States as follows: Nigeria, Sudan, Algeria, Ethiopia and Ghana.

Ghana will be most willing to play host to this conference in Accra. I trust in the interest of peace and goodwill in the Congo, you will agree to the steps which I am proposing as a matter of urgency.

I should like to put these proposals of mine formally to the Extraordinary Meeting of the Council of Ministers of the OAU early next month. I have therefore authorised my ambassador in Leopoldville to hold immediate discussions with you on the proposals.

My proposals were not accepted by the Congolese President. I therefore sent an Aide Mémoire to Prime Minister Tshombe, suggesting a Round Table Conference in Addis Ababa. It seemed more than ever imperative that an *African* solution should be found:

The present situation in the Congo requires serious and urgent attention. It has become quite clear now that military action will not provide a permanent solution. It should be remembered also that under present conditions in the Congo, military action means one group of Congolese people killing another group of Congolese people. This is a most undesirable and regrettable situation which no African State can support or assist.

It is therefore my considered view that immediate steps should be taken to bring about a peaceful solution by:

(a) proclamation of a cease-fire forthwith and neutralisation of all armies in the Congo;

(b) the summoning of a Round Table Conference of the leaders of all the main political parties (including President Kasavubu and yourself) and the warring factions in the Congo to meet in Addis Ababa. This Conference is to agree to the setting up of a Provisional Government, since the present Government appears now to be unacceptable to the various political groups in the Congo. The sole objective of the Round Table Conference will be to organise a fair and peaceful election under the auspices of the Organisation for African Unity;

(c)   for the duration of the Round Table Conference and the general election, the Organisation of African Unity to maintain a Peace Force in the Congo whose main responsibility will be to assist the new Provisional Government with the preservation of law and order. This Peace Force is to be withdrawn as soon as the Round Table Conference and the general election have been concluded, and a truly democratic Government elected by the people is established.

These proposals were put before the OAU at a special meeting held in Addis Ababa in September 1964. Tshombe failed to get the necessary endorsement to allow various African States to give him military aid. He had appealed to Ethiopia, Liberia, the Malagasy Republic, Nigeria and Senegal for troops. But Ghana's Foreign Minister, Kojo Botsio, who was our delegate at the conference, warned members that if troops were sent to the Congo they might be faced with the problem of fighting African nationalists.

At an emergency meeting of Foreign Ministers on 7 September, foreign interference in the Congo was condemned and Kenya's delegate, Joseph Murumbi, suggested that a high-powered delegation from the OAU should be sent to Washington, Peking and Brussels to urge the governments to stop interfering in Congolese affairs. He also supported the idea of a Round Table Conference to find means of political reconciliation. Tshombe, however, objected strongly to such a conference, saying he had gone to Addis Ababa 'for help not criticism'. On the face of it, his appeal for military aid from African States might have seemed acceptable, if only to forestall full-scale western military involvement, but in practice it would have meant bolstering up the loathed Tshombe leadership against Congolese nationalist forces. These forces had just set up in Stanleyville the 'Congolese People's Republic' under the presidency of Christophe Gbenye, who was Minister of the Interior in Lumumba's cabinet in 1960. In a statement delivered to the Conference delegates they claimed that Kasavubu had 'betrayed the national cause' and that their aims were the restoration of the Congolese people's sovereignty, the recovery of national independence and the re-establishment of national liberty and democracy.

Eventually, after long discussions, the OAU agreed the following six-point plan:

1 The ending of recruitment of foreign mercenaries and the expulsion of those already in the Congo.
2 The granting of safety to all those combatants who laid down arms.
3 An appeal to all Congolese political parties for a national reconciliation by the setting up of a Government of Union to ensure order and free elections.
4 An ad hoc committee to help political leaders to achieve national reconciliation, to bring about normal relations between the Congo and her neighbours and to decide on aid to the Congo.
5 A mission to visit capitals of countries interfering in the Congo to ask them to desist.
6 Member states to be asked to cease any action that would aggravate the Congo situation.

When this plan was finally agreed at the end of an all-night meeting of Foreign Ministers, our delegate, Botsio, was so overwhelmed at the happy conclusion that he declared he would not make a speech. Instead, he led the other delegates in the rousing song, often heard in Ghana: 'In the struggle for Africa there is victory for us'. Tshombe shook hands with the Foreign Minister of the Congo (Brazzaville) and everyone clapped.

Yet the conference was not an unqualified success. Six countries, including Nigeria, Sierra Leone and Senegal, abstained from approving the six-point plan. Further, Tshombe had succeeded in preventing Gbenye's supporters from being heard; he had defeated the proposals for a Round Table Conference and a cease-fire.

However, the Congo Conciliation Committee, consisting of nine states under the chairmanship of President Kenyatta, was set up, and this commission contained a majority of States who had voted for the sending of a peace-keeping force to the Congo. The first meeting of the Conciliation Commission was held in Nairobi on 18 September. Representatives from Ethiopia, Nigeria, Guinea, Cameroun, Somalia, UAR, Upper Volta, Tunisia and Ghana attended, and the chairman also invited Tshombe and representatives from Burundi and Congo (Brazzaville).

At the opening meeting on 20 September, Tshombe pledged himself to 'respect scrupulously' resolutions of independent African States on the Congo. He added, however, that he would accept 'no interference in the internal affairs of his country'. True to form, Tshombe was playing a double game, allowing the continuance of foreign intervention and at the same time trying to win support from independent Africa.

On 23 September, the Conciliation Commission urged the U.S.A. to withdraw all its military supplies, equipment and men from the Congo, and to stop further assistance to Tshombe. The Commissioners said that American withdrawal was essential before peace could be restored in the Congo. The Commission's chairman, President Kenyatta, then declared that it had been decided to send a delegation to see President Johnson 'because we find that while the Congo is still supplied with materials of destruction the peace we intend to make in the Congo cannot be made. We are trying to persuade our friends and those interested in the Congo to refrain from supplying war materials to the Congolese.' The American reaction was to accuse China of subversion in the Congo, and to assert that U.S. aid to Tshombe's government was in the best interests of Africa as a whole.

News of the proposed OAU mission to Washington was received in Leopoldville with great alarm. Without consulting Tshombe, who was then in Katanga, Kasavubu announced the Congo's withdrawal from the OAU, on the ground that the mission represented interference in the Congo's internal affairs.

Meanwhile, in Washington, President Johnson snubbed the OAU mission by refusing to hold discussions unless the Congolese Government also took part in them. Eventually, Dean Rusk, American Secretary of State, met members of the mission at a working luncheon and gave vague assurances of America's sympathetic understanding of the peace efforts of the OAU. But basically the position remained the same as before. The attitude of the American President had shown unmistakably just how little importance he attached to the OAU. Without the authority of a Union Government, and an African High Command at its back, he thought the organisation could safely be treated with contempt, or at best, with polite indifference.

Yet in spite of the mission's failure, I remained convinced that the OAU was the body which should devise a solution for the Congo problem, since it alone would act solely in Africa's interest. I made this point strongly at the Conference of Non-Aligned Nations which was held in Cairo in October 1964. The Congo was, I said, still being torn by internal disputes kindled by mercenaries and foreign interference. This disease was threatening the future of the whole

African continent and its cure lay in united action on the part of the independent African States.

Shortly after the Conference opened, Tshombe arrived at Cairo airport to attend the discussions, but he was kept in the El Orouba Guest Palace in suburban Cairo under heavy guard, until he was finally forced to leave the country. His exclusion from the Conference, however, did not prevent him from proceeding on a European tour, where he openly appealed to Europeans to play a greater role in Africa.

In October, the military base of Kamina was securely in the hands of Belgians and South African mercenaries. Elisabethville was also recaptured, and the whole of North Katanga cleared of Soumialot's troops.

Most of the world Press was at this time obsessed with the acts of brutality said to have been committed by the nationalists. But for us it was no surprise to read the record of one of Tshombe's mercenaries as it appeared in a London newspaper:

> I was a hired killer. And now I was sick of killing. So sick that I was prepared to do almost anything to avoid taking even one more life.

He went on to describe how, on the way to Stanleyville, one of the mercenaries' lorries broke down. The soldiers unloaded it and retreated for a time into the bush. When they returned, they found the vehicle completely destroyed. In a fit of rage the young English lieutenant ordered the mercenaries to advance to the nearest village 'and take it apart'. According to this writer it was a familiar enough command. 'It seemed to me we had been taking villages apart, innocent villages of peaceful farming folk who did not want any part of this war, all the way along the track from far down in the south.' He described how the soldiers would arrive at a village unexpectedly, would open fire without warning and burn every hut and shack to the ground regardless of who might be inside. The idea was to terrorise the whole area.

It was just before dark when the mercenaries entered the village near where the lorry had been wrecked. Unsuspecting women were carrying out the last of the day's chores, while their children played around them. Then came the order to fire. Women and children screamed as they were hit by machine gun bullets. Some of the soldiers threw cans of petrol on to the huts before setting fire to them. Others threw phosphorus hand grenades at the villagers, turning them into 'inextinguishable torches of fire'. For a time there was chaos as the mercenaries, many of whom had learned to hate all Africans, ran through the village killing or wounding everyone they saw. For they had been told in the course of their training never to take prisoners. 'Even if men, women and children come running to you, even if they fall on their knees before you, begging for mercy, don't hesitate. Just shoot. To kill.'

The mercenary went on to report how time and again in the weeks that followed they were ordered to shoot down Africans at point-blank range and were not even allowed to make sure that they were dead before leaving them to the mercy of the tropical sun and the vultures wheeling overhead. Some of the mercenaries raped the village girls before shooting them. 'We shrugged it off. Sometimes we killed in a frenzy. Sometimes we killed coldly. Some of our column killed for kicks; killed for fun. We all seemed to have turned into wild rampaging animals. This was the truth, the reality of this Congo war.'

In a struggle such as the Congo went through in 1964, obviously terrible acts of brutality were bound to occur and no side could claim that its troops always behaved as they should. But I have quoted at length from the mercenary's report in order to correct the impression left by the biased accounts in so many newspapers of the 'cruel', 'savage' behaviour of the 'rebels' and the high-minded 'brave' acts of the mercenaries, as though they alone had the monopoly of courage and idealism.

The campaign against Gbenye's government in Stanleyville was reaching a climax as the negotiations for the release of foreign civilians in the capital failed to achieve any result. Throughout September and October efforts were made on both sides to find some kind of settlement, though the chances of reaching an agreement were recognised as being extremely slim. As the mercenaries advanced towards Stanleyville, bombing and destroying villages, naturally the Stanleyville government was all the more inclined to use the presence of foreigners in the city as a bargaining counter. What other course was open to them? Gbenye asked only that the bombing of Stanleyville should cease, the advance of the mercenaries upon the city should stop, and that the Belgians and Americans should end their military support of Tshombe.

Nevertheless, the western Press continued, during November, to print alarmist stories of the impending massacre of American and European men, women and children in Stanleyville. It became obvious that the intention was to prepare public opinion for an American-Belgian rescue operation.

On 21 November came news of the arrival of about 800 Belgian paratroopers on Ascension Island in the South Pacific Ocean. The British Government had given permission for the troops to be stationed there 'solely as a precautionary measure', according to the Belgian Foreign Ministry. Two days later, however, the troops were reported to have arrived in Kamina, the large air base in North Katanga. Under the military aid treaty between Belgium and the Congo, Belgian troops could be sent to Stanleyville only on the invitation of the Congolese Government. It was also necessary for the Head of State, President Kasavubu, to sign a written request.

While the mercenaries advancing on Stanleyville crossed the Lowa River, the last big obstacle before the city and 155 miles south of it, Thomas Kanza, Foreign Minister in the Gbenye Government, arrived in Nairobi to begin talks with President Kenyatta, chairman of the OAU Congo Conciliation Commission, Diallo Telli, the OAU'S Secretary-General, and William Attwood, the American ambassador. At the start of the discussions, Kanza made it quite clear that the hostages would be safe as long as the talks were going on. But it seemed that Attwood had already made up his mind on the necessity for using force to rescue them. His attitude was in line with Tshombe's view that Stanleyville must be taken quickly and with the use of the Belgian paratroops.

At dawn on 24 November, while the OAU was still negotiating, Belgian troops parachuted from giant U.S. aircraft into Stanleyville airport. They quickly captured it. More troops were flown in and soon large areas of Stanleyville were seized. About 30 hostages were killed and 40 wounded when Gbenye's troops opened fire at the Lumumba monument and in front of an hotel. It was surprising the loss of life was not greater in view of the fever pitch at which everyone in Stanleyville had been living for months and the suffering caused by repeated air raids on the city, which must have aroused bitter resentment.

The paratroop operation had been made in spite of the OAU appeal to the Americans and Belgians not to attack Stanleyville, but to agree to a cease-fire to allow a peaceful solution to be negotiated. Full blame for the deaths in Stanleyville must therefore be placed on those who allowed the action to be carried out. All over the world students and others demonstrated against the operation and in many capitals, British, U.S. Belgian, and Congolese embassies were attacked.

Meanwhile, the American State Department piously asserted that American aircraft and Belgian troops were used, and would continue to be used, merely to rescue hostages and not to fight rebel forces. On 27 November came news that they had attacked Paulis, the pretext again being that they were trying to save hostages. At this point, President Kenyatta sought the views of African Heads of State on the Congo situation, which was becoming more and more serious. He made it known that he had been neither consulted nor advised before the news came of the U.S./Belgian paratroop landings in Stanleyville.

I think the strength of anti-American and Belgian feeling caused throughout the world as a result of the Stanleyville action, surprised even the most hardened of Tshombe's supporters, and certainly had bearing on the Belgian Government's decision to withdraw its troops by the end of November. Speaking in Brussels, M. Spaak, the Belgian Foreign Minister, said that the sending of paratroops into Stanleyville was the most harrowing decision he had ever had to make, and that the action was 'strictly humanitarian'. Yet at the time he made the decision he knew that negotiations were proceeding in Nairobi for the repatriation of the hostages through the services of the International Red Cross, and that there was a fair chance of a political solution being found to the Congo deadlock.

It seems that once again, the western powers were determined to block any success the OAU might have had in settling the problem. Doubtless they would have regarded it as a dangerous precedent for an African solution to be found, and on no account did they want to see a strengthened OAU. As far as Tshombe's Government was concerned, it was naturally to their immediate interest to destroy the Gbenye regime, and they had no scruples about making use of foreign soldiers and aircraft to achieve this end. For the second time[1] in less than three months, the ineffectiveness of a weak OAU had been publicly demonstrated.

[1] The first time was in September, when President Johnson refused to see the OAU Mission.

24 The Failure to find a Military Solution

As the last Belgian troops left the Congo on 28 November, it was estimated by Colonel Charles Laurent, commanding the operation, that 1,800 people had been evacuated from Stanleyville and 375 from Paulis. But the Belgo-American operation had done little to help put down the so-called rebellion, which was revealed to be much more extensive than was generally thought. Tshombe's chances of ending it were as hopeless as ever. As soon as his army captured a town and moved on, leaving only a small garrison behind, it was chased out by 'rebels' in a matter of days. Furthermore, the Stanleyville leaders, Gbenye, Olenga, Soumialot and Mulele, had all escaped capture and were reported to be in Juba in the Southern Sudan.

As always, Tshombe turned to Europe for help. This time, he visited Paris for talks with General de Gaulle, much to the alarm of Belgian officials, who accused the French President of 'unfriendliness'. Doubtless Tshombe had been disappointed with the way in which Belgium and America had withdrawn troops and aircraft so soon after the capture of Stanleyville and before the nationalists had been subdued. He had failed to persuade them that a military solution could be found to the Congo's problems, and he sought a new ally.

By then, it was obvious that those who fought against the Central Government were expressing a widespread feeling of discontent and disillusionment and that a negotiated political reconciliation was the only answer. President Kenyatta, on behalf of the OAU Conciliation Commission, urged Tshombe to take members of the opposition into his government and to form a broadly based administration, but the appeal fell on deaf ears. Tshombe was achieving quite a bit of success in Paris and was in no mood to bargain with his enemies. He emerged from a long discussion with de Gaulle saying that he was 'very satisfied'. He and the General had reviewed the whole Congo situation and had discussed co-operation between the two countries, with the result that France was willing to give Tshombe moral support and the massive technical assistance the Congo needed, though there was no question of French military involvement.

Strengthened by the support of France, Tshombe then proceeded to pass a decree under which the Congo was to recover all land conceded to three Belgian holding companies and to collect all royalties paid to the companies by the mining firms, including the giant Union Minière of Katanga. This action was interpreted as a measure to gain the approval of de Gaulle, who was understood to have told Tshombe that France could not take an interest in the Congo unless there was an end to other foreign influence there. Probably, Tshombe also regarded the move timely in view of the conference of Heads of African States due to open in Addis Ababa on 18 December. He was well aware of the fact that most Africans called him an 'imperialist's lackey' and thought that nationalisation might make him more acceptable.

It seemed to me that the position in the Congo had reached such a critical stage that action to save the situation should be taken at once and not await the outcome of the Addis Ababa Conference. I accordingly cabled the Emperor of Ethiopia (29 November):

Have the honour to refer to your telegram of 27 November concerning events in the Congo. With all due respect, I consider that the present situation in the Congo is another example of the weakness of the OAU and how ineffective it can be in an emergency involving the security of our Continent. In my view, a meeting of Heads of State at this time would only delay action and cause the situation to deteriorate. In view of the fact that contrary to his own promise Tshombe has failed to call a halt to the use of mercenaries and U.S. military equipment in the Congo, we must each decide very quickly what aid we can give to the Congo to rescue it from complete collapse. Such a collapse would affect us all in the long run. As far as I can see, only a Union Government of Africa can protect us effectively from these mounting threats to our security in Africa.

A copy of the telegram was sent to President Ben Bella of Algeria and on 8 December he replied that he agreed with me that action should not await the outcome of the Addis Ababa meeting. Yet he thought the meeting should take place as planned and he hoped that I would attend personally.

A note from President Nasser (3 December 1964) reached me a few days before I heard from Ben Bella:

I have received your message dated 24 November regarding the situation in the Congo. While I am deeply concerned about the events going on in the Congo, I feel that it would be a matter for regret if an armed invasion is launched against the Congo at the same time as the OAU ad hoc Commission for the Congo is submitting its proposals for a peaceful and rightful solution for the problem, in which the last word is for the Congolese people themselves.

This in itself means that the powers which imposed the armed invasion on the people of the Congo are not willing to accept a peaceful solution for the problem. Furthermore, what is more serious is that the mere launching of this invasion is a threat to Africa, its security and integrity.

This invasion is strong and clear evidence that the colonial powers will not hesitate to resort to armed force and aggression in order to maintain their policy of robbing Africa of her natural resources.

What is going on in the Congo now is not only a great threat to the small countries which refuse subjection to imperial and foreign domination, but is also an intolerable threat to African Unity, as it implies an attempt to violate the dignity and efficiency of the OAU.

I have sent instructions to my Foreign Minister who is now in New York attending the United Nations General Assembly to hold consultations with his colleagues, the Foreign Ministers of the African States who are there, for concerted action to confront this situation.

I have sent to Mr Diallo Telli, Secretary-General of the OAU, advising my consent to attend the African Summit Conference scheduled in Addis Ababa on the 18th December to be preceded by a preliminary meeting of the Foreign Ministers.

Please accept Your Excellency my highest consideration and esteem with my best personal wishes for your happiness and success.

I replied as follows (9 December 1964):

I thank you for your letter of 3 December which was handed to me this morning by your Ambassador, Mr Kader. I agree with your analysis that the colonialists will not hesitate to use armed force to maintain their economic domination of Africa. The Congo situation is a manifestation of the serious threat which colonialism and imperialism pose to Africa, and the helplessness of the Independent African countries, as at present organised, to deal with this threat.

The only way out of our present predicament and impasse is bold and courageous action to create a Union Government for all Africa which will deal resolutely with the fundamental causes of our recurrent crises. You and I tried to establish an African High Command, and with the emergence of the OAU this had to stop, unfortunately. The invasion of Congo by Americans, Belgians, British, South Africans and other mercenaries, challenges us of the Independent African States to unite in one African Union Government.

As I have informed the Emperor of Ethiopia, I consider the present situation in the Congo another example of the weakness of the OAU and how ineffective it can be in an emergency involving the security of Africa.

As you may well remember, during the recent Non-Aligned Conference in Cairo, we considered ways and means by which aid could be given to the nationalists through Nairobi. Later, however, when all arrangements had been made, the Kenya Government did not see fit to allow planes to land, contrary to the decision we took at Cairo.

A meeting of Heads of State without direct positive and concrete proposals would only delay action. Despite his own promise, Tshombe has failed to call a halt to the use of mercenaries and U.S. military equipment in the Congo. We must therefore decide very quickly what aid we can give to the Congo to rescue it from complete collapse. Such a collapse would affect us all in the long run.

I was glad to learn that Your Excellency is already helping to prevent such a collapse in the Congo. The situation calls for urgent action to save the progressive forces in the Congo from annihilation. We should not wait until the 18th December to take action. If, however, the Heads of State agree to meet in Addis Ababa, I shall be represented. I am very busy just now.

I have noted that apart from the urgent action that is required, you have also asked your Foreign Minister to hold consultations on the subject in New York. I have asked my Foreign Minister to take resolute action in New York. He has already called at the

State Department to underline our opposition to foreign intervention in the Congo. I have also asked King Hassan of Morocco to support the Security Council discussion of the Congo problem.

In my view, while we take such secondary action, we must realise that ultimately the solution lies in our own hands. The Independent African States can only act in their true interests when they are completely united; and such unity can only be found within the collective strength of a Union Government. While we must work for the immediate achievement of this great objective, we must also find a short-term solution which will save the Congo. I strongly suggest that the African States which are in a position to give material aid to the nationalists, should do so now.

In view of the extent of foreign aid to Tshombe's forces and the ruthless methods of the mercenaries, it was amazing that the nationalists were able to continue the struggle so effectively. Even the western press began to report accounts of the savage treatment of nationalists by Belgian troops and Congolese Government forces. The following report appeared in the British newspaper, *The Guardian*, on 26 November 1964:

The streets in Stanleyville are virtually deserted. Belgian troops are . . . killing and arresting suspected rebel supporters, shooting them summarily and apparently without authority. With automatic rifles at the ready, the Belgian troops stopped an African riding through a dusty side street on a bicycle. On his head he balanced a bunch of bananas. 'Are you a Mulelist?' the Belgians demanded. 'No', the African replied. 'You are lying', one of the Belgians said, and shot the man dead. A United Press International photographer, Ed van Kan, said he watched as a group of paratroopers moved through the streets of Stanleyville. 'I saw them kill three Africans just like snapping my fingers. One man was sitting on a tank. Suddenly, one of the Belgians just shot him for no reason.'

Later, on 7 December, came an account in the British *Daily Telegraph* of the terrible reprisals against nationalists in Stanleyville:

12,000 Africans suspected of rebel sympathies have been screened in Stanleyville by Congolese Government military police. 'Trials' were held in the stadium. When a man's name was called out and the watching crowd booed, he was immediately condemned to death, taken beside the river and shot.

But the *Daily Telegraph* printed, on 9 December, an article which clearly showed the contempt with which the writer viewed the Congolese nationalists:

> The Mulelist revolution now defiling the name of humanity in its death throes has demonstrated finally and conclusively that the Congolese cannot exist alone. They must be led, driven and shown by outsiders. . . .

The writer went on to refer to Gbenye, Soumialot and Olenga as leaders who had exploited the superstitious beliefs of their people 'to make the naturally cowardly Congolese fight'. The bulk of the 'rebel' army was made up of 'unthinking low-grade Africans'. As for the OAU, this organisation was, according to this *Daily Telegraph* correspondent, 'the great stumbling block to order in the Congo', its meetings being attended by 'brash, young and politically ignorant Ministers'. The solution suggested for the Congo problem was 'to ignore African opinion and rely on foreigners to fill key positions'.

It was pointed out in the same article that although there was little difference between 'a Congolese with a white band round his head to signify allegiance to the Government, and a rebel wearing the monkey-skin head-dress of a Simba', the West could not wash its hands of the whole business because of the strategic importance of the Congo, and the fact that it was 'one of the economic prizes of the world, with diamonds and tin, copper, timber, cotton, manganese, uranium and dozens of other materials'.

I have referred at some length to this article in the *Daily Telegraph* because it seems to expose so clearly all the basic elements which make up western thinking on the Congo. There is racial contempt in practically every line, greed for the riches of the Congo and a complete absence of any thought for the well-being of the Congolese people themselves. While obviously not every westerner would subscribe to the views expressed in the *Daily Telegraph*, it would be fatal for Africans to disregard this evidence of the unchanging attitudes of western thought.

These attitudes were seen in the speeches of certain delegates at meetings held at UN headquarters in New York during December 1964. Once again the Congo was to the forefront in discussions in the Security Council. On 9 December, the Security Council considered a memorandum from 21 countries, mostly African, asserting that the Belgo-American operation in the Stanleyville region was a threat to the peace and security of Africa. Just before the meeting was due to begin, it was announced that Tshombe had sent a note to the President of the Council accusing various countries, including

Algeria, Ghana, UAR, USSR and China, of interfering in the Congo's affairs. Tshombe was, at that time, about to visit European countries again in search of support for his regime. On 14 December he was reported to be in Rome. Five days later he was in Brussels.

In Belgium, Tshombe was advised to initiate peace discussions with the nationalists, since it was clearly unlikely that a military solution could be achieved. Tshombe, however, insisted that all he needed was large-scale investment in the Congo, so that he could defeat the forces of opposition by a return of prosperity. Tension was mounting in the Leopoldville area and he saw the discontent solely in terms of economic hardship.

At the end of December, the Security Council adopted an African-sponsored resolution calling for a cease-fire in the Congo and demanding the immediate withdrawal of all mercenaries. Significantly, France abstained in the vote but all other ten members of the Council supported the resolution. Further, the OAU was asked to pursue its efforts towards restoring harmony between the warring Congolese factions and the Council requested all countries to refrain from intervening in the Congo's domestic affairs. But the resolution contained no criticism of the American-Belgian military intervention in the Stanleyville area.

In view of Tshombe's attitude towards the nationalists, a settlement in the Congo seemed as far away as ever. Speaking in Brussels on 20 December before flying to Leopoldville, he said, 'There is no question of negotiating with the rebels. If they want to lay down their arms, we will accept.' On the same day, incidentally, came the report of a Lisbon correspondent, pointing out the fact that an understanding had existed for some time 'between the Congo and Portuguese Government on the idea of a pro-western bloc in Angola and the Congo, which Mr Tshombe has described as "the last hope of the free world in Africa".' When assessing a man it is helpful to take a look at the quality of his friends. In Tshombe's case they were mostly foreigners. He had hardly a true friend among the independent African States.

On 5 January 1965, the ex-Prime Minister of the Congo, Cyrille Adoula, wrote to me, enclosing a detailed plan for solving the Congo problem. He was then living in Rome, I quote the letter and his proposals in full:

(Translation)

The tragic situation my country is facing today, is a threat not only to its own future, but also to the future of Africa as a whole and the peace of the world. A further worsening of the situation in the Congo would only lead to its 'Vietnamisation' and bring the cold war into the very heart of Africa, with all the dangers that it entails for the stability and development of our African States.

Apart from these dangers which are not the least, having regard to the geographical position of the Congo between free Africa and Africa still in bondage, there would be the further danger that the freedom of the countries forming the southern loop of Africa would be retarded and Africa's unity compromised.

In order to prevent such gloomy prospects from materialising, I have after serious thought drawn up a plan which might provide, if not a basis, at least a starting point for the solution of the Congolese problem. If I failed to take this step earlier, it is because any action on my part would certainly have been interpreted as a tendentious démarche by the outgoing Government vis-à-vis the authorities in power. However, I think the state of anarchy and deterioration that exists at present in the Congo, compels me to break my silence, particularly as Mr Tshombe gave himself three months to bring his task to a successful conclusion, and that period is now greatly exceeded.

Please find enclosed herewith a copy of a plan I have drawn up in the hope that it may contribute something, however small, to the Congolese problem. I propose, after sending it to all the Heads of the African States, to release it to the public in the next few days. I should be pleased to know what you think about it. If any suggestions meet with your approval, I should very much like you to give them your support by a move in public after I have made them known to the world.

Aware as I am of the interest you have always shown in the Congo, and your devotion to the cause of Africa, I am convinced that you will spare no pains to see that a solution is found, capable of preserving the future of the Congo, and at the same time serving the cause of the whole of Africa.

Adoula's proposals for a solution to the Congolese problem were as follows:

The tragic situation the Congo is facing today is a threat to its future, the future of Africa and the peace of the world. It is important to find an immediate solution so as to prevent the situation from worsening, remove any dangers present in it and pave the way for a lasting solution to the Congolese problem. With this aim in view I propose the following plan which is based upon an analysis of the situation as follows:

(a) Any solution which does not reckon with the so-called rebels, even if the insurrection were to be crushed, would be a mere dream. It would only widen the gap between the Congolese, and hold within itself the seeds of a new encounter. We are in a vicious circle which must be broken at all costs.

(b) Insurrection can only be crushed with the help of more mercenaries, more loss of human life, more suffering and more misery. This would, in one way or another, make the Congo more dependent on other countries than it is at present.

(c) The way in which the situation has developed shows that the possibility of crushing insurrection is uncertain, if not impossible, particularly since the African states have decided to give massive help to the insurgents.

Such help is justified by the fact that Mr Tshombe is combating the insurrection with the help of Africa's declared enemies such as South Africa and Portugal, and is thus hindering the decolonisation of Africa, which is one of the pivots written into the Charter of the OAU of which the Congo is a party.

From a practical standpoint, the fact that both sides are receiving outside help, can only mean the 'Vietnamisation' of the Congo, which must be avoided at all costs in the interests of the Congo, Africa and the peace of the world.

This being so, I make the following proposals:

1 There will be a confrontation between the President of the Democratic Republic of the Congo—who in virtue of the new Constitution is also the Head of Government—embodying the legally constituted authority of the Congo, and the representative of all shades of opinion in the Congo, especially the combatants. The object of this confrontation would be to form a transitional government.

Such a confrontation should exclude Mr Tshombe, who has deliberately stood aside from any framework of national reconciliation and bears the responsibility for the present situation.

On the eve of his return to the Congo, Mr Tshombe had declared that the disturbances there were a popular (people's) revolution. Now he describes the leaders of the insurrection as assassins. Mr Tshombe has therefore failed in his attempt to achieve national reconciliation.

Mr Tshombe promised a new Congo within three months of his setting up a Government of Public Safety. Everyone knows how this promise has been fulfilled. Mr Tshombe has therefore also failed to restore law and order in the Congo.

Intrinsically, all this is not really serious, since no man is infallible. What is serious is the fact that Mr Tshombe has brought South African mercenaries, and Portuguese mercenaries, into the Congo and has carried out a policy which has made thousands of victims among nationals of the Congo as well as among people living in the Congo, sown the seeds of anarchy in the Congo, and ostracised our country from African society, the developing countries and all the progressive forces in the world.

We cannot forget this, still less can we condone it. Tshombe has relied upon our enemies and we must fight him just as we would fight a Verwoerd or a Salazar.

2 The tasks facing the transitional Government are to:

(a) Eliminate all the forces of foreign intervention in the Congo without distinction, mercenaries, Belgian and American troops and any others, and replace them immediately by forces exclusively African. These forces would be sent to the Congo under the auspices of the Organisation of African Unity, and would be placed under its control.

(b) Assess the situation which the (provisional) transitional Government has inherited from Mr Tshombe, so that no blame for such a situation may rest upon it.

(c) Hold a meeting which would include all shades of opinion in order to draw up a minimum programme. What is required is a discussion to discover the common denominators present in all the varying shades of opinion, to make possible the elaboration of a minimum programme.

If there is to be a firm understanding among the Congolese, it can only come about through a programme based upon the people and not upon individuals as has been the case in the numerous attempts at national reconciliation earlier, all of which failed.

There do exist common denominators for the drawing up of this minimum programme. Every Congolese would like to see his country return to peace; every Congolese would like to see freedom of expression and his own personal safety assured; every Congolese would like to see his country enjoy economic expansion; every one of them is conscious of the fact that there are no effective means at present to meet the needs of the people. The majority of our countrymen would like the Congo to take its place in the stream of African Unity and carry out a policy of non-alignment. The drawing up of this minimum programme which all shades of opinion would undertake to carry out independently of individual personalities in power, should take place before the elections. The Congo must face the elections in a spirit of true reconciliation. Otherwise, if these elections were carried out in a spirit of recrimination, those who happen to be defeated would seek to avenge themselves on those in power and nothing would be solved. At the very least, those who happened to be defeated would harass the men in power who would then be unable to devote themselves wholeheartedly to the gigantic task entailed in the effort to put the Congo's house in order. The task of the meeting after it has drawn up a minimum pro- gramme would be to propose to the Government a date for the holding of elections.

(d) Organise the elections.

3 Let Africa have a share in the settlement of the Congolese problem through the OAU. The OAU should provide the Congo with forces which would replace all foreign forces at present in the Congo, help to organise the meeting embracing all shades of opinion in the Congo, supervise the elections, and help to restore the administration of the Congo.

It is stated as a duty in the Charter of the Organisation of African Unity, that it should come to the help of any African State in difficulty. In addition, every African State has a direct interest in the stability and unity of the Congo, which is a condition for the elimination of all forms of foreign intervention. Here questions of a practical nature which must not be shirked come into play, if we are to be realistic. Neither the OAU nor the African States have the resources in money or men to carry out this task. They can and must find the means for undertaking this task by approaching the UNO, in accord with all the Great Powers, if need be through special financing with the prior approval

of the USSR, France and Belgium, if the error committed
in the First Congo operation is not to be repeated.

Once the question of financing is disposed of (and in this
connection I think it can be given not as an investment
where the funds would be irrecoverable, but as a loan spread
over 10 or 12 years, made to the Republic of the Congo)
the OAU would appoint with the approval of the President
of the Republic and the Congolese Government:

(a) a responsible military officer to keep order in the Congo
for a period of about two years, to give a new structure
to the Congolese army. Assistance in this respect would
be strictly African.

(b) a responsible civilian who might be a Congolese and
would be assisted by civil servants recruited in Africa as
well as from UNO and countries prepared to help the
Congo and equipped for this purpose. Their task would
be to reorganise and supervise the Congolese administration during the transitional period indicated above. In
this way there would be a healthy effort on three parallel
fronts: law and order, administration and the political
structure.

4 Shedding light on the Lumumba Affair.

With a view to avoiding any return to the tragic situation
we have been experiencing, it is important that the
circumstances surrounding the death of Patrice Lumumba
should be clarified. Until this is done, there will always be
people in the Congo or outside it, of good or bad faith,
who will use that name, which of all the names of our
national heroes, has the greatest pull. The Lumumba
affair is a grave shadow that hangs heavily over the
political stability of our country, and it is important that
this heavy burden should be removed, but this should not
be done in a spirit of revenge.

What is wanted is not to indict anyone, because that
would stir up hate and plunge the country in a new set of
disturbances. The transitional government would undertake to shed light upon this matter, and announce its
findings. This enquiry would be carried out in conjunction
with a Commission appointed by the OAU. This could be
done in the course of a ceremony during which one of our
towns will be called LUMUMBA TOWN, and in it a
monument would be raised to his honour.

These are the steps which we recommend to extricate the Congo from the deadlock it has fallen into. It was our duty to make this appropriate contribution which is in harmony with the aspirations of our people and is capable of winning the approval of the great powers who are interested in the Congo. We should be amply rewarded if these suggestions may contribute something, however small, towards rescuing the Congo from its present tragic situation.

Adoula's proposals were practically the same as I had advocated for so long and I felt bound to point this out in my reply of 22 January 1965:

I have received your letter of 5 January 1965, forwarding your proposals for a solution to the Congo problem. But may I remind you that the proposals which you are now putting forward are more or less those that I have been advocating for so long, including the period of your service as Prime Minister of the Congo.

If only you and other Congolese leaders had paid heed to me, the Congo would have been saved from experiencing the present chaos, confusion and foreign intervention. I have no doubt also that you will recall how at the Belgrade Conference of Non-Aligned States held in 1961 I opened out my heart to you and to Antoine Gizenga like a brother, but how eventually you decided to ignore my brotherly caution and advice, for reasons best known to you. And what do we see in the Congo now?

Let us hope, therefore, that we have learnt from experience and that you sincerely wish to co-operate with those who have the true interests of the Congo and Africa at heart and will work energetically and loyally for the restoration of peace and harmony within the framework of a truly independent Congo free from neo-colonialism and within the greater framework of an all African Union Government.

Adoula wrote again on 10 February:

(*Translation*)

I was deeply touched by the terms of your letter by which you acknowledged receipt of the proposals which I put forward with a view to solving the Congo crisis. I am very happy to realise that you consider my proposals as similar to yours and I do not doubt that you will use your influence to bring nearer, on the basis of these proposals, the time for solving the Congo problem.

Why did I not put up these proposals earlier? You know more than anybody else, Mr President, the condition in which I governed. You are aware that I faced the realities which confronted me, even if sometimes this did not often agree with my views and with my personal wishes. By this I tried, nevertheless, as you would agree, to change gradually the political orientation of my country and to associate it more and more with the important African problems. Perhaps, this may be the very reason for my resigning from the Government. You can sincerely believe that I am very happy about this, since this decision permits me to recover my freedom of opinion and action.

All this, as you will agree, Mr President, is very complex. I shall be very happy if the opportunity presents itself to explain everything in detail to you viva voce. Perhaps this will contribute to clearing once and for all, every misunderstanding, and thereby help you in your untiring efforts so that the Congo may recover peace and make its contribution to the advancement of Africa.

On receiving Adoula's note, I instructed the Ghanaian Ambassador in Rome to make arrangements for Adoula to come and see me, but this visit did not materialise.

For a short time, Adoula seemed to rally some support for his plan. But the key to any success lay in gaining the confidence of western interests, and these were not then sufficiently sure that Adoula was the right man to succeed Tshombe. It has always been a tragic reminder of the weakness of independent Africa, that throughout the Congo struggle it was to foreigners, and not to Africans, that Congolese leaders found themselves forced to appeal.

25 The Dismissal of Tshombe

WHEN Adoula put forward his plan for the Congo a very large part of the territory was in revolt in Kwilu, Kivu, around Leopoldville, Coquilhatville, in South Kasai and in North Katanga. It was officially recognised that at least eight out of the 21 provinces were no longer under the control of the government. Even in the towns, a revolutionary situation existed. And it is no exaggeration to use the word 'revolutionary', since opposition to the Government began to take on the appearance of a rising of a whole people seeking genuine independence, the destruction of the servitude to the Union Minière, Unilever, Forminière, Société Générale and the other neo-colonialist interests and the end of inefficient rule by the bureaucracy.

The following excerpt from an article in the February/March 1965 edition of *Under the Banner of Socialism*, gives some idea of the kind of conditions the people of the Congo were protesting against:

The people have risen up against those who are responsible for the famine which has covered all those areas outside the fields of the big trusts; the epidemics; the exactions of the Army and of the police. The big trusts continue to do good business and have even had an increase in production and profits. Independence has been cornered by a new layer of corrupted bureaucrats who have sold their people to imperialism for a lush life and enormous salaries.

The 1962 budget devoted 80% of its 19 billion Congolese francs to the payment of functionaries' salaries. A Minister earns from 600 to 750 thousand Congolese francs, while a Deputy earns more than 500,000. Deputies are also high functionaries (at an equally high salary) and high employees in semi-public firms. Moreover, loans without any precise limitation are granted to them by the State (30 million C.F. on 15 June 1962). With the replacement of the six colonial provinces by the 21 present provinces the Ministers and Deputies received salaries of 700,000 C.F.

When the austerity budget was voted in 1962, a 200% increase in Deputies' salaries was also voted at the same time! And all that without mentioning the smuggling, exportation of currency, bribes, etc. A well paid worker in a Leopoldville factory earns 50,000 C.F. a year, while a peasant—6,000!

Yet Tshombe, in the face of such obvious widespread discontent, was prepared to continue the civil war. It was reckoned that one million Congolese had been killed since 1960. The Minister of Foreign Affairs of Burundi, Mbazumutima, revealed at the UN Security Council that there had been between 30,000 and 40,000 deaths since the taking of Stanleyville by Government forces in November 1964.

Clearly, the continuing military struggle did not suit imperialist interests in the Congo. If Tshombe could not win the war then he would have to be replaced by a man more suited to the situation, who would be prepared to work at a political reconciliation. For a short time, at the beginning of 1965, it was thought that this man might be Adoula. According to the *Financial Times* (15 January 1965), 'Tshombe's western backers may well have decided that they have backed the wrong horse.'

In the U.S.A. opinion was rising against further American involvement in the war. It was realised that to continue and extend the war would mean entering into a new Vietnam. The nationalists could not be defeated by losing a major battle; they could only be challenged by the adoption of counter-guerrilla tactics and this in an immense country of 2,400,000 square kilometres, half of which is covered with forest. They sought, therefore, a political solution by urging Tshombe to accept a cease-fire and to allow more moderate elements into his Government; and at the same time they encouraged the Independent African States to bring pressure to bear on the Congolese nationalist leaders to enter into negotiations with either Tshombe or Adoula.

When Tshombe visited Belgium in January he was received very coldly. M. Spaak was annoyed that the Congolese Prime Minister had not acted on the advice, given him in December 1964, to include Adoula and Bomboko in his cabinet. The Belgian Foreign Minister offered to set off the Congo's colonial debt of £328 million against Congolese securities worth £336 million still held in Belgium, the difference of £7 million to be paid in the form of 'technical assistance'.

At the same time, he demanded that the Congo should hold itself liable, up to an unspecified amount, for material and moral damage suffered by Belgian citizens in the Congo since Independence. The Congolese Government should also restore to the Belgian chartered companies their rights to mineral and other royalties that were taken over in the decree of 29 November 1964. But this was entirely unacceptable to Tshombe.

The most important part of the decree had the effect of transferring control of the Union Minière from Belgian banking and other interests to the Congolese Government without compensation. The decree allotted to the Congolese Government the entire portfolio of 315,675 shares in the Union Minière held by the Comité Spécial du Katanga, a concession-granting concern, two-thirds of which is owned by the Congolese Government and one-third by Belgian interests. The Belgian Government considered that 123,725 of these shares belonged to the Compagnie du Katanga, which was an offshoot of the Société Générale de Belgique. The effect of the appropriation was that the voting strength of the Société Générale and its associate, Tanganyika Concessions Ltd in the Union Minière, was reduced from 40 per cent to less than 29 per cent. The Congolese Government's votes were raised from 24 per cent to nearly 36 per cent. The weakness of Tshombe's position was that the Belgian Government held the entire portfolio in trust; but his strength lay in the expiry of Union Minière's lease in 1990. Its value to Belgium was reflected in the fact that in 1959, the last year before independence, the Company declared a net profit of £25 millions, compared with the £35 millions aid granted to the Congo by the Belgian Government in four years.

As a result of the talks in Brussels, Tshombe was able to return triumphantly to Leopoldville with 150 letters authorising him to collect the Congo's portfolio of shares and titles worth £120 millions. He also carried a cheque for £660,000 handed to him by the Union Minière at a reception at the Congolese Embassy. The cheque represented royalties and dividends on the Congo's 210,450 shares in the Union Minière, which gave it 24 per cent of the voting rights in the company. With this success to his credit, Tshombe felt in a much stronger position to deal with his enemies.

He launched a new national party, the Confederation of Congolese Associations (CONACO), in order to rally electoral support in the elections due to take place in March. Previously, Tshombe had been merely president of Conakat, a purely Katangese party.

While Tshombe was in Europe, Soumialot was visiting various

African countries to appeal for support. In Cairo, he asked the Arab countries to supply him with troops and arms. In the Cairo press, Soumialot was described as 'Colonel Soumialot, Defence Minister of the Revolutionary Government of the Eastern Sector of the Congo'. Soumialot's colleague in the revolutionary struggle, Christophe Gbenye, was also actively engaged in gaining support for the anti-Government cause. On 15 January he was reported to have had a long discussion on the Congo problem with Presidents Kenyatta and Nyerere, and Prime Minister Obote at Mbale, Uganda.

In the meantime, Adoula was on the move, travelling to Brussels and Frankfurt where he had talks with various officials and explained his plan for the setting up of a transitional government in the Congo, excluding Tshombe. The transitional government would, he said, remove all foreign troops from the Congo and replace them with OAU forces.

If this were to be done, it would have to be done quickly. As each day passed, news came of fresh efforts by Tshombe to recruit more mercenaries. The mercenary leader, Major Hoare, on leave in South Africa, said that he was experiencing trouble with his troops because their pay was in arrears. In Stanleyville, one complete commando unit refused to go into action when about a hundred nationalists attacked a position on the outskirts of the town. They said they would not fight again until they were paid. The morale of the mercenaries was, however, soon restored when their pay and conditions were regularised; and there was apparently no lack of recruits in South Africa or Rhodesia. On 1 February I received a note from Thomas R. Kanza, Minister of Foreign Affairs of the Congo Revolutionary Government, enclosing a copy of Gbenye's six-point plan to solve the Congo problem:

1 Immediate liberation of M. Antoine Gizenga and 'all other political hostages held by the Leopoldville régime'.
2 Immediate withdrawal of mercenaries and all Belgian and American armed forces.
3 Immediate sending by the OAU ad hoc Commission of representatives to Katanga 'to enquire into manoeuvres by the Belgians and Americans to provoke a new secession by Katanga'.
4 Constitution of a commission to carry out 'sanctions against the assassins of Patrice Lumumba and some of Lumumba's associates'.
5 Widening of the Revolutionary Government by the introduction of 'other Congolese brothers who are in non-liberated regions but who continue to enjoy the confidence of the people'.

6 Holding of elections with OAU observers present which should be held six months after such a widening of the Government.

Gbenye said that he rejected Adoula's plan for a solution. 'We cannot negotiate with traitors.'

It was evident that Government forces in the Congo had lost for the time being the initiative against the nationalists. There were concentrations of anti-Government troops near every Government-held town, and nationalist raids became more frequent and more daring. This view of the military situation was confirmed by the three members of the OAU sub-committee who visited the Congo at the beginning of February. The members, who came from Ghana, Guinea and Nigeria, spent three days in Leopoldville in talks with government officials and then went on to Brazzaville and to Bujumbura in Burundi, before returning to Nairobi to report to the OAU ad hoc Commission on the Congo.

After several postponements, the ad hoc Commission finally met in Nairobi on 25 February under the chairmanship of President Kenyatta. In his opening address, Kenyatta told delegates that the Commission had been unsuccessful in its efforts in the Congo and that things had gone from bad to worse. The recruitment of white mercenaries seemed to have been increased, in spite of his appeal for their withdrawal.

Unfortunately, representatives of the Congolese revolutionary forces were prevented from attending the Conference, although the Sudanese Foreign Minister, Mr Mahgoub, suggested that they should be asked into the plenary session to answer certain questions. Thirteen countries voted in favour of the Sudan's suggestion and seven against, with 14 abstaining. The reluctance to agree to the Sudan's proposal was probably due to the feeling that once the revolutionaries were allowed in, pressure would be exerted to recognise their regime as legitimate. The fact that they were dis-united also undoubtedly operated against their admittance.

Tshombe, who represented the Congolese Government at the discussions, regarded the exclusion of the revolutionary leaders from the Conference as a personal triumph. He announced that a general election would take place in the Congo in a fortnight's time and the earlier suggestion of a round-table conference was therefore unnecessary. He suggested that the OAU should send a team of observers to the Congo and said that he would allow the team free-dom of movement provided that the revolutionaries had laid down their arms.

After five days of discussions, the 35-strong Council of Ministers of the OAU broke up on 9 March, agreeing only to refer the Congo question to the African Heads of State, due to meet in September. In effect this was an agreement to put the Congo question into cold storage for six months. On the closing day of the conference, two motions were heavily defeated. The first, from Cameroun, suggested that the OAU should send a peace-keeping force to the Congo. The second, from Ethiopia and Tunisia, asked all states not to aggravate the situation; a moderate enough motion but impossible to pass at that stage of the proceedings, when feelings were running very high.

Probably one of the most significant results of the meetings in Nairobi, was, however, the indication given of Tshombe's new supporters among the French-speaking African States. Most of these states sided with Tshombe against the rest of independent Africa, and it was not to be long before Tshombe would bring the Congo actively into the 'French club'.

But before then, came the general election. Tshombe, at the head of the Convention Nationale Congolaise Parti, which he had formed in February by linking 49 party groupings, was confident of victory. His party was particularly strong in Katanga, Kivu and Kasai, while President Kasavubu's party, ABACO, was thought likely to win most of the seats in the Leopoldville area. The main opposition party, Mouvement Nationale Congolaise Lumumba (MNCL) was less well organised and was not expected to be in a strong enough position to present a serious challenge to Tshombe.

It was arranged that the election should take place over six weeks, the voting being done province by province. Some 166 deputies were to be elected to the National Assembly, 132 senators, and deputies and senators for each of the 21 provinces.

Many people doubted whether any true expression of opinion was possible in the Congo at that time. On 29 March the Congolese Government postponed the elections in Leopoldville because of administrative breakdowns. The two senior electoral officials and several workers at printing shops where the ballot papers were to have been printed were arrested. In many parts of the Congo there were reports of a shortage of election stationery, stripped ballot boxes and missing electoral lists. In Bandalungwa voting district, 15 of the 65 lists of candidates were missing. In other places, all the necessary papers were available, but no ballot boxes.

According to a Government communiqué, 'certain political parties' deliberately sabotaged the election. But after many delays, the elections were eventually completed, though Kasavubu was forced to postpone the opening of Parliament after the courts had annulled the returns from three provinces, Kwilu, Central Basin and Central Kivu, after hearing complaints of irregularites.

In the meantime, fighting continued in various parts of the Congo. On 27 April news came of a surprise attack on Stanleyville. The insurgents tried to mass for an attack in the city's north-eastern area near Camp Kitele, one of the main army installations in the city. But they were beaten off.

At the time of the Stanleyville attack, Soumialot was forming in Cairo the 'Supreme Council for the Revolution'. This, it was said, would be the paramount organisation of the Congo insurgents. But it would not supersede the revolutionary government headed by Gbenye. The president of the 20-member Council was Soumialot, who gave up his post of Defence Minister in Gbenye's government. Pierre Mulele, Commander of the Western zone forces and Laurent Kabila, Eastern zone commander, were named the first and second vice-presidents. It soon became apparent, however, that Mulele and Gbenye, who did not take part in the discussions in Cairo, were not prepared to serve under Soumialot.

The divisions among the Congolese opposed to the Central Government were, throughout the next few months, matched only by the increasingly obviously rift between Kasavubu and Tshombe. This amounted to a bitter struggle for power between the two leaders, which was to end just before the opening of the OAU Accra Summit in October with the dismissal of Tshombe.

In an effort to win support Tshombe had in May 1965 taken the Congo (Leopoldville) into the Afro-Malagasy Common Organisation (OCAM), to become the 15th member of the Organisation. The Congo was admitted after an Extraordinary Meeting of OCAM held in Abidjan on 25 May 1965. The President of OCAM, President Moktar Ould Daddah of Mauritania, did not attend the meeting.

In a letter sent previously by Tshombe to President Daddah and to all members of OCAM, asking if Congo (Leopoldville) could become a member of the organisation, Tshombe said that he wanted to obtain military help from OCAM countries in order to safeguard his government. He also stated his willingness to respect all decisions and resolutions which OCAM adopted and to adhere unreservedly to the final draft of the Charter of the Organisation which would probably be established during the next official meeting in Tananarive in January 1966. Tshombe's request was received favourably in Abidjan and Dakar. President Houphouet Boigny advocated the sending of troops to help Tshombe, but his suggestion was opposed by Mauritania, Cameroun and Congo (Brazzaville). President Daddah informed the members of OCAM that he would not accept Tshombe's adherance to the Organisation, nor would he support the particpation of OCAM troops in the fighting in the Congo.

The admittance of Congo (Leopoldville) into OCAM helped Tshombe's relations with de Gaulle, and also enabled him to call on aid from member states in the economic, financial, military and administrative spheres. It was no coincidence that the African leaders who were most loyal to de Gaulle were also the most determined defenders of Tshombe. General de Gaulle had not given up his old idea, expressed to the Belgian Government when independence was declared, of putting a pacified Congo in the lap of French-speaking Africa; in other words, under French economic and cultural influence. With this in mind, the French Government depended on Tshombe and was always opposed to Hammarskjöld's plan to establish in Leopoldville a central government under the unofficial tutorship of the UN. At that time, France depended also on the support of two neighbouring states, Gabon and Congo (Brazzaville).

To General de Gaulle the entry of the Congo into OCAM must have seemed a step in the right direction and Tshombe was welcomed to Paris at the end of May when he visited France to ask for economic and technical assistance. Observers considered de Gaulle would seize the chance of challenging the Belgo-American alliance in the Congo. On leaving Paris for Brussels, Tshombe told a press conference, 'The admission of the Congo last week to the Afro-Malagasy Common Organisation (OCAM) has brought the country out of its isolation. It belongs now to the community of realistic countries in Africa.'

He was at that point very optimistic about the situation in the Congo. The revolutionary movement seemed to have been brought under control, and his Party (CONACO) commanded a majority in the new Parliament. In the northern Congo, government forces had at the end of May moved to within 60 miles of the town of Buta. A few days later, they captured the town.

But in the economic sphere, the position of the central government was less happy. A greatly increased deficit was forecast and the danger of inflation appeared imminent. External national accounts were also unsatisfactory. Since the first of January, exports had declined and that meant a considerable decrease in foreign currency. For agricultural products alone, this decrease was estimated at four million dollars a month. Even taking into account the rise in the price of cobalt at the beginning of 1965 and the increased production of copper in Katanga (which was up by 5,000 tons on the previous year's production) a drop in exports of about 10 per cent was expected compared with the 1964 figure.

At the root of the trouble lay the continuing anarchy in certain parts of the Congo, a deficient and ineffectual administration and a growing struggle for power in Leopoldville between President Kasavubu and Tshombe.

In a speech made in Leopoldville on 29 June, Kasavubu declared that it was his prerogative to dismiss Tshombe and to present a successor to the newly-elected Parliament for approval. Kasavubu's term of office was scheduled to expire six months after the opening of Parliament. He wanted, therefore, to install Tshombe's successor, as soon as Parliament met. Tshombe, on the other hand, claimed that his government could remain in office until the election of Kasavubu's successor as President. The new Parliament should have met during the last week of June, but failed to do so because the elections in three provinces were declared void. Its opening was therefore postponed until August.

On 7 July, Kasavubu dismissed Tshombe's Minister of the Interior and right-hand man, Godefroid Munongo, and appointed him governor of East Katanga. The dismissal was contained in a Presidential decree, and apparently it took Tshombe by surprise. Kasavubu followed up his decree with a request that Tshombe should enlarge his 10-man cabinet to include two of the President's supporters. But Tshombe avoided doing this by filling the vacant ministries (Interior and Civil Service Administration) himself. He now headed eight of the 20 ministries in his government. In addition to his new posts and the premiership, Tshombe held the Ministries of Foreign Affairs, Information, Posts and Telegraphs, Economic Development and Planning, Labour and Social Security, and Foreign Trade.

Yet as events later proved, Tshombe's position was in fact weaker than it had ever been. In August he once again visited Europe, supported by an impressive delegation of 16, including his Finance Minister, M. Ndinga, and the general manager of Air Congo, M. Essandja. In Brussels, he asked the Belgian Government to proceed as quickly as possible with the issue of the Congo conversion loan $3\frac{1}{2}$ per cent bonds which, under the agreement signed in February, would finally deal with the Congo's unguaranteed external debt on terms which would cost his country only a 40-year annuity of just over £2 million. In Bonn, Tshombe had talks at the Federal Ministry of Economic Co-operation about the prospect of increasing West German development aid to the Congo. He was promised a loan of over 10 million marks and a credit agreement was signed for 3,700,000 marks to reconstruct two bridges near Congolo and Kebanya-Kaji.

But his success in Bonn was quickly overshadowed by the deterioration in his position at home. While he was in Europe the elections in Maniema, where his followers obtained all the seats were declared invalid owing to an electoral fraud; and in the three provinces where elections were held again after the cancelling of previous elections, his party was heavily defeated. Moreover, the new Minister of the Interior, Victor Nendaka, convened the deputies of the North East provinces belonging to Tshombe's party for the purpose of forming a new parliamentary group and this threatened Tshombe's majority in Parliament.

It was reported that Kasavubu was busily engaged trying to restrict Tshombe's political influence wherever possible. It was said that the President was determined to attend the Summit Conference of the OAU due to open in Accra in October. In fact, throughout August and September, there was much speculation about who should represent the Congo at the Accra summit. At the beginning of August, Congo nationalist leaders met in Cairo to try to settle the leadership problem. Gbenye came to see me and to explain the latest developments. But on 9 August, the French news agency reported that the Congo revolutionary movement had split into two opposing camps when Soumialot formed a new 'government' and announced the dissolution of the 'government' of Gbenye.

The end of Tshombe's premiership was very near. On 13 October, Kasavubu forced Tshombe to resign as Prime Minister and asked M. Kimba, Minister for Foreign Affairs in secessionist Katanga, to form a new government. He led the Balubakat Party, which had only two seats out of 166 in the Chamber of Deputies, and six in the 132-seat Senate. But Kimba's party had joined the newly-formed Front Démocratique Congolais, headed by Nendaka.

The dismissal came just in time to allow Kasavubu to come to Accra for the OAU Summit and we were all glad to welcome him. In his speech, he said that the Congo (Leopoldville) had made a new start and was determined to solve the problem of the mercenaries in the interests of the Congo and Africa as a whole. He also said that the Congo realised the need for Africa to unite under a continental government. 'While the Congo needs Africa, I realise that Africa needs the Congo.'

His words seemed to sum up the whole tragedy of the Congo's first five years of independence; years which should have been full of progress and development but which had been, in fact, years of frustration and bloodshed. As he spoke, news of Tshombe's dismissal was fresh in our minds and the future of the Congo appeared brighter than it had been for a long time. But deep down, many of us wondered just how far the Congo's problems were really settled. Would Kasavubu be able to get rid of the mercenaries and had the position of foreign interests in the Congo been weakened in any way? Would these interests allow the Congo to be really independent and to take its place in the OAU as a firm supporter of union government? These questions were answered in part by General Mobutu's dramatic 'coup', soon after the Accra Summit ended and the dismissal of Kasavubu.

26 Mobutu's Coup d'Etat

UNTIL his 'coup' of November 1965, Mobutu's role in the politics of the Congo had not been such as to commend him to progressive African opinion. Between Mobutu and Lumumba there was no love lost, a state of affairs which was well known in the Congo and which was not calculated to endear Mobutu to the Congolese militants dedicated to the life and policies of Patrice Lumumba. There has also never been much doubt about Mobutu's special leanings towards the western powers. He had demonstrated his partisanship towards the west by his intense hostility to Lumumba. With such a background in Congolese politics, Mobutu and his emergence as President of the Congo Republic need some explanation.

After the return of Tshombe to the Congo as Prime Minister, Mobutu had been quick to sense the uneasy link that existed between Tshombe and Kasavubu. The strain between Tshombe and Kasavubu came to a head with the presentation before Parliament of Kimba's Government for a vote of confidence on 14 November 1965. It will be recalled that Mr Evariste Kimba had been appointed Prime Minister by President Kasavubu after his dismissal of Tshombe from the office of Prime Minister. Smarting under this political show-down, Tshombe had taken every precaution, by preening the wings of his Conaco Party and corrupting his adherents and cohorts and other half-hearted supporters, to ensure that he was not robbed of victory a second time. Accordingly when the vote was taken in Parliament, Kimba's Government failed to win the approval of the Senate and the House of Deputies. It received only 121 votes as against 134 for Tshombe's Conaco Party, with 7 abstentions. The Government was therefore defeated by a majority of 13 votes.

This unexpected defeat meant that Tshombe was working his way steadily to Presidential power. The exercise was indeed more of a rehearsal for the Presidential elections due to take place in three months' time and the whole atmosphere was charged with rumours about Tshombe's corruption of the Parliamentarians. It had been reported that three cheques to the value of one million Congolese francs each had been cashed by members of Parliament the following day, Monday, 15 November 1965. The stage was thus set for a direct and head-on collision between Tshombe and Kasavubu.

There were mass demonstrations in Leopoldville on 22 November 1965, in which the demonstrators carried placards condemning Belgium for its involvement in the planned overthrow of Premier Kimba and his Government. In front of the Belgian Embassy the demonstrators set fire to the Belgian national flag. At the British Embassy they condemned Britain for being in fraudulent collusion with the illegal minority settler régime in Rhodesia. Portugal was called upon to liberate Angola, Mozambique and its other African colonies.

Next day the demonstrations reached their climax before Parliament House where the head of King Leopold II's equestrian statue was draped in black with a rope tied round its neck! The youths shouted anti-Tshombe slogans amid long cheers and applause for 'Kasavubu, Massemba-Debat, Nkrumah and The Revolution'.

Meanwhile, in order to ensure that Tshombe retained the political initiative he appeared to have won over Kasavubu, his western supporters warned Mobutu against leaning unduly towards Kasavubu. They even went so far as to drop a calculated hint that the Katangese gendarmes and white mercenaries would rise in revolt if Mobutu did this. The western supporters thus left no stone unturned in their efforts to prop up Tshombe against President Kasavubu. They were sure that with their support and Tshombe's almost unlimited financial resources, which gave him a vast capacity for bribery and corruption, it was only a matter of time before he ousted Kasavubu from the Presidency.

However, Congolese patriots spearheaded by the Front Démocratique Congolais were not unmindful of these moves and manoeuvres. Secret and delicate negotiations were going on between them and Mobutu as to the best means of circumventing and eclipsing the manoeuvres of Tshombe and his foreign mentors, associates and advisers. It was therefore agreed that Mobutu with the support of the FDC should intervene by a military coup so as to forestall the attempts being made with the assistance of foreign powers to install Tshombe as President of the Congo in place of Kasavubu.

Accordingly, during the night of 23 November 1965, Mobutu called a meeting in his residence of the Heads of Military Staff of the ANC and presented them with a statement which declared the removal of Kasavubu from the Presidency, the appointment of himself (Mobutu) as Head of State and Colonel Leonard Mulamba, the military Governor in Stanleyville, as Prime Minister. Twelve military men signed the statement.

Shortly afterwards, Kasavubu was placed 'under protection' in Mobutu's headquarters, a para-commando camp on the outskirts of Leopoldville. Within 36 hours, Mulamba had formed a government which was presented by Mobutu himself to the National Assembly, where it was approved by acclamation, 259 out of 299 members of Parliament being present. A 'coup' had been staged in Leopoldville. It was a premeditated action, aimed at removing Tshombe and outwitting his foreign supporters. In this sense it was no 'coup', except that President Kasavubu was suddenly relieved of his post.

Following the assumption of power by Mobutu, an announcement of the change of government was broadcast by Leopoldville Radio. In the broadcast, Mobutu was named Head of State and Mulamba the new Prime Minister. General Bobozo was declared Chief of Staff for the duration of Mobutu's rule. It was further said that the new government would respect all agreements signed by former governments of the Congo and that the Congo would remain a member of UNO and OAU. It would also continue its membership of OCAM if the agreement signed by a former government was ratified by Parliament. The new government's policy would be first and foremost to promote the welfare of the Congo and of Africa. No interference of any kind from outside would be tolerated.

To emphasise his pro-African tendency and policies, almost the first international act of Mobutu's was to send a trusted envoy on a special mission to Ghana. In his letter to me on this occasion Mobutu among other things wrote as follows:

As you will see from the document, we have been led to take action because of our constant and overriding concern for the true interests of the Congo, which are closely linked with the interests of Africa. It is time to put an end to the race for power which could only benefit the interests of foreign financiers, neo-colonialists and imperialists.

The Democratic Republic of the Congo sincerely hopes that the ties that exist between our two countries will become closer and stronger, as a result of this testing period. As far as the Democratic

Republic of the Congo is concerned, it will not hesitate within the full limits of its possibilities, to support and defend the friendly stand taken by the Republic of Ghana.

In order to understand Ghana's position vis-à-vis Mobutu's government, reference must be made to the circumstances which led to Tshombe's return to the Congo after his self-imposed exile in Europe. It will be remembered that President Kasavubu, in an effort to bring an end to the Katanga rebellion, authorised Tshombe's return in June 1964.

Once in power, Tshombe unhappily disappointed the hopes of all who had reposed confidence in him by using the opportunity offered him to further his own ends and gratify his almost insatiable love of personal power. For this reason, corruption became rampant in the administration, the whole machinery of Government was bent to his will and a race for power among ministers was heightened by the expectation of the Presidential elections.

Tshombe was reported to have maintained as many as 53 personal foreign advisers, including a number who prepared the blueprints for action in his Katanga days. Since he personally held an unusual number of ministerial portfolios, as well as being Prime Minister, these non-Congolese collaborators became deeply involved in the making of policies and were virtually secret heads of Government departments. It was clear to all that far from recovering from its instability due to excessive intervention in its affairs by foreign powers, the Congo was again the unfortunate victim of neo-colonialist pressures.

To save the Congo from these dangerous trends the FDC (Front Démocratique Congolais) had no alternative but to act quickly to block Tshombe's selfish designs by supporting Mobutu. The end result of the 'coup' was that, far from Kasavubu losing face in the struggle for ascendancy between him and Tshombe, it was the latter who in fact suffered defeat. By announcing that his regime would head the administration for the next five years, Mobutu had in fact seen to it that the menace of Tshombe would be kept in cold storage for at least that period. This must have accounted for Kasavubu's declared willingness to continue to serve the nation in support of the new regime by assuming his other role as Senator.

The new Congolese Government gave an undertaking to put Africa first in all its dealings. In a letter to Mobutu, I had this to say:

I thank you for the message which you conveyed to me through your special envoy, Mr Marcel Lengema, Member of Parliament, on 3 December 1965. I am sure that Mr Lengema has now given you a full account of our discussions and the views I expressed about the situation in the Congo.

I have always believed that the Congo can never have peace and stability unless all foreign intervention is removed. Because of its geographical position, lying as it were in the very heart of Africa and owing to its vast potential mineral and agricultural resources, the Congo has tended to become an important centre of attraction for foreign powers.

This being the case, it is absolutely necessary that the Central Government of the Democratic Republic of Congo (Leopoldville) should be completely non-aligned in its foreign policy. Such a policy is the best guarantee for the ultimate safety and security of the Congo.

If the Congo maintains a policy of non-alignment, it will be in a much stronger position to identify itself with the African Revolution and maintain a vigorous position in the ranks of the progressive African States in order to assist effectively in the crusade for the total liberation and unity of Africa. This is why I was happy to learn from your envoy that your Government supports the objectives of the OAU and the aspirations of the peoples of Africa, namely, effective African Unity through the establishment of a Union Government of Africa. I trust therefore that in that spirit of solidarity with the cause of Africa's emancipation you will be able to give serious thought to the declaration of a general amnesty for those who have taken up arms against their own country in the earnest belief that, in doing so, they are seeking the ends of true independence and freedom for the Congolese people.

This in my view would be the most positive means of giving practical effect to the undertaking you gave upon your assumption of office as President, namely, that you would do everything possible to achieve national reconciliation in the interests of progress and peace in the Congo. To this end, I would like to appeal to you to take the earliest possible steps for the removal of all mercenaries from the Congo so as to end the reign of terror established by foreign interests in that part of our continent.

As I indicated to your envoy, the Government of Ghana is ready to assist in any direction which will hasten the establishment of peaceful conditions in the Congo, especially when your efforts are directed towards bringing about peace and mutual understanding between you and the warring factions in the Congo. Ghana would truly be pleased to see the day when the whole of the Congo is effectively united under the Leopoldville administration. This has been my constant plea and the reason for my readiness to give advice and support to the Government and people of the Congo all these years. The tragic history of the past five years in the Congo calls for redress and rehabilitation. Africa does not want to witness a repetition of this tragic and unhappy experience in the Congo.

The people of the Republic of the Congo will undoubtedly decide their own future free from foreign interference. Difficulties and uncertainties will have to be faced. But of one thing I am sure. The victors in the final battle for the Congo's emancipation will spring from the blood of Lumumba.

Bibliography

Belgian Government, *Handbook of the Congo,* 1959

Blackstock, Paul W., *The Strategy of Subversion: Manipulating the Politics of Other Nations,* Chicago, 1964

Boyd, A., *United Nations: Piety, Myth and Truth,* Penguin, London, 1962

Calder, Ritchie, *The Agony of the Congo,* Gollanz, London, 1961

Casement, Roger, *Report on the Congo,* London, 1904

Chomé, Jules, *La Crise Congolaise,* Brussels, 1959

Davister, Pierre, *Katanga Enjeu du Monde,* Brussels, 1960

Doyle, Arthur Conan, *The Crime of the Congo,* London, 1910.

Ganshof Van der Meersch, *Fin de la Souveraineté Belge au Congo,* Institut Royal Des Relations Internationales, Brussels, 1965

Gavshon, Arthur, *The Mysterious Death of Dag Hammarskjöld,* New York, 1962

Hoskyns, Catherine, *The Congo: A Chronology of Events, January 1960–December 1961,* Royal Institute of International Affairs, London, 1962

– *The Congo since Independence,* Oxford University Press, London, 1964

Joye, Pierre and Levine, Rosine, *Les Trusts au Congo,* Brussels, 1961

Lagos Study Circle, *The Tragedy of the Congo,* 1964

Lash, Joseph P., *Dag Hammerskjöld,* Cassell, London, 1962

Leclercq, Claude, *L'O.N.U. et l'Affaire du Congo,* Payot, Paris, 1965

Lemarchand, René, *Political Awakening in the Congo,* California–Cambridge, 1965

Lumumba, Patrice, *Congo My Country,* English translation of *Le Congo—Terre d'Avenir—Est-il Menacé?,* Pall Mall Press, London, 1962

Morel, E. D., *Red Rubber, the Story of the Rubber Slave Trade of the Congo,* T. Fisher Unwin, London, 1906

O'Brien, C. C., *To Katanga and Back,* Hutchinson, London, 1962

Slade, Ruth, *King Leopold's Congo,* Oxford University Press, London, 1962

Young, Crawford, *Politics in the Congo: Decolonisation and Independence,* Princeton University Press, 1965

Reference is made to the following records of the United Nations Organisation:

Security Council Official Records
Fifteenth year, Supplements for July–December 1961
Sixteenth year, supplements for January–December 1961
Seventeenth year, Supplements for January–September 1962

Reports of the Security Council to the General Assembly
Seventeenth Session, 16 July 1961–15 July 1962
Eighteenth Session, 16 July 1962–15 July 1963

General Assembly Official Records
Congo documentation for 15th–18th Sessions
(General Committee, Plenary Committees, and Annexes)

Resolutions adopted by the General Assembly during
Fourth Emergency Special Session, 17–19 September 1960
Fifteenth Session, Vol. 1, 20 September–20 December 1960
Fifteenth Session, Vol. 2, 7 March–21 April 1961
Sixteenth Session, Vol. 1, 19 September 1961–23 February 1962
Seventeenth Session, 18 September–20 December 1962
Eighteenth Session, 17 September–17 December 1963

Reference *passim* to the following newspapers and periodicals:

Christian Science Monitor, Daily Telegraph, Financial Times, Le Progrès, Libre Belgique, New Left Review (No. 31, May–June 1965), *New York Times, Pourquoi Pas, The Guardian, Observer, Sunday Telegraph, Under the Banner of Socialism* (February–March 1965), *U.S. News and World Report.*

Index